Working with Loss, Death and Bereavement

Working with Loss, Death and Bereavement

A Guide for Social Workers

Jeremy Weinstein

SAGE Publications

Los Angeles ▪ London ▪ New Delhi ▪ Singapore

SAGE Publications Ltd
1 Oliver's Yard
55 City Road
London EC1Y 1SP

SAGE Publications Inc.
2455 Teller Road
Thousand Oaks, California 91320

SAGE Publications India Pvt Ltd
B 1/I 1 Mohan Cooperative Industrial Area
Mathura Road, New Delhi 110 044
India

SAGE Publications Asia-Pacific Pte Ltd
33 Pekin Street #02-01
Far East Square
Singapore 048763

Library of Congress Control Number: 2007923828

British Library Cataloguing in Publication data

A catalogue record for this book is available from the
British Library

ISBN 978-1-4129-2390-3
ISBN 978-1-4129-2391-0 (pbk)

Typeset by C&M Digitals (P) Ltd., Chennai, India
Printed in Great Britain by The Cromwell Press Ltd, Trowbridge, Wiltshire
Printed on paper from sustainable resources

With thanks to:

Jenny for unswerving love, support and constructive criticism

Jutta who gave me back my confidence in supervision

Stephen whose sudden death reminded me of how little I actually know

Contents

1 Introduction

Chapter contents

- Basic definitions
- The importance of the social worker as the reflective practitioner
- Examples from contemporary dramas: novels, film and television, biographical accounts
- Scenarios that will be drawn upon throughout the text
- The major ways of assessing loss, including issues of difference and anti-discriminatory/anti-oppressive practice
- Core theme of 'living psychologically beyond our means'
- The structure of this book

This chapter introduces the reader to this text, setting out how it is organized and its contents. It starts out with some key definitions, an overview of basic concepts including understanding and assessing the experience of loss, incorporating the impact of gender and race/ethnicity and from this point exploring the meaning of anti-discriminatory and anti-oppressive practice. Underlying all this is the text's core aim: how we can be helped to recognize, rescue and revive the social work role within our work with loss, death and bereavement.

In focusing on social workers this is not to deny that there are, of course, a host of other professionals and lay people with important parts to play. Health care workers, teachers, bereavement counsellors, those involved in pastoral responsibilities: all take on the caring/curing role, working alongside social workers in the wider community and multidisciplinary teams. Hopefully this text will be useful to all or any of these groups but there is already a body of writing intended for this audience. This is less so for *social workers*, those individuals whose precise roles may change across agencies, different service user groups and countries, whose titles might shift and slide between *social care worker*, *mental health worker* or *care manager*, but who share a body of theories, skills, values and roles which are broadly similar.

Concentrating on what may be called *mainstream social work* means paying attention to the needs of service users when someone important to them has died, or they face losses related to disability, life limiting conditions, the onslaught of mental ill-health, ageing and the disasters that befall family life and child care. The discussion will draw on, but not seek to compete with, the more specialist texts that are already available on palliative care (Berzoff and Silverman, 2004; Firth et al., 2005; Beresford et al., 2006,) or the experience of those who are dying (Armstrong-Coster, 2004).

Integrated into the text are various case scenarios linking the experience of both service users and workers with the theories, research studies, professional values and practical skills that we can draw upon. Examples will also be taken from films, novels and personal accounts while self-tests, points for practice and advice on further reading help readers to stay in touch with your own processes, check and advance your knowledge and indicate where else you might go to consolidate and broaden your understandings. Readers are always encouraged to return to the various texts and authors that are cited, to check your own understandings and develop your own criticisms rather than relying on what other people, including this writer, have said they said.

To start with, however, what follows are some general working definitions.

Some Working Definitions

Loss   is wider than a response to a death, important as that is. It is any separation from someone or something whose significance is such that it impacts on our physical or emotional well-being, role and status. The experience and manifestation of loss can be more or less difficult depending on other important variables. This is explored in fuller detail in Chapter 2.

Dying   Bob Dylan expressed it well when he sang: 'he not busy being born is busy dying' (1965). Professional definitions tend to be more prosaic: *Medical practitioners* usually draw distinctions between *chronic illness/disabilities* which are *life limiting* and *diagnosed terminal conditions* such as cancer or motor neurone disease, needing *palliative care. Sociologists* discuss the various degrees of *aware dying* ranging from *closed* through to *open* awareness (Glaser and Strauss, 1965).

(Continued)

(Continued)

Writing as a *social worker*, Currer sees dying as involving '1) a degree of physical deterioration, 2) an emotional or individual component concerning the self (possibly incorporating a spiritual dimension) and 3) a social dimension about interaction with others' (2001: 38).

Death   outside of strictly medical terminology can prove difficult. Broadly speaking there is:

Living death or a *social death* e.g. lying in a coma, suffering from dementia, imprisonment. Individuals are physically alive but their situation isolates them from their former familial or social links.

Psychosocial death (Doka and Aber, 2002) where someone's *psychological essence* or prior *sense of self* is perceived as having died. This may be through drug dependency, mental illness, coming out as gay, joining a cult, undergoing a religious conversion or, the opposite, losing one's belief, e.g. some orthodox Jewish parents will formally mourn, sit *shiva*, for a child who marries out of the religion and the community.

Bereavement   is the response to a loss. It is a core human experience, common to, and also varying across, all cultures and historical periods. *Grief* is the *intrapersonal* or *psychological* expression of the bereavement. *Mourning* is the *interpersonal* or *social* expression, taking its cues from the attitudes and values of the surrounding context, religious, cultural etc. Both the intra and inter dimensions serve to sanction, or disallow and disenfranchise people's reactions.

Within these general definitions there are those specific to the role of the social worker.

There is discussion about the word we use for those who turn to social workers for support, whether the traditional term, *client,* or even *patient* in some specific work settings or more recent phrases like *service user.* The latter is the most popular currently so it is this I will use in the text, except, of course, where citing other sources.

Once engaged with service users Currer draws attention to the need to combine in our work 'the Emotional and the Practical' (2001: 78); Berzoff and Silverman refer to the need to draw on 'the physical, psychological, social, spiritual and existential' (2004: 8); Farber et al. comment on how social workers need to be 'consultants, collaborators and guides' to those private individuals newly caught up in the uncertainties of significant loss (2004: 115).

This text highlights the importance of the social worker as *a critical and reflective practitioner.* There are many definitions of this concept, certainly it incorporates the skills, theories, values and evidence base of our work and this text seeks to integrate, implicitly and explicitly, these aspects throughout. It also incorporates the all important elements of action and analysis and the need for practice to develop through a commitment to questionning of what we do and why rather than being defensive. Adams uses the phrases 'engaging with ourselves', 'engaging with knowledge', 'engaging with practice' and 'engaging with paradoxes and dilemmas in developing our own critical practice' to represent the various processes (2002). Fook suggests the phrase *critical reflection* to embed within practice:

> the intuition and artistry involved in professional practice ... the importance of context and interpretation in influencing action ... each person engages in a process of theory-building by reflecting on their own practice. What is also vital to a critical approach – which is not necessarily articulated in a reflective stance – is the *emancipatory* project, the capacity to analyse social situations and to transform social relations on the basis of this analysis (emphasis in the original) (1999: 201–2).

Telling Tales: Dramatic Tales of Loss, Death and Bereavement

The above discussions illustrate how our understandings of loss, death and bereavement cannot be captured in a neat turn of phrase. Perhaps we can be brought nearer to its essence by stepping back from the strictly professional arena and looking to literature and other cultural forms. Dinnage (1992) draws on poets such as Coleridge, Browning and Owen, Silverman (2004) turns to the classic images of Antigone by Sophocles and Michelangelo's Pietà while for many music is the compelling medium: funerals, cremations or memorials accompanied by hymns, selections from the great composers or more contemporary choices, such as 'I Did It My Way' and 'Knocking on Heaven's Door'. In Canada a university focuses entirely on novels and autobiographies by way of introducing palliative care to health students (Hall et al., 2006).

This medium has its limitations, of course. Freud notes the attraction of fiction and theatre as a way of fulfilling our need to 'find people who still know how to die ... . We satisfy our wish that life itself should be preserved as a serious stake in life.' Further, fiction offers us all a 'second chance ... We die with the hero: yet we survive him, and possibly die again, just as safely, with a second hero on another occasion' (Freud, 1915/1993). Modern commentators are also cautious. Gibson (2001) believes that cinematic death bed scenes can emotionally distance audiences while Davies comments that, for all our familiarity with death on the television and cinema screen, this 'is largely devoid of serious impact' (2005: 16) since it does not relate to intimate deaths of people close to us.

Nonetheless, such dramatic stories do serve an important role. Bettelheim, in his classic study of fairy stories, argues that they help the child 'make some coherent sense out of the turmoil of his feelings. He needs ideas on how to bring his inner house into order' (1991: 5). The following examples suggest that the stories, or narratives as they are increasingly termed, expressed in contemporary film, television and novels help bring order to the inner house of today's adults.

Scenes From Contemporary Dramas

Interestingly many successful British films use death as a powerful counterpoint to humour. *Four Weddings and A Funeral* (Newell, 1994) sets the funeral scene against the celebrations and portrays the depth and range of passion and pain which is felt by the various mourners: parents, friends, gay lover. *Love Actually* (Curtis, 2003) starts with scenes set in an airport, people hugging their greetings, as a contrast to all those who never arrived because on 9/11 their planes crashed into the twin towers, the lesson of their deaths is to love more. In *Calendar Girls* (Cole, 2003) a group of middle aged women pose nude as a charity stunt. Since this is also a memorial to a husband it shows, amid the humour, something of the obsessions of mourning and the disruption it can cause within friendship groups.

Death is a metaphor in more seriously intended, iconic, films such as *Field of Dreams* (Robinson, 1989) where legendary, and long dead, baseball players gather for one last game and assert the survival of American values as well as providing the opportunity for personal and political healing. Death comes as a climax in *One Flew Over the Cuckoo's Nest* (Forman, 1975) when Chief Bromden kills the rebel hero McMurphy, whom the mental hospital professionals have already mentally murdered by means of a lobotomy. Loss is represented not just in this death, it is there in the loss of liberty, either enforced since McMurphy is detained under an order, or surrendered, since most of the fellow patients are there in a voluntary capacity. Chief Bromden, a native American, is an elective mute, becoming voiceless when, despite the verbal protests of the elders, the tribe is forcibly moved to a reservation. Loss is played out on many levels in this story, as is the redemption in Bromden's escape to freedom.

A more prosaic style is chosen for the film *Last Orders* (Schepsi, 2002), based on the award winning Swift novel (1996) which follows the misadventures of a group of South London working-class men struggling with their own clumsy feelings about grief while following their dead friend's last request to have his ashes scattered into the sea. Mourning is portrayed in *Truly, Madly, Deeply* (Minghella, 1991), where the partner of a young woman, Nina, dies suddenly. This is, in some ways, a very realistic presentation of the pain of her loss, deeply felt in her counselling sessions and repressed in the face of the sheer ineptitude of family and friends who want to help but have no idea about how to reach her. The non-straightforward aspect lies in the way that Nina moves from the 'normal' sensing of the lover's continued presence around the home to his becoming a very real manifestation. They play, bicker and make love, much as they had before his death, until Nina escapes the thrall of this all too fleshy ghost and is ready to move on with another relationship.

This theme is played out more fully in television series. As I write the weekly schedules include repeats of *Six Feet Under* (Ball, 2001–2005), about a family business of undertakers, and two programmes featuring reluctant mediums, *Ghost Whisperers* (Fox, 2006) and *Afterlife* (Volk, 2005–2006) whose strap line is: 'You don't contact them, they contact you'. Similarly in the best selling novel *The Lovely Bones* (Sebold, 2002) the dead are as real as the living characters. Throughout these stories the dead are continually interfering, not always benevolently, in earthly events, offering wry comments and advice, like more modern and so acceptable versions of those voices that mediums provide at séances. Staying with séances, the novel *Beyond Black* (Mantel, 2005) is an always engaging story of a modern day sensitive.

Another important dimension is the impact of loss on those who are professionally involved. *Bringing Out The Dead* (Scorsese, 1999) is stark in the detail of a weekend night duty of a New York paramedic, Frank. The shift is fuelled by pizzas, blood, adrenaline and the urgent calls from the ambulance radio summoning him to the next crisis. Frank wants to save lives, in those moments it is as if 'God has passed through you ... God was you' but most of his time is as 'a grief mop', witnessing people's deaths, seeing 'the spirits leaving the body and not wanting to go back'. He comments that there are a lot of 'spirits angry at the awkward places death has left them'. One such spirit is Rosa, a young woman who collapsed and died on the sidewalk and who Frank now sees again on the faces of passing strangers, the homeless and the prostitutes. Rosa's face is reproachful, sometimes words go with the accusing stare and he hears her demand 'why did you kill me?' Frank finds no way to answer her.

The main character in the film *The Son's Room* (Moretti, 2001) is a psychotherapist and the film follows the impact upon him, personally and professionally, of the accidental death of his son. Apart from the seismic shifts within his family he is also put in a very different place with his clients as he contrasts his own trauma with what now appears to him as the lesser complaints of 'the walking wounded'. The film ends with him apparently abandoning his practice, the loss of his son entailing also the loss of his profession.

This discussion cannot ignore those books which are personal memoirs, or confessionals, which have proved immensely popular. A few examples include the accounts by Diamond (1998) and Picardie (1998), both dying from cancer, reflections by an orphaned son (Morrison, 1998) and a widowed wife (Didion, 2006), and Bayley (1999) and Grant (1998) on living with dementia in the family. These are difficult books, condemned by some as part of 'the sentimentalisaton of modern society' (Anderson and Mullen, 1998) and it does seem that many need these accounts, all by already established writers, to reflect back and give words to their own experiences.

Exercise 1.1

Impact of television, films or books on you?

1. Reflecting on a film, novel or television drama is there a particular scene that has stayed with you and helped you think differently about loss, death and bereavement?
2. How and why has this moved you?
3. Has the dramatic impact of death meant that less consideration is paid to other forms of loss?
4. These mainstream films and books reflect a variety of experiences but all are rooted within the white population. Can you think of more ethnically diverse examples and how different might these stories be?

The Scenarios

The stories above serve as an introduction to the discussion, those below are a bridge into the rest of the text for our central concern must be the experience of service users, represented through the scenarios, which are expanded upon in the subsequent chapters. There will be two major scenarios in each chapter, one relating specifically to death-related loss and one to loss in its wider context.

All the scenarios are based on real situations known to me personally or professionally or shared with me by colleagues but all identifying details have been changed to ensure confidentiality:

1. *Kuldip,* or Kay to her work colleagues, came to the UK from Pakistan as a child. Her mother was dead, her father a political exile. Now 38 and single, she looks after her sick father while also holding down a demanding job in publishing. She is Muslim, in cultural rather than religious terms, an identity she felt happy with until she felt the tensions around her grow after 9/11 and 7/7. Eight months ago she collapsed at work and despite many subsequent tests and examinations there is no clear diagnosis, just a viral infection, cause unknown.

2. *Marcia* is 17, is a bright young girl from a family not previously known to social services although there have been increasing concerns from school about her deteriorating standard of work. Marcia is now due to appear in court following her involvement, with a group of girls, in a series of violent, drink fuelled incidents. A year previously her father had died of throat cancer and she had been a primary carer. Her mother is a nurse and she has a younger brother.

3. *Mat,* 34, is in the terminal stages of an AIDS-related illness and *Douglas,* an ex-lover, moved back to be the primary carer. When Mat's mother, *Mary,* comes to the city where the couple live she insists that it is her role to look after her only son. Not previously knowing about Mat's sexuality she now refuses to accept that he is 'really' gay or that he is dying. Douglas, and other gay friends, are banned from the house and denied any role in planning the funeral.

4. *Lou,* 77, had been married to *George* for 59 years. He suffered from Alzheimer's Disease for ten years and Lou had been nursing him at home up to a few months ago when their children eventually persuaded her that he ought to go into hospital for an assessment. He died there very quickly. Lou now lives alone, is in ill health and isolated. Although her four children are in the area they are preoccupied with their own families.

5. *Susan* is 37, pregnant by her husband *Daniel* and with two daughters, *Denise,* aged 10 and, *Sarah,* 8, from an earlier relationship. Despite the pregnancy being difficult Susan has taken as much care of herself as she can manage. In hospital, however, the baby has to be delivered by a Caesarean operation and when Susan wakes up from the anaesthetic, in a side room on the maternity ward, she learns that her baby, a son, died shortly after birth.

6. *Lorraine* and *Michael* are in their early forties with an only child, *Wanda,* aged 12 who has Cystic Fibrosis. They try to be very positive

about Wanda, love her deeply but are becoming increasingly concerned as she becomes an adolescent and suddenly begins to resist the treatment vital for her continuing health. They wonder what life will hold for her and feel sad at what they fear she, and they, will miss out on.

7. *Dorothy* is 45, married with two sons in late adolescence and a husband, *Max*. They have just celebrated their 25th wedding anniversary. If asked to comment Dorothy describes herself as 'contented and conventional', 'at peace with myself after a difficult adolescence'. Quite unexpectedly she has heard from an agency that a son that she had when 15, who was then adopted, is now wanting to meet her.

8. *Peter* is 55, black British, living alone in the inner city. He is unemployed, apart from occasional cash-in-hand casual work. In his late adolescence, shortly after the sudden death of his father, he had a breakdown and was sectioned but has not been hospitalized for the last ten years. He feels his life has been wasted and his only comfort lies in his music and his sense of being a spiritual person.

9. *Sam* is 72, working class, described by neighbours as previously 'a well turned out, quite dapper gentleman' until six months ago when his wife, *Mavis*, died of lung cancer in the local hospice. He has children but they live out of the area. Sam is now wandering the streets, looks quite dishevelled and seems distressed but is unwilling to talk to anyone who approaches him.

Exercise 1.2

Your reactions to the scenarios

- Select the scenario that most impacts on you.
- Reflect on the impact of the losses on the individual(s) involved.
- Reflect on your own emotional and cognitive responses, first on a personal level, then as someone who could, potentially, be called upon to help professionally.

Understanding and Assessing Loss

Because these scenarios are so varied, although loss is a central motif, what emerges is a need for further clarity about how the phenomenon can be assessed. Practitioners and researchers have reached for some understanding and some of the key themes are outlined below.

Major Ways of Assessing Loss

- The nature of the attachment
- Sudden or anticipated death
- Traumatic bereavement
- Personality of the bereaved
- Life complicated by a crisis other than the bereavement
- Social factors
- Age
- Religious belief
- Unsupportive families
- Unsupportive communities
- Issues of diversity, disadvantage and discrimination such as race and gender

---

The nature of the attachment: as will be explored in Chapter 2, Bowlby (1991) reminds us how much flows from the part the deceased, or the other forms of loss, whether of employment, intimate relationship or country, played in the emotional well-being of the survivor.

Sudden or anticipated loss: anticipation can reduce the trauma of loss or bereavement (Parkes, 1980) while being unprepared can be 'a predicator of risk of psychological or physical disability' (Stroebe and Stroebe, 1987: 239). A loss needs to be integrated into an already *existing world-view*, allowing either a fatalistic acceptance or the need to 'gradually reformulate their (the bereaved's) view of the world to incorporate the event' (Wortman and Silver, 1989: 364).

Traumatic bereavement: a traumatic dying can cause angry and self-reproachful behaviour (Parkes, 1975, Raphael, 1977) while distress can be caused if religious funerary rituals, e.g. involving preparing the body, are ignored (Eisenbruch, 1984).

Personality of the bereaved: a grief reaction can highlight other problems in the individual's personality, reawakening feelings of *learned helplessness* (Seligman, 1992), previous patterns of relationships (Pincus, 1978) and losses (Bowlby, 1991, Marris, 1996), reactivating mental illness or addictions to alcohol or drugs (Worden, 1991).

Life complicated by a crisis other than the bereavement: various writers (Worden, 1991, Parkes, 1998) indicate clearly the degree to which loss may require difficult and sudden changes in life style, such as loss of income or moving home. This features often in the research of widows (Raphael, 1977; Van den Hoonaard, 2001).

Social factors: class allegiances, membership of religious groups or ethnic communities can provide guidelines and rituals to follow. Losses can seriously affect material circumstances, causing homelessness, poverty or other economic difficulties.

Age: the *young* bereaved often experience greatly increased physical distress and drug use for symptom relief (Parkes, 1975; Stroebe and Stroebe, 1987). Wortman and Silver (1989) suggest that the initial impact on younger spouses is greater but they recover more quickly than older widows/widowers. *Older people* are often assumed, because of their age, to have grown used to losses and deaths and are psychologically 'disengaging' from life. But these ageist attitudes 'mask the grief symptoms from the eyes of onlookers' (Barker, 1983: 15) and the ability to grieve 'may be lessened because of many losses in an abbreviated time period' (Worden, 1991: 128).

Religious belief: Stroebe and Stroebe see no evidence of religious belief helping individuals cope any better with their loss (1987: 218) but one third of the widows in Van den Hoonaard's study found that religion was very important, providing the comforts of both a personal faith in God and a 'powerful connection to the community and a church family' (2001: 123).

Unsupportive families: widows were clearly adversely effected when families were physically and/or psychologically unavailable (Parkes, 1975, Raphael, 1977) and mourners were restrained from expressing their feelings, especially negative ones (Barker, 1983).

Unsupportive communities: Young and Cullen refer to the need for the bereaved individual to draw on 'communal existence' (1996: 161), where the story of the death can be heard and 'human solidarity' offered (1996: 183). This reinforces the idea of grief as a 'social process' with the need of the community to come together to construct 'an enduring and shared memory of the dead' (Walter, 1996: 14).

Difference and Discrimination: the Need for Anti-discriminatory/ Anti-oppressive Practice

One of the distinctive qualities of contemporary social work is its open recognition of the divisions in society and the way that these impact on the way, firstly, that individuals become service users and, secondly, how we as professionals need to respond. There are quite profound problems, however, in how we phrase this understanding, whether we prefer the phrases 'ethnic sensitivity' and 'cultural competence' over 'anti-discriminatory practice' and then again whether this is synonymous with 'anti-oppressive practice'. There are sharp debates as to whether the major signifiers in a service user's experience come down to their gender or their ethnicity or their class or their age: questions that can face us with what has been called 'a hierarchy of oppressions'. The scenarios above will have touched on how these concerns can be felt when we work with loss, death and bereavement, the subsequent chapters will allow for a fuller exploration while the paragraphs below serve as a short introduction to the major themes.

Bereavement and Gender

Gender is an obvious issue when reflecting on loss, and immediately illustrates the difficulty in finding common ground. For the feminist writer, Cline, raising the subject of 'women, death and dying' 'breaks through our most sacred taboo' so hidden is the 'specific relationship women have to the dying process' (1995: 1). Walter makes an opposite point; it is not women's experiences which are peripheral but men's since most theories of grief are based on researching women, especially widows (1996: 21).

What does seem uncontroversial is that men and women tend to grieve differently. Riches researches bereaved parents, noticing the 'gendered patterning' of grieving (2002: 80) with women attending to the 'emotional labour' of grieving while men intellectualise their loss or take on practical tasks, trying to maintain continuity in their life, as the wage earner, or involved in loss related activities such as fund raising for cancer charities. Men/fathers who admit grieving express their emotions in private, with support groups, counselling sessions or visits to clairvoyants left to their female partners (2002: 85).

Cline reminds us of the cultural context for this: how, historically, tending for the dead and dying has been 'a communal and female event (undertaken by) traditional female specialists' (1995: 44) and that a socially constructed emphasis on women's caring and expressive roles is further reinforced by biology, the potential of pregnancy involving simultaneously a life growing in the womb and 'the spectre of death' which 'may be the core of women's perception of death from "inside"' (1995: 24). In today's society it may be that women have retained the caring role but without any of that community support, thus Young and Cullen's (1996) warning that where a patient is terminally ill the demands on the main carer, usually women, are considerable in terms of increased isolation and dependence on, and preoccupation with, the dying person.

Drawing on extensive research, Stroebe and Schut (1999) conclude that widowers are relatively worse off than widows, with higher rates of depression and other health consequences, including mortality rates.

Men's past dependency on their wives can then leave them socially and emotionally isolated. Research further suggests that men are more likely to see bereavement as a problem to be resolved by drawing on their own resources and thus 'turning ... to distracting activities' (Stroebe and Schut 1999: 86). This provides immediate relief but men are more likely to become depressed subsequently. Women are more immediately expressive, confronting their feelings, seeking out support but neglecting the other practical needs which also need addressing. Stroebe and Schut conclude that what is needed is 'a healthy mix of both male and female ways of coping, a confrontation and avoidance of both emotions and problems, an oscillation in attention to these dimensions' (1999: 86). Many social workers have come to see this *dual process model* as an enormously helpful way of working with the bereaved.

Bereavement and Race/Ethnicity

While gender is a widely acknowledged and debated aspect of loss, death and bereavement, there is far less material on race and ethnicity.

Stroebe and Stroebe, reviewing the research on health and risk factors in bereavement, are unable to reach any meaningful conclusions concerning ethnic differences given 'the limited evidence and the problems of interpretation' (1987: 191). This is a revealing comment and certainly race and ethnicity are more usually considered in terms of anthropological studies of distinct and often distant societies (Stroebe and Stroebe, 1987; Robben, 2004) or descriptions of different religious practices (Neuberger, 2004).

It is important that social workers remain alert to this gap in the knowledge and draw on what is known. Kalish and Reynolds suggest that 'Anglos' are more 'death-avoidant' and less in contact with the dying and with death than other ethnic groups (1981: 27). It does seem that minority communities are more likely to retain religious beliefs and cultural patterns that support the mourning process, the Irish wake, the Jewish shiva, the rituals in Islam and Hinduism, but acculturation and assimilation means that when influenced by the majority culture these customs fade. The novel *Disobedience* (Alderman, 2006) gives a poignant picture of the supportive process of mourning within an orthodox Jewish community and the disruptions caused to this by the return of the deceased rabbi's 'heathen' daughter. Grieving considered to be excessive by Eurocentric standards can also lead to inappropriate diagnosis by mental health professionals (Littlewood and Lipsedge, 1997) and Eisenbruch (1984) suggests the following questions that can increase professional understanding.

Ethnic and Cross Cultural Variations in the Development of Bereavement Practices (Based on Eisenbruch, 1984)

1. What is the individual's perception of the best way to die?
2. How does the individual perceive different types of death, for example, that of a child or a suicide?
3. What are the procedures involving the body of the deceased and any other burial rites?
4. Who are the principal mourners and how are they expected to behave, what is expected or prohibited in the days, weeks or months of the specified period of mourning or at anniversaries?
5. How might these practices be influenced or diluted by the expectations of the Western host society?
6. How is the dead person perceived in terms of their spirit, possessions?

Such aids can help social workers become more culturally competent, the term that is becoming increasingly common within health and social care. This is important for as Raiff and Shore remind us when writing on community care:

> Minority group members are latecomers to many different systems of care. They are less served by preventative services, more often routed to punitive, custodial settings and are more frequently ignored. They are ... invisible. (1993: 66)

And 'culture' does not just relate to different ethnic groupings. Returning to the scenarios it may be that 17-year-old Marcia whose father had died, Wanda who has Cystic Fibrosis and is on the edge of adolescence or the two young daughters of Susan, Denise and Sarah, just 10 and 8, whose half-brother is stillborn, may, for all their obvious differences, share a common experience of being young people confronting unanticipated losses with feelings that society is uncomfortable allowing them to express. Ageism may be apparent also at the opposite end of the spectrum in the experience of 77-year-old Lou.

There is a further layer when disability activists defy discussion that sees their situation as a deficit model compared to 'normal' people and so they make claim to a community that is based on a shared culture. Readers will be returned to these themes when we meet Kuldip, suddenly struck down by a virus, Mat and Douglas, caught up in the AIDS crisis and Peter, living with what has been termed an enduring mental health problem.

In all of these arenas it is important that the social worker is able to enter the world of the individuals concerned, to see what differences belong with the wider cultural expectations and the strengths this may bring in the face of adversity. This is the gift of *cultural competency*, 'a dynamic process of framing assumptions, knowledge and meanings from a culture different from our own' (Bartol and Richardson, 1998: 23) and we can never be complacent. As Gilroy reminds us, talking of the black communities but with, I suggest, wider implications: cultures are 'never fixed, finished or final. It is fluid, it is actively and continually made and re-made' (1992: 57). Desai and Bevan (2002) remind us also of the need for a wider perspective, one that recognizes how insidious and persistent racism eats away at an individual's sense of self-esteem and identity, leading to a cumulative sense of loss, alienation and exile. Holland (1992) suggests that 'loss' is too small a word in these circumstances, it is 'expropriation'.

This brings us then from working with 'difference', a relatively neutral term, to an appreciation of the wider dimension of discrimination and oppression, from understanding the diversity of people and groups to 'a focus on combating institutionalised discrimination in society, which represents the interests of powerful groups' (Payne, 2005: 269). Payne provides a full and careful history of what these terms mean in the context of social work and we are fortunate that we have theories and models that can integrate what may otherwise seem confusing or contradictory. Especially helpful is Thompson's PCS (personal, cultural, structural) model first presented in 2001 for a general social work audience and its applicability argued for loss in 2002.

Thompson's PCS Model (2001, 2002)

P stands for *personal* and it can be extended to *practice* and also to *psychological.* It focuses on the individual: feelings, attitudes and actions.

C is for *cultural,* those 'shared assumptions and meanings ... the framework of values, beliefs, codes and so on that become part of our individual and group identity' (2002: 10) so it further includes *community.*

(Continued)

(Continued)

S represents *structural,* the impact of society and the power relations embodied in the social divisions that include race, gender and class.

These are not either/or considerations but must be interrelated and offer a holistic overview.

Various contributors to the Thompson text (2002) specifically flesh out this model to help underpin their discussions of gender and race. I certainly encourage readers to return to Thompson and see how useful his ideas are in both their clarity and comprehensiveness. In this text I use the model implicitly rather than explicitly as the discussion moves through the psychological theories, mainly as it connects to the individual (Chapters 2 and 5) and then to wider social and cultural/collective considerations (Chapters 3 and 6).

I take up two main threads throughout this text to inform my understanding of *anti-discriminatory practice*. One of these is *disenfranchised grief*, recognizing and valuing those forms of losses that are often disregarded within the wider society. The other is *narrative* which builds on the conventional strengths of social work, namely to hear the story that the service user brings, but develops this to make it a more active process where the individual is helped to see that they do not just have a voice but that it is as equally, or even more, important than that of the professionals whose views are normally given more prominence. It seeks to help the individual become the subject, not the object, of their story. At times this perspective allows the individual to become part of a collective outside of their immediate family and community and to actually campaign and change aspects of their experience. The scenarios offer glimpses of this, whether it is challenging social workers removing children from their racial communities, on forcing medical systems to value and fully mourn stillbirths and developing forums where older people and service users can become involved in local and national advocacy groups. It is in these latter examples that I see the potential for *anti-oppressive work* and recognize that this normally arises from outside the profession rather than as a result of our own initiatives.

A Core Theme: 'Living Psychologically Beyond our Means'

The discussions above touch on a range of issues and, for all their brevity, do serve to indicate the many ways that 'grief ... adds a new dimension to a person's life' (Davies, 2005: 16). Indeed, the feelings can be of such power that Freud suggests that:

> In our civilized attitude to death we are living psychologically beyond our means … Would it not be better to give death the place in reality and in our thoughts that is its due and to give more prominence to the unconscious attitude towards death that we have hitherto so carefully suppressed? (1915/1993: 38)

By 'civilized' I understand Freud to mean all the ways that he saw people denying or sublimating the reality of death and, since he was speaking in the shadows of the killing fields of the First World War, he was probably reflecting on the gap between the images of brave soldiers going off to war and fighting heroically and the reality of boys dying horribly in the trenches or stretched out in no man's land. While such war torn contrasts are still with us, other 'suppressions' are revealed in our habitual ways of thinking and behaving. Whatever our feelings about the deceased we automatically refer to them as 'a loved one' and adhere to the old adage 'don't speak ill of the dead'. Many still say 'the c word' rather than 'cancer' and find euphemisms for AIDS while memorial notices describe people 'passing away' or 'gone to sleep' or dying after a 'brave fight'.

There are good reasons, of course, for this reluctance to look death in the eye. Latner talks of 'the terrible despair of mourning': we risk being close to another human then their death suddenly brings us into 'contact with emptiness. We look into the abyss' (1986: 67). We are also reminded of our own mortality which is a terrible puzzle for, as Becker reminds us, we each have 'a mind that soars out to speculate about atoms and infinity… At the same time man is a worm and food of worms. This is the paradox: he is out of nature and hopelessly in it' (1973: 26).

Even when we think we have reached some sort of peace with death and dying this can be revealed as most precarious. Deborah Hutton interviewed by a *Guardian* correspondent about her book (2005) offered advice on how people with terminal cancer, like herself, can be supported by friends and relatives:

> Halfway through … her husband interrupts to tell us that people are feared dead following bomb blasts. It means that her book launch … that evening will be cancelled … She doesn't react immediately, but later tells me that she savours life more than before her illness … 'I feel that each moment is exquisitely precious. I love the rain, I love the clouds, I love the sun. Each day feels like a gift, and of course it is. And now out of the blue, all those people who expected to have infinite time won't be going home this evening'. (the *Guardian*: (Jeffries, 2005) 12 July 2005)

Professionals, Helping or Hindering?

Professionals can also struggle in such existentially shocking situations, especially, perhaps, when we are expected to be 'the experts' at times when we feel as unsure as our service users. These feelings belong to a range of professions. Certainly in *medicine,* as shown in one person's experience following the onset of an increasingly serious and inexplicable paralysis:

> 'I don't want to alarm you ... there's nothing to be frightened of ... er ... you don't have to worry a wee bit ...'. He interrupted himself and turned to one of his colleagues. With words such as alarm, fear and worry thrown in one incomplete sentence, he could not have sought a more dramatic effect! He succeeded in doing precisely what he had been trying hard to prevent: he scared the living daylights out of me! (Laungani, 1992: 13)

Research studies highlight the way *counsellors* are perceived as discomforted and evasive when bereaved clients have tried to tell them about their sense of the continuing presence of the dead (Taylor, 2005) or want to share their spiritual beliefs (Danbury, 1996).

As *social workers,* we will have our own defence mechanisms. Grenier (2005) notes that, when undertaking risk assessments of older people, social workers seek to pin down all the uncertainties, of health, frailty, family support, but avoid confronting the one thing that is certain: the mortality faced by the service user. Perhaps this is linked to the frustration of social workers who:

> may seem, at first sight, to be useless in the face of such remorseless finality ... what the social worker might elsewhere attempt to achieve needs not so much to be reversed as set aside ... activity and optimism are not required but rather pain and sorrow, even despair ... have to be worked with. (Philpot, 1989: 11–12)

Cooper and Lousada relate this quite specifically to the increasing pressure for social work practice to be outcome-led which can lead to 'shallowness in welfare', an avoidance of 'difficult, painful, conflictual, affective work' (2005: 7). Yet our strength lies precisely in those moments when 'the suffering of the other connects to our suffering' (Browning, 2004: 29). If this is blocked, put out of our awareness in our daily practice, then social workers cannot be fully present to those who seek us out. Instead we hinder rather than help, seek to look after and reassure ourselves, not our client.

The Structure of This Book

Moving on from these broad themes, what follows are summaries of the chapters to show how the discussion will be developed.

Chapter 2, Psychological Theories, explores the internal, or intrapersonal dimensions of individuals who have experienced loss and how this is categorized: physical/practical, symbolic, psychosocial and with special emphasis on disenfranchised loss. Links are made with the case work tradition within social work. The key theoretical traditions are identified as psychoanalytical; loss and attachment; existentialism and the humanistic school represented by gestalt and their competing and complementary perspectives are explored through their insights into the perceived potency of death and other significant forms of loss, consequently the importance of separating the living from the dead and how the process of separation is posed in terms of the 'stages' and 'tasks' of 'normal' and 'abnormal' mourning. And there is the significance of staying with the intensity of loss and the importance of 'continuing bonds', of 're-membering' rather than dismembering. The case scenarios of *Marcia* and *Kuldip/Kay* are featured,

There is always an interplay between the intrapersonal and interpersonal since feelings are both timeless and rooted in the changing attitudes of the wider society and Chapter 3 looks at the social and cultural dimensions whether this is 'death denying' (Ariès, 1981) or a period of witnessing 'the revival' or 'resurrection of death' (Dickinson, 2005; Walter, 2005). Essential to this is today's cultural currency of the 'Good Death' and the contradictory nature of this is illustrated through *Sam*, whose wife's death from cancer confronts him, on many levels, with the stories people tell about dying and how he finds his own voice. The importance of narrative is continued in the scenario of *Dorothy*, who is sought out by the son she placed for adoption which highlights how the changes in our view of children and parenting touches individuals and whole communities.

Chapter 4, Social Work Values, focuses on the social work values as they relate to loss, death and bereavement. On the surface, and as expressed in the GSCC Codes of Practice (2002), these seem uncontroversial, nonetheless our values systems, on personal, cultural and professional levels may bring us into conflict situations, not just with our agencies and service users but within ourselves. This chapter explores these dilemmas, as linked to the changing value systems within the profession.

Two themes are identified. The first, *support versus surveillance*, is looked at through the case scenario of Susan and her family, and the *death of a baby through a stillbirth*. The second, *outcomes versus process*, is seen in the context of *life limiting* and *chronic illness*, specifically Wanda, a child with Cystic Fibrosis.

In Chapter 5, Social Work Skills, Methods and Theories in Work with Individuals, we acknowledge the growing repertoire of theories and interventions open to social workers in working with individuals. These are discused through the case scenarios of *Lou,* whose now dead husband had Alzheimer's Disease and *Peter* who has enduring mental health problems.

Core issues for social workers are addressed with a special emphasis on assessment, drawing on earlier discussions concerning how we understand loss and ways of working is explored through cognitive behavioural approaches and working with the sense of the self, drawing on psychodynamic concepts. The discussion returns us to the two key themes of the text, the use of narrative and its usefulness in helping us understand the dynamics of disenfranchised loss.

Chapter 6, Social Work Skills, Methods and Theories in Work with Families, Groups and the Wider Community, continues the emphasis on social work skills and consolidates the learning from previous chapters. The discussion moves from the focus on the individual per se to the wider world they inhabit: family, groups and the wider communities. These are illustrated through previously presented scenarios. The tasks and skills of working with families are explored both through the direct work with the whole family where there has been a stillbirth (Susan, Daniel and the daughters) and the indirect work where an individual service user (Marcia) brings to the social worker's office her experience of her family. The potential of group work is explored through Wanda and her parents as they struggle with a life limiting illness. Working with communities is expanded through the experiences of Lou, an older woman who is widowed and is now finding a new place for herself in the wider world.

Chapter 7, The Evidence Base, continues the focus on the reflective practitioner through a consideration of the nature of *evidence* and *research mindedness,* how we can unknow what we think we know, to 'make strange what is utterly familiar' (Reimann, 2005: 90). The chapter examines the competing and complementary arguments about qualitative versus quantitative research, wondering if territorial disputes are actually necessary. The discussion returns to various studies cited in the text, posing questions about methodology, problems and potential and the researcher's value base and also using a particular approach, 'narrative theory' as a case study of how research can nourish the development of new ideas. Finally this writer introduces some of his own work, a small scale study originally focused on the effectiveness of bereavement counselling, to unpack the research process.

Finally, Chapter 8, Social Workers within our Agencies: the Need for 'Relentless Self-care' looks at the degree to which our employing agencies struggle to support and offer containment to their workers. This discussion builds on the insights of Menzies Lyth (1959/1988) into how a hospital sought, and failed, to defend nurses against anxiety, and relates this to social work's experience of stress, and how this relates to the fear of feeling deep within the culture of modern state welfare (Cooper and Lousada, 2005). The concept of relentless self-care (Renzenbrick, 2004) is adopted and linked to how this might be found within our organizational, professional and personal support systems. Emphasis is given to the importance of supervision and 'the seven eyed model' developed by Hawkins and Shohet (2006) is followed. The chapter ends by revisiting the scenarios and advocating the place of hope in our work.

In concluding this chapter I want to acknowledge the contribution made by previous and present generations of students who have helped shape my views, those peers who have responded to my papers and conference presentations (sections of which have been refined and represented here) and the social workers, practitioners, managers and academics, from a range of settings, who have shared their thoughts, skills and feelings around this work. Above all, thanks to those service users whose stories, implicitly or explicitly, contribute to this study, especially those who did not fit readily into any 'category', those:

> who do not fit our formulae and patterns, the ones who fight us and make life difficult for us. Let us count our blessings for making mistakes, for these are the moments when we get thrown back into chaos and disarray, when we lose our foothold and are forced to stretch beyond already acquired knowledge and insight. (Duerzen-Smith, 1995: 45)

Points for practice

- Most service users that social workers encounter have to deal with loss in some form or another.
- They may have lost a loved one or they may have lost their job, home status, physical or mental health, parents, or child/ren – not necessarily through death but through misfortune.

(Continued)

(Continued)

- Social workers must therefore be aware of the social and emotional impact of loss and help service users understand how this has affected them and what they need in the way of support.
- Responses to loss are not just experienced internally but will be shaped by the wider society.
- Suggestions might include helping the person to talk about feelings of loss such as anger or grief, linking the person with others who have suffered similar loss, helping the person to maintain positive memories if the loss is of a loved one.

2 Psychological Theories

Chapter contents

- The ways that losses are defined
- The core psychological theories
- What is meant by 'normal' and 'abnormal' grief
- How theories relate specifically to death-related loss and to loss in all its aspects
- The move from the intrapersonal to the interpersonal

Introduction

This chapter builds on the discussion initiated in the Introduction, drawing out the psychological theories as they relate to the internal, or intrapersonal world of individuals who have experienced loss. There is a description of how loss is categorized, such as physical/practical, symbolic, psychosocial and with special emphasis on disenfranchised loss.

Links are made with the case work tradition within social work. The key theoretical traditions are identified as psychoanalysis; loss and attachment; existentialism and the humanistic school represented by gestalt. Their competing and complementary perspectives are explored through their insights into the perceived potency of death and other significant forms of loss, consequently the importance of separating the living from the dead and how the process of separation is posed in terms of the 'stages' and 'tasks' of 'normal' and 'abnormal' mourning. And there is the significance of staying with the intensity of loss and the importance of 'continuing bonds', of 're-membering' rather than dismembering.

The case scenarios of *Marcia* and *Kuldip/Kay* are featured.

Loss as a Generic and Deeply Personal Term

The ways we respond to those who have had a loss are very telling. After a death, there might be the all encompassing 'I am sorry for your loss', emphasising empathy while, at Jewish funerals, the phrase, 'I wish you long life', carefully contrasts the end of one life with the need for the mourners to focus on their own continuing lives. This echoes the expression, 'May your life be spared', heard at Sunni Muslim funerals in Turkey (Gork, 2006) while the words of comfort at an Iraqi funeral have a different resonance, 'May their life come into yours' (McCarthy, 2006), suggesting instead the wish for 'continuing bonds'. These different attitudes will be explored shortly.

Another indicator of wider attitudes are to be seen in greeting cards, not just for bereavements but increasingly for other events such as moving home and divorce. In these latter examples the emphasis tends to be remorselessly positive, offering hopes for a happy future rather than dwelling too much on the past. Cards marking a retirement or a move to a new job stress the loss to those still left behind and offer congratulations to the person moving on. Printed pictures and verses are not available for other, less obvious or difficult to acknowledge situations, consequently there are cards for successful exam results but not for students who fail. Zinner (2002) calls this 'the Hallmark test', if this trademark firm does not market a card for the occasion then this cannot be deemed a legitimate loss.

'Loss' is, then, both a generic term and a deeply personal one, as can be seen from the scenarios offered in the introduction and the comments above. Its definitions cover a complex range of circumstances so, not surprisingly, as social work professionals and members of a wider society, we struggle to find not just a string of words that can rise to the occasion but to understand its whole process.

Categorizing Loss

One strategy is to measure the various components of loss, thus the continuing popularity of the *social readjustment rating scale* which allocates various Life Crisis Units to specific events. On a scale of 1–100, a child leaving home scores 29, loss of a job, 47, the death of a marital partner, 100 (with no reference to a non-marital partner) compared to 63 for the death of a close family member and 37 for that of a close friend. Although this scale is widely available on the net there are rare references to the fact that it was compiled nearly 40 years ago and the scales based on the very specific responses of US servicemen (Holmes and Rahe, 1967). Payne et al. offer a fuller critique of the 'stress' model (1999: 33–9).

Loss can be felt on an *existential* plane with the shattering of dreams or illusions of hope, safety and purpose, echoed in Freud's moving reflections on how the death of his grandson left him profoundly sad, mourning that specific child and all children to the degree that he was 'indifferent' even to his own impending death from cancer (cited in Silverman and Klass, 1996: 7). For many the sudden, bloody eruption of the bombs on a London Underground train or the natural disasters of flood or fire destroy more than lives and structures but also the previously assumed solidity of daily life and one's core sense of self.

Psychosocial grief is for losses that directly impact on the individual's role and status in the social world, such as the process of exile, retirement or redundancy, examples described and discussed more fully below.

Some losses have the opportunity for public recognition, others may be invisible to and unacknowledged by the wider society or even by the individual concerned; this is *disenfranchised* grief (Doka: 2002).

Examples of Disenfranchised Grief

Lou is told by her son that she should be less upset by her husband's death, because of his Alzheimer's Disease 'he hadn't recognized any of us for years, he wasn't the dad we knew'. She should get over it and try to get out and about.

Susan is told by friends that 'there is no point in dwelling on things', she should just 'try for another baby' as quickly as possible. Daniel, the father, is locked away in a depression and cannot bear to talk and the children are assumed not to be affected. The baby's ashes are in a cupboard at home awaiting a decision as to what to do with them.

Douglas is banished from his ex-lover's home, not allowed to care for Mat or to have any role in the pending funeral since the mother now has primary mourner status. The fact that Mat is dying, and what he is dying from, AIDS, is not allowed to be spoken out loud in front of Mat.

Other losses are *ambiguous*, occurring in situations where an individual 'ought' to be celebrating an occasion, a birth or a marriage or a new job and instead they are surprised by feelings of anti-climax linked to disallowed feelings of loss in the passing of previous status and skills. The standard response about 'losing a loved one' can be a caricature of the authentic feelings. Imagine a father who sexually abused the daughter who is now expected to be distressed at his death.

And some are *necessary* losses, perhaps linked to developmental stages, such as puberty or retirement or the death of a parent and these are useful, transformational even, in their inevitability and necessity 'because we grow by losing and leaving and letting go' (Viorst, 1987: 3).

Exercise 2.1

Understanding your own losses

- Write a list of losses that you have experienced.
- Check your losses against some of the other terms referred to above, 'disenfranchised', 'ambiguous' or 'necessary' etc.
- Are these categories helpful?

Now consider the following case scenarios

Marcia, a Bereaved Daughter

Marcia is 17, with a younger brother, Carl, aged 14. Her mother is a nurse and her father had been a fire fighter who died the previous year from throat cancer. The family has not previously been known to social services although the school, having seen Marcia as bright and expected to go to university, comment on her deteriorating work. Marcia is due to appear in court following a Saturday night of violent, drink fuelled incidents with a group of friends.

Marcia readily admits the offences, also similar 'tantrums' directed mainly at her mother who just 'goes on at me all the time, for watching too much television, smoking, not doing my homework, having the wrong friends, for everything'. She reacts to the forthcoming court appearance with a mixture of defiance and fear.

Talking about her family she says her parents were devoted but fought all the time, mainly about her father's heavy drinking. She recalls huddling together with her brother listening to their nightly fights and, on one occasion, after he had hit her mother, she, aged 12, ordered her father out the house and bolted the door behind him. When she was 15 he did leave, and her relationship with him begun to improve. After

(Continued)

(Continued)

contracting cancer he moved back in to be cared for by Marcia and her mother. Carl refused to be involved. She describes how her mother, as a nurse, prepared her, step-by-step, for the illness and then his dying.

Immediately after the death her mother sent her to bereavement counselling but she refused to return after the first session. Talking now to the social worker a constant reference point is 'my dad's death'. She describes how, being so rehearsed in preparing for his death, she was left with no space 'to do it my way'. She is angry that having just started to get to know and love her dad she loses him again to his illness. But she shrugs off the sacrifice of caring for him, losing her old friends and getting in with a new crowd, risking a criminal record and the chances of getting to university.

Kuldip/Kay, Newly Disabled

Kuldip, 38, came as a child to the UK from Pakistan. Her mother was dead and her father a political exile. Kuldip did well at school and when she left university she entered publishing where she is successful but this has come at a price; it is a highly competitive world and a merger with another company is likely. When she allows herself some space to think Kuldip is worried about her future. 'I'm a woman, and an Asian woman, so I've got to work twice as hard as anyone else if I'm to survive, three times as hard to get promotion.'

Kuldip is single, she jokes that she is married to the job and she also looks after her father, aged 68, who never fully recovered from a period in prison in Pakistan. There are two younger brothers but they have their own families so she has always assumed the primary carer role.

Kuldip is a Muslim but sees this more in terms of identity than religion. She had never considered this a problem at work: she fitted in, told her colleagues to call her 'Kay' because 'it's easier for them to say'. When she went socializing she did drink; it was easier than trying to explain that it was against her religion.

(Continued)

(Continued)

Things became more difficult after 9/11, and then the 7/7 London bombings, 'not that anyone said anything directly but the mood got tense, people went quiet around me, I knew I was being blamed'.

Eight months ago, Kuldip started having bad headaches, occasional dizzy spells and some numbness in her hands. She knew she ought to visit her local GP group practice to check out her symptoms but 'never had the time'. She then collapsed at work, her legs gave way, her arms went into spasm. Despite lengthy periods in hospital, many tests and examinations by various consultants Kuldip is no clearer as to a diagnosis. It is some sort of viral infection, cause unknown but similar in its effect to multiple sclerosis. Her medical condition is subject to some variations but she is currently wheel chair bound, and has little control over her hands. The medical prognosis is that while she may not get any worse neither do they expect much improvement. Kuldip is currently on long-term sick leave.

Exercise 2.2

Understanding Marcia and Kuldip's losses

- List the losses Marcia and Kuldip have experienced.
- Now list these under the headings, physical/practical, psychosocial/symbolic.
- Are these categories helpful?
- Check their losses against some of the other terms referred to above, 'disenfranchised', 'invisible', 'ambiguous' or 'necessary'.
- Are these categories helpful?

Possible Responses to Marcia and Kuldip/Kay

For Marcia, *caring* for her father entailed *physical and practical losses* leaving her less time for her own interests, going out with friends, school work etc. Now it is more *psychosocial/symbolic*, she has lost her father but also her mother in that they became

(Continued)

(Continued)

almost sisterly during the illness and now Marcia is not letting her mother back into her parental role. She has lost the sibling she does have, Carl. She is in danger of losing her early promise of educational success. Her losses are *disenfranchised* in that the rest of her family wants, apparently, to move on. Being 'sent' to counselling may have conveyed the message: 'don't talk about it here' so she acts out her distress in other ways, or holds it for the family. Her loss may be *ambiguous* in that she had very mixed feelings about her father and these were put on hold during the period of physical, but not necessarily, emotional intimacy with him. The loss is *necessary* in that it is expected that parents die before children but Marcia is young, she still needs her father.

For Kuldip the *practical/physical* seems paramount, focusing on getting a diagnosis, managing finances, negotiating with her workplace. The *psychosocial/symbolic* lies in her history, trying to prove to those around her that she can do well, justifying herself as an only daughter to her father, to the Muslim community as a woman, to the white community as an Asian immigrant. The fact that the illness is unnamed suggests it is *invisible* to the doctors, even *disenfranchised* if there are thoughts that it is a psychosomatic, phantom condition. There may be a level of *ambiguity,* it is threatening to Kuldip's career and it provides some relief in taking her out of an intolerable work situation.

The Psychoanalytical/Casework Tradition in Social Work

What is clear is the degree to which the physical/practical and the psychosocial/symbolic aspects of loss are complementary but this may go relatively unrecognized when traditional thinking about loss and bereavement emphasizes Freudian ideas about the intrapsychic life of the individual. This is especially important for social workers given the role of psychoanalytically influenced *casework* in the origins of the profession (Biestek, 1961, Hollis, 1964), focusing on the importance of the worker–client relationship, work with individuals and a psychodynamic understanding of human behaviour.

The degree to which this influence continued within social work is represented by the Barclay Report (1982) inquiring into the role and tasks of social workers and which included counselling, loosely defined as any personal contact with individuals, as a core component, alongside social care planning. Pinker's Minority Report in that same document stressed that social work's survival depended on the essential element of work with individuals and families via 'professionalised casework'. A decade on Lousada defended the profession against a rising tide of outcome based core assessment forms and the overriding expectations of other, more powerful disciplines, such as medicine. His argument, that psychodynamic work with the individual, their family and the immediate environment is 'the heart of social work' (1993: 105), is echoed in Statham's advocacy for the 're-emergence of relationship and process in social work' (1996, cited in Seden, 1999: 141) and the championing by the London based Tavistock Clinic and the *Journal of Social Work Practice*, of 'relationship based social work'. Psychoanalytical based concepts have made deep inroads into social work through Bowlby's attachment theory, subsequently developed by others, such as Marris (1974, 1996), to incorporate a more societal dimension.

Other approaches have been important within social work in terms of counselling skills, e.g. Rogers' person centred model (1951, 1961), but this makes no specific contribution to debates around loss and bereavement. Nevertheless, references can be found within the broadly humanistic tradition, in Yalom's existentialism (1980) and in modern variations of gestalt therapy.

As a way of identifying the differences and the commonalties between the different schools for understanding loss, death and bereavement, the following discussion focuses on five main themes:

1 The Potency of Death and Other Significant Forms of Loss

Perhaps the most striking aspect of 'death' is its absence from many of the psychological theories outside of Freudian psychoanalysis, while 'loss' is so pervasive that its distinctiveness is in danger of being diffused.

In the *person centred approach* of Rogers his key texts (1951,1961) make no mention of 'death' and 'mourning' which is, perhaps, not surprising given his statement in one of his later works, that 'I think little about death ... The current popular interest in it surprises me' (1980: 49). Staying within the *humanistic tradition,* gestalt is relatively silent. For Perls, 'death' is a metaphor (1969: 55–6) for the process of discovering, through therapy, new ways of being, thus 'death', or 'the fear of death' is the ultimate layer in the neurotic character structure where can be found the true and basic animal anxieties through which we discover our 'authentic self'. Another gestalt writer, Latner, faces death more centrally when he uses such phrases as 'looking into the abyss' and 'the terrible despair of mourning ... (where) the contact we have opened ourselves up to is suddenly a contact with emptiness. We look into the abyss and we become filled with grief and loss' (1986: 67). But there is no further analysis, indeed he cautions against raising 'questions about the meaning or worth of our living ... Our questioning interferes with the awareness of our present existence ... replacing the flow of the dialectic with preconceptions' (1986: 60–1).

This is not say that those trained within these models cannot work well with loss and bereavement, see McLaren (2005) as an example of a skilled Rogerian, person centred counsellor and Zinker, a gestalt therapist, and his work with a bereaved family (1994) but they do so without explicit guidance from the main body of theory.

Psychoanalysis is a real contrast given Freud's willingness to engage with the issues. Nonetheless his contribution is problematic since, in the course of his extensive writings, he can be contradictory, a tendency exaggerated as each generation picks from Freud what they need to reflect and reinforce their own views (Richards, 1989). Traditionally Freud has been identified with the case for 'breaking the bonds', linked to his warnings against the seductive power of death, but a new generation of writers are finding within the texts Freud's argument for 'continuing bonds' (Klass et al., 1996). This is discussed more fully below.

To explore Freud we need to start with 'Mourning and Melancholia' (1917/1984). Although Freud's prime interest is in 'melancholia', as a form of obsessional neurosis, the essay is important in that it is 'the first time mourning became an object of scientific investigation' (Spiegel, 1977: 29). His preoccupation with death was also provoked, as was noted in the Introduction, by the First World War which prompted the comment that in reflecting on death we are 'living psychologically beyond our means' (1915/1993: 38). In this lecture for lay people he argues that essentially individuals seek to deny emotionally the reality of their own mortality. If death comes it is the fault of others, or the inevitability of our own death is put off to the unforeseeable future or the terror of death is mediated by the invention of the soul, spirits and heaven.

Freud also developed the concept of The Death Instinct, or Thanatos, a sort of internal drive or biological self-destructive tendency, *'an urge inherent in organic life to restore an earlier state of things'* (emphasis in the original) (1920/1984: 308) and as illustrated in the Oedipus complex, the violence against the father repressed through fear of retaliation and ambivalence. Essentially '(T)he Death Instinct becomes part of the psyche set against itself' (Jones, 1957: 295).

An element of caution is needed here. Freud admits that he is 'throwing out a line of thought' (Freud, 1920/1984: 332) and the Death Instinct is never seen as having a phenomenological basis, instead it 'operated quietly within the individual ... not obvious even to psychoanalytical investigation' (Greenberg and Mitchell, 1983: 62) while, of his significant successors, only Klein takes the idea further. It does, nevertheless, continue to exert influence in the popular term 'death wish', the poet Philip Larkin notes that 'Beneath it all, desire of oblivion runs' (1988) while *Corpse Bride* (Burton, 2005) is not a straight to video horror film but rather a tapping into European folklore in its story of the Land of the Dead which is so much more vibrant than the world above the ground.

Returning to service-users, individuals might present as unduly fascinated with death, thus the term *microsuicide* to describe those whose drug or alcohol dependence takes them to the point of endangering their lives, or who present as physically or emotionally withdrawn from life (Firestone and Seiden, 1987).

Examples of the Death Instinct or Miscrosuicide

From the 'Talking cure' television documentaries.
Psychoanalyst working with bereaved parents:
Therapist addressing the father: I feel you're almost dedicated to the idea that this is your life now, now that Paul's gone. You are the man who's lost Paul, the father who's lost Paul. And you can't see a future that holds anything else, other than that ... I don't want Mr Green to put himself in the tomb with Paul (Holgate: 1999).

Society invents a spurious convoluted logic tae absorb and change people (who want tae use smack). The fact is ye jist simply choose tae reject whit they huv to offer. Choose us. Choose life. Choose mortgage payments; choose washing machines; ... choose rotting away, pishing and shiting yersel in a home, a total fucking embarrassment tae the selfish fucked-up brats ye've produced. Choose life. Well, ah choose no tae choose life. If the cunts cannae handle that, it's their fucking problem' (*Trainspotting*, Welsh, 1993: 187–8).

Exercise 2.3

Understanding the 'Death Instinct' in your life

- What do the terms the 'Death Instinct' or 'microsuicide' mean to you?
- Do you see it reflected in any aspect of your life, or that of your family, friends or wider community networks?
- Do you recognize it in any aspect of Kuldip or Marcia and their responses to their circumstances?

2 The Importance of Separating the Living From the Dead

If death is this alluring then it is imperative that we separate ourselves from the dead, and the rituals associated with religious beliefs often do precisely this, acknowledging, to the bereaved and to the wider society, an important rite of passage and, as communal events, countering the generally isolated and privatized sense of much modern living. They further indicate the degree to which both the bereaved and the deceased are betwixt and between:

> The dead are no longer alive, nor wholly passed over into the land of the dead; the bereaved are likewise caught between the worlds of the living and that of the dead ... (the) rituals move both the deceased and the bereaved into, through and beyond the marginal state. (Walter, 1999: 28)

Freud stresses the degree to which, in mourning, 'each single one of the memories and situations of expectancy which demonstrates the libido's attachment to the lost object is met by the verdict of the reality that the object no longer exists' (Freud, 1917/1984: 265). Bereavement is slow and painful, marked by ambivalent feelings as the individual struggles with the tension between separation and attachment, the mourner having to see what is 'other' about the person who died, the deceased is 'object' rather than part of the self of the mourner. Following this, those who work professionally with bereavement have a particular goal: the recognition of loss and the emotional detachment from the dead person.

Generally mourning is not regarded as pathological since it is assumed to pass or diminish with time and indeed 'any interference with it (would be regarded) as useless or even harmful' (Freud, 1917/1984: 252). And we may prove 'reluctant mourners' (Richards, 1989: 39), prepared to stay with the initial, totally self-absorbing experience and resist moving on. Indeed so intense can this be that mourners continue to see, hear and otherwise experience the dead, a form of 'hallucinatory wishful psychosis' (Freud, 1917/1984: 253).

Although Freudian theory is an important strand within social work Bowlby and attachment theory probably provides a more recognizable form of psychoanalytical ideas. Bowlby turns away from Freud's 'drive' theory, with its perceived reduction of human needs to biological urges such as sex. Instead, drawing on what he witnessed of children's trauma at the loss of a parent, he puts at the heart of our lives the paradox that we need, for our safety and security, to develop strong affectional bonds with others, but the stronger these bonds the more painful it is when they are broken, by any significant loss and ultimately death itself (Bowlby, 1991). He also reasserted the concept of mourning as being less an individualized crisis or illness than a normal part of the life cycle (Silverman, 2004).

Bowlby's strength lies in the sheer detail of his writing and the range of theories he draws upon, such as developmental biology and cognitive psychology. On reflecting on our losses in adult life he sees the persistence of our earliest attachments; how the pattern of protest, despair, yearning, apathy and detachment that follows a baby's separation from a parent figure can be reactivated and presented in full force in adult loss. The ability of the adult to cope with attachment in intimate relationships, to negotiate independence, dependency and interdependency, and to manage loss is all about how successfully they coped with separation as an infant or child. As a baby they had to retain their sense of their mother even in her absence and now again, as part of the mourning process, they strengthen their own identity with the support of the internalized object.

The importance of early trauma and its resolution is reinforced by Erikson's (1965) examination of early developmental crisis, trust vs. mistrust, and by Miller's insistence on the importance for children of being allowed to freely express all their emotions otherwise '(T)he denied trauma is a wound that can never form a scar and which can at any time begin to bleed again' (cited in Leick and Davidsen-Nielsen, 1991: 15). Bowlby, however, is not unduly deterministic since, in his view, even persistent patterns of behaviour can also 'remain sensitive in some degree to later experience and, as a result, can change either in a more favourable direction, or in an even less favourable one' (1991: 217–18).

Other writers have valued attachment theory for its *psychosocial dimension*, recognizing the potential for attachment anxiety in any situation that involves changes in the individual's role and status in the world, such as divorce, deterioration in physical and/or mental capacities and any group loss, especially perhaps within and inflicted upon minority communities (Eisenbruch, 1984). It challenges our *assumptive world*, those habitual, unconscious ways that we live our lives, structure our thoughts, feelings and actions. When a major change occurs we confront 'a host of discrepancies between our internal world and the world that now exists for us' (Parkes, 1998: 91).

Marris describes the *conservatism* that is at the heart of the individual's struggle with the pain of loss despite, on a conscious level, desiring change. This is the 'impulse to defend the predictability of life (which) is a fundamental and universal principle of human psychology' (1974: 2). For him the key period is childhood, that point at which:

> we attach meaning to the things and people about us. We transfer experience from one situation to another, perceived to be essentially alike, and so the circumstances of life become increasingly manageable, as more and more of them can be put into familiar categories ... We survive partly because we impose one meaning with great determination, if need be contradicting facts which to others seem obvious ... it is slow, painful and difficult for an adult to reconstruct a radically different way of seeing life, however needlessly miserable his preconceptions make him. (1974: 8–9)

Marris (1974), exploring such losses as slum clearance, decolonization, entering higher education as well as death, reminds us that uncertainty is present throughout our lives and it is also subject to a process of subordination and marginalization. 'The social control of uncertainty is competitive, often protecting the more powerful at the cost of greater uncertainties for the less powerful' (Marris, 1996: 81). One example he cites is the factory closure where the worker, despite being a model employee, is made unemployed while the manager is promoted and moved to another job. Consequently one group sees the world as 'understandable and manipulable, and their ambitions are enriched by their confidence' while the others see themselves:

> governed by remote and largely unintelligible systems over which they have no control, and the meaning of their life is correspondingly narrowed by their vulnerability ... the range of choices open to them is so narrow and so insecure that sustaining any worthwhile purpose is a constant anxiety. (1996: 87)

Exercise 2.4

Attachment patterns in Marcia and Kuldip's lives

- Referring back to the case studies what might be the attachment patterns of Marcia and Kuldip?
- How might this be impacting on the way they are managing their loss?
- What are the aspects of their assumptive world that they are reluctant to relinquish?

Possible Responses

Marcia's attachment patterns appear complex. With the domestic arguments she steps in to protect her mother, then, just as she was about to establish a father/daughter relationship she has to again parent her parent. Her attachment to her brother is cut across by whatever is going on for him. Her original friends are lost during her preoccupation with her father's dying. She has learnt that the world is arbitrary and unsafe: parents do not protect, violence can occur at any point, terminal illness comes out of nowhere so there is relief in the new friendship group which bonds so easily around a drunken night out and makes no demands on her.

Kuldip has lost many of her early attachments, to her homeland and her mother. Her attachment to her father has been a caring one but now her own disability puts this at risk. She has worked hard to make attachments at work but real friendships are not possible given the fierce competition. Kuldip, in the highly charged post 9/11 political atmosphere, is also not sure how to square her attachment to her country and to her religion. Her work, her home and her health all seem vulnerable.

We do not know anything about Marcia or Kuldip as babies but attachment issues seem significant and offer us insights into what might be going on.

3 The Process of Separation: the 'Stages' and 'Tasks' of 'Normal' and 'Abnormal' Mourning

It s perhaps inevitable that when constructing patterns about how people respond this is linked to ideas of what is *normal* and *abnormal* when, in terms often applied to mourning, someone should *reach closure* or *resolve* their grief. The phrase *dysfunctional* is often used despite systems theory (see discussion in Chapter 6) helping us to understand how even what appears initially as the most strange behaviour serves a purpose. But for the moment this discussion stays with ideas of normal/abnormal, because such formulations are part of 'the common sense' of how people frame the world around them.

The concept of 'normal/abnormal' grieving originates in the large-scale research conducted by Lindemann (1944) into the reactions of those who had lost a family member in a nightclub fire. He detected certain pathognomic characteristics of normal or acute grief:

- Somatic or bodily distress of some type.
- Preoccupation with the image of the dead.
- Guilt relating to the deceased or the circumstances of the death.
- Feelings of anger and hostility.
- Inability to carry on functioning after the loss.

Worden's (1991) highly influential text follows this line of thinking in his 'four tasks' model, which is also explicitly faithful to Freudian based ideas about 'breaking the bonds':

1. To accept the reality of the loss.
2. To work through the pain of grief.
3. To adjust to an environment in which the deceased is missing.
4. To emotionally relocate to an environment in which the deceased is missing.

The first task is *to accept the reality of the loss,* cognitively and emotionally, which counters the common, initial response of disbelief that someone has died, even where it might 'reasonably' be anticipated, for example, in the case of terminal illness. Indicators of 'denial' may include the persistent belief that the deceased is still present and they are glimpsed in the street or heard around the house: Queen Victoria is often remembered for laying out the clothes and shaving cream for her long-dead husband or a child is seen to be 'just like' someone who had died so that the deceased is immortalized. Worden recognizes that these are protective mechanisms and names them 'wish fulfillment', 'distortion', 'delusion' (1991: 11).

Next is the need *to work through to the pain of grief,* individuals are suffering physically and emotionally but, for reasons of personal protection and supported by a conspiracy of silence from friends, relatives and the wider society, may deny this need. They 'short circuit' or 'hinder' (Worden, 1991: 13–14) this process by only allowing good thoughts of the deceased or minimizing their lasting importance or by 'keeping busy' in work or partying. Freud was not immune to this. He reflects on how 'shaken' he had been after the death of a beloved daughter but '"(T)he unvarying circle of a soldier's duties" and the "sweet habit of existence" will see to it that things go on as before' (cited in Silverman and Klass, 1996: 6). Worden draws on other sources, such as Bowlby, to warn that if the pain is repressed and not fully experienced at this point, then it is all the more difficult to access and work with subsequently.

Task three is *to adjust to an environment in which the deceased is missing* and here the multi-layered nature of the loss needs exploring. The deceased may have played many parts in the life of the mourner and it takes time to realize and then explore each aspect of that loss, and how it impacts on the mourner, the changes needed, for example, to change from 'wife' to 'widow'. Losses can challenge core beliefs, in religion or the everyday nature of life. This task might be blocked through 'promoting their own helplessness, by not developing the skills they need to cope, or by withdrawing from the world' (Worden, 1991: 16).

The final task is *to emotionally relocate the deceased and move on with life*. Worden is explicit here in expressing his debt to Freud while also being clear of the need to remain sensitive to the continued importance of the deceased, honouring the intensity of the feelings and allowing the individual to love again.

Worden answers his own question, 'when is mourning finished?' by suggesting that, while no date can be set, it is associated with being able to think of the deceased 'without pain', there is sadness but it is not 'wrenching' and the mourner can reengage with life.

Throughout his discussion there are references to the work that needs to be done and the defences that can be mounted. There is also a further explicit discussion of what he refers to as *abnormal*, or unresolved grieving. Thus responses might be *delayed*, the immediate reactions to the loss put on hold only to then emerge, possibly all the stronger, some years later, when precipitated perhaps by a sudden memory of the deceased or an apparently unrelated loss, of a pet for example. The opposite of this is *chronic* mourning, sustained over many years or exaggerated ways as epitomized by Queen Victoria.

The *masked* or *inhibited* response entails not expressing the grief but acting it out in other ways, such as the physical symptoms of illness, what Freud terms as feelings being *somatized*. This urgent sense that work needs to be completed with some strategies being right, others wrong, belongs not just with Freudian psychoanalysis. Tobin, an early figure in gestalt therapy, sees *unfinished business* belonging to early childhood patterns of suppressing the physical experience of pain, as explaining how individuals fail to move on in their bereavement. There may be secondary gains in staying in mourning since it wins easy sympathy, justifies feelings of self-pity and avoids the dangers of establishing a new relationship. Whatever the reasons, the effect can be that the dead are as 'an introjected lump of dead matter that comes between the person and his world' (1975: 122) with those over identifying with dead people appearing as 'walking zombies ... they report feeling physically numb' (1975: 122). This sharp language reveals an impatience for people to move on, to complete *a stage* rather than recognizing that mourning consists of a number of processes to which individuals may return at different points of their life.

We can see the usefulness of such models, encompassing *stages* or a *series of tasks*, for social workers and other professionals, indeed they have entered the lay world's understandings of death and dying. The problems lie, despite the warnings of their creators, in them being interpreted as prescriptive rather than descriptive. The use of Kübler-Ross' (1969) well-known model is a case in point, given that the stages she presents of *denial, anger, bargaining, depression* and ultimately *acceptance*, are often applied to bereavement even though her research was based on those who were dying. People who have a disability may also be expected to follow this same process and so 'come to terms' with their circumstances although there are important differences here from 'ordinary' grief processes. The disability can continue to cause new losses in both the private and public arenas meaning that the pain is ongoing. 'The problems must be faced, evaluated, re-defined, and readapted to, again and again and again ... "My Polio" and "My Accident" were not just my past; they were part of my present and my future' (Oliver, 1990: 64).

Exercise 2.5

Stages of grieving in Marcia and Kuldip's lives

Returning to the case studies what 'stages' are Marcia or Kuldip at? Marcia in coping with her father's death, Kuldip with the losses she is experiencing in her life right now?
Can you identify whether the responses to the losses are 'unresolved', if so, in what ways?
How might these responses be helpful or unhelpful to the individuals themselves and their impact on the wider family and networks?

Possible Responses

Marcia might be seen as still struggling to 'work through to the pain of grief'. As discussed above her family do not seem available to her and with her broken school record she cannot easily return to that form of 'keeping busy' which had previously given her value. With her feelings *disenfranchised* she seems to be acting these out in anger at the family, which might be meant for the father, and in the drunkenness and bravado she may be unconsciously imitating her father's behaviour. Certainly her grief seems unresolved and is in danger of having huge repercussions for her and her family. Fortunately her comments to the social worker allow the potential to work with this (see Chapter 6).

Kuldip will need help to grieve for her lost physical well-being and, as indicated in the main text, this is hard in circumstances of such continuing uncertainty. Both Kuldip, her father, and her family will need to find a way to adjust to her as she is now, rather than her as a diminishment of her past self. If her condition is a somatic response to her cumulative losses then her response is of a different order. The dynamics of disability is explored further in Chapters 3 and 4).

4 The Significance of Staying with the Intensity of Loss

Another important element to be found within Freudian thinking is the importance of staying with death and the whole experience of loss: the pain is real and instructive and from that place we can find hope. 'It enjoins us to be resigned to our condition, but not necessarily to our fate' (Richards, 1989: 35) while Freud uses the evocative phrase 'if you want to endure life, prepare yourself for death' (1915/1993: 39).

Freud is less interested in loss as a reactive response, provoked by an external stimulus such as a particular incident or death, but more with it as an intrapsychic phenomenon, a state of mind which is core to the developmental process and an acknowledgement that the hope for oneness with the world, with fusion, is an illusion. This has echoes in writers in other traditions. Zinker, the gestaltist, acknowledges death as 'that most painful and powerful mystery of human existence' (1994: 272) seeing, in the way that individuals and families face that experience, the broader 'good form' and aesthetics of life. This aspect is explored fully by Yalom, the existentialist psychotherapist whose extensive essays and case studies illustrate his belief that 'conflict flows from the individual's confrontation with the givens of existence' (1980: 8), one of which is 'death', along with 'freedom', 'isolation' and 'meaninglessness'.

Yalom's importance lies in his wealth of research and the clarity and honesty of his case material which make him as accessible as Bowlby. Where Yalom differs from the 'attachment school' is his preoccupation less with the relationships that individuals forge with the outside world and more with the nature of the relationship that they have with themselves. Yalom rejects the Death Instinct and Freud's refusal to work with death issues in his patient's material, instead he draws on the 'existential dualism' of eastern philosophical traditions.

Yalom starts from the position that 'The fear of death plays a major role in our internal experience; it haunts as does nothing else; it rumbles continuously under the surface; it is a dark, unsettling presence at the rim of consciousness' (1980: 27). Childhood, as with other theorists, is identified as a key period, for it is then that such views are learnt and subsequently sanctioned by society and subject also to all manner of displacements. By this he means that even while fears and feelings about death are rarely fully expressed 'explicit death anxiety is always to be found' (1980: 188), emerging through dreams and fantasies, concerns about deaths in the wider family or social networks or the 'many small deaths' (1980: 57) represented by the ageing process. More neurotic individuals retain feelings of personal omnipotence or find the need to dedicate themselves to being, or waiting for, 'the ultimate rescuer' who will give life its meaning. Where life is not lived for its own sake, but in the service of the more dominant object or goal, it can lead to dependency and depression when the dominant other proves fallible, when political leaders prove corrupt, ideologies collapse or individuals die so these have the potential to 'propel the individual into a confrontation with one's existential situation in the world' (1980: 159). A core understanding within this school of thought is that each of us dies alone, even mourns alone despite funeral crowds. For all our talk of 'personal freedom' we do, in fact, live our lives within the tight restraints of interpersonal relationships.

5 The Importance of 'Continuing Bonds', 'Re-membering' not 'Dismembering'

The ultimate test of theory is its ability to relate and respond to daily experience, and perhaps the sharpest debate within current thinking about loss involves the challenge to the prevailing 'common sense' that we attain 'closure' by 'psychologically letting go' and moving on. This is expressed in the argument about 'continuing' rather than 'breaking the bonds' and can be linked to various theories clustered around *post modernism* and *social constructivism* which question the idea that there can be any 'essentialist' or 'universal' ways of managing loss. Instead it is for each individual to find their own meaning, *construct their own narrative*.

The sociologist, Walter, has made a major contribution to this debate, advocating the *biographical* model and the need to maintain an *enduring sense* of the deceased as *ancestor*, acting as role model, guide, upholder of the values of the mourner and/or taking a valued place in their own biography (1996). This is further supported by practitioners such as Hedtke and Winslade who advocate the use of *conversations* that help to *re-member* lives, a restorative, purposeful process as opposed to *dis-membering* them. These *stories* and *constructive conversations* can hold meanings about the person who has died and allow them a *continuing membership* within the family/community, providing space to hold 'what might continue rather than what might be lost' (2003: 5).

Hellinger (1998, 2002, 2003) expands gestalt approaches to work with individuals and their families into what he terms *family constellation work* and loss, whether from illness, death or bereavement, informs the very core of the work. Staying with bereavement Hellinger challenges:

> A lot of people act as if the dead were gone. But where can they go? Obviously, they're physically absent, but they're also present in their continuing effect on the living. When they have their appropriate place in the family, deceased persons have a friendly effect. Otherwise, they cause anxiety. When they get their proper place, they support the living in living instead of supporting them in the illusion that they should die. (Hellinger et al., 1998: 185–6)

If this is another way of expressing the need for the bereaved to find ways to integrate the deceased into our lives, a process of *internalization*, or inner representation of the dead, then this brings us back to Freud and the various writers and researchers from within the psycho-analytical tradition who are revaluating his work from this perspective. In 'Continuing Bonds' (Klass et al., 1996) draw on a wealth of research of individuals experiencing significant losses, of child, spouse or parent, through death or family breakup and adoption. A consistent theme that emerges is of intense and dynamic connections, whether through dreams, a sense of being watched over or conversations with the dead. One example is women whose parent(s) had died when they were chil-dren and find that the relationship 'had developed over time … was developmentally appropriate' (1996: xvii). Further, this experience is 'normal' both in the statistical sense of how wide ranging it is being reported, and in the psychological sense that the individuals betrayed no signs of psychopathology.

The introductory essay in Klass et al. (Silverman and Klass, 1996) provides a closely argued survey of the various strands within analytic writings, noting that the process by which the mourner internalizes aspects of the deceased into their lives is a core theme, even though the exact nature of the process is contested. Originally seen as a necessary but passing stage, preliminary to the subsequent relinquishing of the deceased, it can also represent a stuck place, the sense of the dead person as fixed introjects. Others, such as Pincus (1978), focusing on surviving family dynamics, are more positive seeing internalization as a creative, shifting relationship. The deceased leaves a 'living legacy' and the survivors allow themselves to be open to important aspects of the deceased which make for change in their continuing lives.

Commenting on these debates, Silverman and Klass see an underlying tension between those who value autonomy and individuation, with its encouragement on 'breaking the bonds', and a more relational and interdependent approach which recognizes the degree to which 'bonds formed in the past can inform our present and our future' (1996: 17) and that families, communities and society are often the site for this.

Points for practice

- If you are assessing someone who has suffered some level of loss, you need to think theoretically about what stage the person is at in their grief process.
- If you are working with a child who has suffered the loss of a parent, consider whether the child had a good quality attachment prior to the loss and reflect on how the benefit of that attachment can be maximized.
- If you are working with a child who missed out on a positive attachment, you may need to think carefully about explaining the potential implications of this to future carers of the child.
- If someone is grieving, it is ok to stay with them in their grief rather than trying to 'cheer them up' or 'take their mind off it'.
- Anti-discriminatory practice is illustrated by the emphasis on disenfranchised grief.

Further reading

Bowlby, J. (1991) *Loss,* volume three of *Sadness and Depression.*
Freud, S. (1917/1984) *Mourning and Melancholia.*
Howe, D. (1995) *Attachment Theory for Social Workers.*
Walter, T. (1996) 'A New Model of Grief: Bereavement and
    Biography', *Mortality,* 1(1): 7–25.
Worden, W.J. (1991) *Grief Counselling and Grief Therapy: A
    Handbook for the Mental Health Practitioner.*
Yalom, I. (1989) *Love's Executioner and Other Tales of
    Psychotherapy.*

For the psychoanalytical approach:
The website of the Tavistock clinic, www.tavi-port.org.uk
Journal of Social Work Practice.

For the attachment based psychoanalysis:
www.attachment.org.uk
Attachment and Human Development.

3 Social and Cultural Dimensions

Chapter contents

- The focus on the interpersonal and the outer networks
- The use of storytelling, or narrative, as a conceptual framework
- The historical and sociological changes that have impacted on how loss is seen
- The current debates as to whether loss is 'invisible' or 'celebrated'
- Debates related to case scenarios on the 'Good Death' and child care/adoption

Introduction

In any form of loss there is a meeting of 'the inner forces of self-identity and the outer networks' (Davies, 2005: 31), consequently we now move from the previous chapter's concern with the intrapersonal to an exploration of the interpersonal, where the individual meets the wider world. In doing so we need to recognize the way that, while the feelings of grief are timeless, they are also contoured by changing societal attitudes. We explore the degree to which our society is 'death denying' (Ariès, 1981) or, alternatively, witnessing 'the revival' or 'resurrection of death', (Dickinson, 2005; Walter, 2005).

Another core and widely accepted concept is that of the 'Good Death' and the contradictory nature of this is illustrated through *Sam:* his wife's death from cancer confronts him, on many levels, with the stories people tell about dying and how he finds his own voice. The importance of narrative is continued in the scenario of *Dorothy,* who is sought out by the son she placed for adoption. This highlights how the changes in our views about children and parenting touch individuals and whole communities.

Narrative and Social Work

Storytelling is, of course, not new in social work. We know it as *reminiscence* when used with older people (Rattenbury and Stones, 1989) or *life story work* with children (Shah and Argent, 2006) so it is important to be cautious about a new phrase like *narrative* and to question whether it is simply a matter of old wine in new bottles. Taking the concept further it does, however, seem to consolidate and theorize our previous thinking and to offer some important new perspectives. It emphasizes the degree to which the importance of a story lies not in its chronology but the way that it is told, 'the way themes emerge and in the telling take on new meanings' (Wilks, 2005: 1264). It is, then, an open ended process: there are 'always other stories that can be told about the same events or experiences' and the most powerful element lies in how the stories 'are always co-constructed, are told in the presence of a real or implied audience' (McLeod, 2000: 344). The dialogic aspect offers the opportunity for individuals to develop their own perspective, to *re-author* their story and this is especially important at a time when there have been disruptions in one's life, when 'the present is not what the past was supposed to lead up to and the future is scarcely thinkable' (Frank, 1995: 55 cited in Farber et al., 2004: 120). Armstrong-Coster elaborates this in her study of how cancer patients construct for themselves the lead role as a dying hero, shielding, on practical and social levels, those they care for (and who are caring for them) from the harsh realities of their illness and pain (2004).

Narrative approaches have the potential to be anti-discriminatory once the power dynamics within these dialogues are fully recognized, and the individuals experiencing loss are allowed to tell their own story rather than be swamped by what is called the dominant narrative, the language of 'oughts' and 'shoulds' representing the world view of professionals, including social workers. Neimayer and Jordan link this very specifically to working with disenfranchised grief since it gives a voice to what may otherwise 'go unrecognized, unarticulated and unvalued, perhaps even by ourselves' (2002: 96). Research has helped identify 'the active ingredients' which can bring out 'the healing power of narration', with some participants 'helped to work towards profound transformation of the tragedies about which they are writing' (Neimeyer and Anderson, 2002: 56).

Before moving onto *Sam* and then *Dorothy,* and her unexpected confrontation with her son *John,* I want to explore the potential of narrative by returning to *Kuldip,* whose sudden disability was focused on in the previous chapter.

Exercise 3.1   Kuldip: the other stories that can be told

In Kuldip's case scenario (see previous chapter):

- What are the 'other stories' that are being played out in this situation?
- Whose are the 'dominant narratives' and how might these be challenged by Kuldip's own story about herself?

The illness narrative is very powerful in every area of disability, tellingly reflected in such language as 'becoming a patient', waiting on a diagnosis and treatment does indeed demand patience, or 'being under the doctor'. This passivity may be further reinforced if the social worker works too exclusively within the medical model, and care packages to facilitate only the practical side of things.

The therapy narrative may be framed within the various psychological models of grieving, looking for Kuldip to move from anger with, through to adaptation to her condition. A more psychodynamic interpretation might wonder if her condition, so resistant to a medial diagnosis, is a somatic response to stress, a new form of hysteria (Showalter, 1997). Social workers might draw on an understanding of systems to see how a new balance, or homeostasis, can be reached within this family.

The religious narrative. Despite the profession's origins in Victorian Christian philanthropy, mainstream social work is now, for the most part, a secular occupation reflecting the mores of the wider society. This may prevent the social worker from fully hearing or respecting the profoundly held religious beliefs of service users, especially, if like Kuldip, they are outside of the dominant culture, even though they allow her to be part of a strong faith community.

The ethnic/black identity narrative. There are tensions as she vacillates between being Kuldip and Kay but strength could come once she allows her sense of self as a proud black woman. She might then no longer over compensate in response to the underlying racism within society that caricatures immigrants as 'sponging' and 'work shy', and, in the current period of 'The War on Terror' as dangerous Muslim fundamentalists.

The narrative of 'disablement' rather than 'disability'. While the medical model focuses on the individual characteristics of the disability the social model will highlight the process of *disablement*, the pressures of the market driven forces threatening her job, the lack of formal support for the ill father which in turn may have made her ill. Once Kuldip's condition stabilizes she might take on a more active role in various disability campaigns, contributing to the developing agenda within welfare of service user involvement.

In this brief example we can readily see the shifts between the different perspectives, not just through others involved in the event but by the same person at different points of their reflections and this can depend on whom the story is being told to, whether this be family, her faith/cultural community, health and social care professionals or, potentially, disability campaigners. This is expanded in the following scenario.

Exercise 3.2   Mat: the other stories that can be told

Mat, 24, is in the terminal stages of an AIDS-related illness and Douglas, an ex-lover, moved back to be the primary carer. When Mat's mother, Mary, comes to the city where the couple live she insists that it is her role to look after her only son. Not previously knowing about Mat's sexuality she now refuses to accept that he is 'really' gay or that he is dying. Douglas, and other gay friends, are banned from the house and denied any role in planning the funeral.

- What are the 'other stories' that are being played out in this situation?
- Whose are the 'dominant narratives' and how might these be challenged by Mat's own story about himself?

The disability and illness narrative. Both Mat and Kuldip have a disability and illness and so share some similarities, especially given the early history of AIDS when the condition was equally mysterious and dependent on diagnosis and treatment. If, however, illness is a metaphor (Sontag, 1993) then the differences are legion. There may be sympathy for Kuldip, victim of a mysterious virus, but AIDS offers no such comfort to those infected since it is a sexually transmitted disease identified first with gay men, a double stigma, and now increasingly with heterosexuals, but mainly Africans and Asians, so racism is added to the brew, or through the infected needles shared by drug users.

Mat's gay narrative. Being young and terminally ill is difficult enough, for Mat and those close to him, but there are layers beyond this as his story gets snared up in the changing history of AIDS and of sexuality.

His condition was less unusual in the 1980s when HIV and AIDS was first diagnosed and labelled 'a gay plague' since it was this group most obviously dying, and in such large numbers. One response from the gay community was defiance: campaigns blossomed committed to fund research, provide appropriate palliative care, raise awareness of 'safer sex' and fight the vicious homophobia which arose in the wake of the illness. Solidarity was shown through wearing red ribbons and projects like the quilts whose thousands of individually sewn panels memorialized those who had died.

The situation changed with the availability, within North America and Europe, of dramatic and life saving cocktails of drugs which meant that those who had been preparing themselves for death could live again. This had a profound psychological as well as physical impact, what Thompson (2003) has termed the *Lazarus Phenomena*, while for new generations of gay men the 'safe sex' message seemed less important.

So Mat has to struggle with his feelings. There was the joy he had felt on moving away from home, losing his shame and isolation by 'coming out' and finding his place in an exciting and accepting community. But this had led him to being complacent, first in getting infected and then not seeking treatment. He is now getting important support from his ex-lover and the circle of gay friends but this is threatened by his mother coming to town. She offers him love and support, but on very different terms.

Mary's family narrative. She is no less devastated by what has overtaken her son. She has not been exposed to the diversity or openness of modern city life, she turns away from the occasional same sex kiss on the TV soaps and takes it for granted that sodomy is a sin. In this situation Mary has, then, lost all that she holds to be normal. Her son is dying which is out of the natural order of things. Mary manages this by not seeing how mortally ill he is and believing in the recuperative powers of mother love. She is also determined to deny his gay sexuality but this is challenged every time she sees Douglas and the other gay friends, which is why she banishes them.

What is being played out here is a modern day version of that medieval drama of the Devil and an Angel fighting over the soul of the dying man and it will be hard for an already weak and vulnerable Mat to find his own voice.

Changing Cultural Currencies Regarding Death

The examples above serve to illustrate societal attitudes towards illness, disability and death, and how the stories told about them change over time, sometimes centuries, sometimes decades. Interestingly, this is a form of stages theory which, like the classic psychological stages of loss and grieving explored in the previous chapter, offers both insights and problems if applied mechanistically.

Invisible Death

Ariès is the most notable advocate of *stages*, taking a long view as he explores changes in his native France from the Middle Ages through to the mid-twentieth century. He needs this broad time scale since he argues that attitudes move very slowly and, as such, they 'exceed the capacity of the collective memory' (1981: xvi). One period he identifies is The Tamed Death of the early Middle Ages, when death was not struggled with, nor sought, but accepted and prepared for in its own time with careful final goodbyes, proceeding to a peaceful end and an afterlife. This he sharply contrasts with the current period where death is rendered *invisible*, a medical process taking place in hospitals away from the family and community and clouded in a sense of privacy ever 'more rigorous, more demanding' (1981: 611).

That this was the prevailing wisdom of the era can be seen in Pincus' argument that we lack 'a climate in which grief and mourning are accepted, supported and valued' (1978: 254) and Bowlby's concerns that, '(L)eft without the support of sanctioned customs, the bereaved and their friends are bewildered and hardly know how to behave towards each other. This can only contribute to unhappiness and pathology' (1991: 190).

How Walter describes the changes is that in the Middle Ages the focus was on the soul of the deceased, this then shifted to the preoccupation with the corpse with its attendant elaborate funereal rites, and in the last 100 years, as dying has increasingly moved from the home to the hospital and cemeteries from the centres of town to their outskirts, the emphasis has turned to the psychological state of the bereaved (1999: 135). The systems that have habitually offered comfort have, however, largely disappeared: religion has succumbed to the secularization of the age, family networks have dispersed and been weakened through increased marital breakdowns, leading to one estimate that one third of all those bereaved need to seek help from outside the immediate network of family and friends (Raphael et al., 1993).

The Revival of Death

These ideas, about both the rate of change and the degree to which death is marginalized, are being questioned with some contemporary commentators arguing that in fast moving societies one can detect quite sharp shifts, even from one generation to another, especially when provoked by national crisis such as war.

Changes of Perception During a Single American Century
Strauss and Howe in Stillion (1995)

The Lost Generation. The 'old, old', aged 90 plus, identified as 'the Lost Generation' having come of age at the time of massive losses, first in the Great War and then in the devastating outbreak of influenza. These factors shape their attitude to life, and death, leaving them reactive and stoical, feeling that they can do little to prolong their lives.

The GI Can-Do Generation matured in a very different period. Regarding themselves as the victors of the Second World War, then buoyed up by a subsequent period of economic growth, they developed a 'can-do' approach. In line with this, and through developments in technology and medicine intended to prolong life, death becomes another enemy to confront and better.

The Silent Generation has, as their backdrop, the non-heroic Korean War which bequeathed a general sense of seriousness and the wish to seek compromise, as reflected in the striving for 'fairness' during the debates about universal health care.

The Baby Boomers' war was Vietnam, which they opposed and ended through their acts of collective protest. This is an idealistic generation now reaching maturity and demanding better health care alongside a commitment to healthy living. As Stillion comments: 'It is almost as though their youthful, anti-war slogan, "Hell, no, we wont go!", is now being directed toward aging and death' (1995: 308).

An emerging theme is of a 're-writing' of the traditional scripts about dying to the point where there is a 'resurrection' of death. Dickinson (2005), as evidence, cites the phenomenon, in the UK, Australia, Ireland, Scandinavia etc., of floral tributes placed by the roadside to mark a fatal accident, and the mass wakes following high profile deaths, whether of known celebrities such as Princess Diana or following a notorious murder or accident. These are examples of death being brought out of the closed off cemeteries and into very public places.

Dickinson gives further, rather dramatic examples, of the growth of individualized funerals, especially in the USA.

The ashes of the deceased can:

- be mixed in paint for artwork which is then displayed,
- orbited around the world in a space capsule,
- inserted into a concrete, artificial reef.

From the body:

- a fingerprint can be taken and then imprinted on a gold or silver three-dimensional wax model, or 'thumbie',
- a diamond can be made from carbine in the brain.

Caskets or coffins can:

- be customized, decorated with gardening or hunting scenes or shaped like a golf cart depending on the interests of the deceased,
- be bought in advance and used, pending a death, as a bookcase or sofa.

Some funeral homes offer webcasts of the ceremony for those unable to attend.

Exercise 3.3

Your reaction to customized funerals

- Note your reaction to these suggestions. Are you shocked or excited?
- How often have you felt that a funeral you have attended genuinely represented the person who died?
- Have you planned your own funeral or thought about what you would want as a memorial of your life?

Change and Continuity in Societal Attitudes

The arguments cited above provide fascinating insights, but in their sweep do an injustice to the variations, even within the generations and societies studied, of gender, race and class. If we are living through significant changes then, remembering Ariès' warning that we need a historian's perspective, we may be too close to see fully what is transient and what is enduring. Nonetheless we can identify elements of continuity and change.

There is a continuing need to believe not just in an afterlife but our ability to reach out to the dead, a need fed, as suggested in the Introduction, by the widespread popularity of films, novels and television series that take for granted the continued involvement of the dead in the land of the living. This can also be seen in the still thriving spiritualist societies, churches and séances, although the material manifestations of a previous generation have given way to general reassurance of another world, evidenced through 'homely and comforting messages' (Walter, 2005: 398). Mantel (2005) offers a fictionalized account of a contemporary 'sensitive', while the all too real complexities of this experience are movingly charted in Picardie's (2001) confessional account of her stumbling and rather embarrassed attempts to make contact with her dead sister in defiance of her previous, rationalist rejections of such beliefs.

The importance of spiritualists can be seen if they are included in what Walter terms 'mediator death workers', that body of people such as pathologists, coroners, obituary writers, leaders of funeral services and even social workers who help us 'interpret, reconstruct, construct, them [the dead] for us' (2005: 408). Their role is to be directly involved with mourners and so channel information, 'interpreting the dead to the living' (2005: 385) and sometimes editing that story to make it more palatable. The importance of these death mediators lies in their 'familiarity' with death, a familiarity which is denied to or shunned by others.

Drawing on all of this, there does seem some evidence that the moment has passed when death is only *invisible* or *denied*, and that may equally apply to other losses. Walter, however, argues that individuals are driven to find new ways of mourning not because things are changing, but as a response to those forces trying to keep things the same, to maintain the prevailing ideology that keeps the dead and dying 'unfamiliar' to the living. For every commentator celebrating the 'post modern' death, which overthrows tradition and makes up its own rules, there will be another who critiques 'conspicuous compassion' (West, 2004) or the 'cultivation of vulnerability' (Furedi, 2004) and yearns for a return to the stoicism and stiff upper lip of established customs.

The case scenarios used throughout this text reveal the complexity of the present period and the tensions within each situation. These are further highlighted below where we see a variety of mediators at work with the newly widowed Sam and we continue to test out the usefulness of their interpretations within the context of narrative theory.

'The Good Death': Dying of Cancer

Case Scenario Sam, Widowed by Cancer

Sam is 72. Neighbours who once saw him as 'well turned out' and 'a gentleman' now report their concerns to social services. He is wondering the streets, dishevelled and distressed looking and refusing help. They do not know that his wife died six months earlier.

His wife, Mavis, had lung cancer but delayed diagnosi meant it was untreatable and her death 'came so fast'. Sam and she did not talk together about the illness, ''it was just too painful, we

(Continued)

(Continued)

put it in a bottom drawer, like it didn't exist.' Mavis refused to let Sam tell her children to avoid upsetting them or their pitying her.

Sam is furious with the hospital, about the misdiagnosis and the treatment she received, the insistence on endless blood samples, 'she was not a person, just a number'. Once in the hospice Sam loves how she changes, 'her old self and her dignity got back... she started smiling again, she sits up in bed and feels better, the pain under control, she starts talking about the future.'

The death leaves Sam distraught, exhausted and full of regrets, about failing to get a quicker diagnosis, not telling the children who are angry with him, not saying a proper 'goodbye' to Mavis. This includes 'the mockery' of the funeral: the presiding priest is a stranger to Mavis and Sam is an atheist. He refers to how he 'lost the plot' which seems spot on.

Social services involvement quickly helps Sam with his physical care but he remains in psychological turmoil, threatening suicide. Although reluctant to accept counselling, 'it's a load of bollocks', he is persuaded to let someone in from the hospice and he finds that counsellor helpful, 'very matter of fact'. She helps Sam return to the hospice for the Evening of Remembering and he also goes frequently to pray in the chapel and walk the gardens which Mavis had loved. He meets a widow at the Evening of Remembering and they start a relationship, satisfying because Sam can talk about his wife as she can about her husband and both can honour their losses. It is important for Sam that the woman knows that Mavis 'is still a very big part of my life, my wife, but life goes on'.

Remembering the concept of 'narrative', what are the 'other stories' that are being played out in this situation? Whose are the 'dominant narratives' and how might these be challenged by Sam's own story about himself?

Sam is a respondent in some hospice based research (Weinstein, 2005, 2007) whose findings suggest that he represents a very familiar process whereby individuals are turned into extras in their own dramas and have to struggle to emerge, or *re-author* it. The narrative themes that I identified can be summarized as follows:

'Well Person' Becomes 'a Cancer Patient'

Our assumption, the dominant narrative, is that we are physically well and the possibility of serious illness or mortality is pushed well out of consciousness. Consequently a diagnosis of a potentially terminal illness invariably carries a sense of shock, the dis-ease of disease, a mood well captured by Sam in his phrase 'we put the news into the bottom drawer' and the distancing from family and neighbours. This could be seen as a classic Freudian defence mechanism or simply a description of how, in such situations, 'words fail': the previously taken for granted vocabulary of the ordinary person is no longer adequate, can no longer 'match' experience (Powis, 2005). What happens instead is that the patient and family find themselves increasingly caught up in the medical process, reliant on doctors and diagnosis and losing their own identity. This is especially true in the case of cancer where the narrative is usually about searching for cures, fighting the illness, even when, as with Mavis, the medical interventions no longer seem relevant. Interestingly the doctors' fighting the illness is mirrored in Sam battling the doctors.

Entering the Hospice, Negotiating 'the Good Death'

Once the patient and the carer is referred to palliative care the battle for a cure becomes redundant and makes way for another narrative, namely that of 'the Good Death' which has become the all pervasive 'cultural currency' conveying 'an image of dying in which others wish to believe' (Lawton, 2000: 15). It envisages all concerned, the dying person, their family and the professionals, managing 'a dignified and aware death', including the opportunity to reflect on their life and get their affairs, both practical and psychological, in good order. Sam, however, illustrates the problems in this. It works in that the hospice proves very supportive and, with the medical team accepting the reality of the death, he can let go of the fighting and also accept. But Mavis' continued insistence on keeping her dying in 'the bottom drawer', denies her family the comforts of an acknowledged goodbye or making plans for her funeral. And in this challenge, conscious or unconscious, to the ideology of 'the Good Death' she is not necessarily alone. Lawton's hospice based research gives example after example of similar resistance, such as visitors treating the dying patient as already 'socially dead'. She describes the hospice worker, known to be especially committed to wanting patients 'to talk openly and frankly about the incurable nature of their illness', and how patients do everything possible to avoid her. When she appears 'a wave of tension used to hit the room' (2000: 68).

The Person Reclaimed, 'The Person' Being Both the Deceased and the Bereaved

For Sam, the distress and disorientation continues after the death: he had lost Mavis to the patient role, briefly retrieved her in the hospice when her 'old self got back' but then she disappears in the unsatisfactory ritual of the funeral. Something starts to shift when the counsellor gives him the space and support to reclaim her, and the life they lived together. Photographs of holidays and family events prompt his reminiscences. The hospice based events, both the arranged Evening of Remembering and the more spontaneous visits to the gardens where they had walked together, also fill out the memories. He is helped to make up with the children and regain contact with neighbours while the widow meets his need to honour the memory of his wife and to find a new relationship.

Child Care and 'The Stolen Generations'

Discussions about 'the Good Death' and individualized funeral rites have emerged relatively recently and publicly but issues relating to child care are subject to a slower pace and are less overt but no less sharp and complex in how they are acted out.

Exercise 3.4   *Rabbit Proof Fence*

The film *Rabbit Proof Fence* (Noyce, 2002) is set in New South Wales, Australia and is based on a true story. We see three girls, the oldest 12, who are part of the indigenous community but because they were fathered by white men the authorities designate them as 'half castes'. The girls are seized from their families and removed over a 1,000 miles away to a centre where their skin is colour coded, their original clothes, food, language and religion denied them and they are trained in basic domestic duties. As the official, called without irony the 'Chief Protector of Aborigines', explains in the film, the

(Continued)

(Continued)

purpose is to prevent the 'creation of an unwanted third race' and, by allowing them only to marry white people, the intention is to 'breed the black out' and let them 'advance to white status'.

The film is set in 1931 but the policy continued until 1975 with an estimated 10,000 children becoming members of this stolen generation. Subsequent campaigning has helped raise awareness in Australia about their colonial history and following a report commissioned by the Commonwealth Attorney-General social workers, through their professional association, formally apologized for their role in what is described as the genocidal policy of forcible removal of children (see Briskman, 2003, Dawes, 2002).

- What is your response to this story?
- Can you see any similarities with other child care stories in other countries, at other times?

Historical Perspectives on Child Care

Almost every aspect of what is currently called *child protection* has been subject to consistently changing attitudes – popular, professional and party political – regarding how children, who can no longer remain with their biological families, should be cared for by, in that inelegant phrase, corporate parents.

Child care policy at the turn of the twentieth century has been described as 'poorly informed unconcern' (Teague, 1989: 117) and its influence stretched across many oceans. In the UK a large voluntary agency celebrated its centenary with posters showing two forlorn children staring into the camera. One was in sepia colours, clearly depicting a Victorian urchin, the other was a more modern portrait and the strap line declares: 'a hundred years on, the faces change, the bruises don't'. But this beguiling argument about the timelessness of the abuse children face is misleading. It emphasizes physical abuse over sexual or emotional abuse and/or neglect. It assumes abuse within families rather than that of a society and political system which condones levels of inequality, ill-health and poverty which then impact on morbidity and mortality rates. In her exploration of the related field of family violence in the USA Gordon comments, 'the lack of a history' means inevitable 'distortions' in public discussion (1989: 2).

Drawing on American case files Gordon characterizes this period, at the end of the nineteenth century, as deeply moralistic, blaming the lower class Italian and Irish immigrants and African-Americans, who dominated the client group, as cruel men and ignorant women, both genders liable to sexual impropriety and alcoholism, more depraved than deprived. The case records are free with phrases like 'primitive', 'limited', 'typical low-grade' (1989: 14–15). Sympathy for the mother 'would have been condescending ... [social workers] would not have helped her seek economic independence as a route to safety but would more likely have offered two choices: either reforming the husband through a combination of moralizing and punishment or institutional-izing her children' (1989: 21).

In the UK, right up to the 1960s, children were being separated from their parents and sent to the colonies for 'a better life', very much in the spirit of the Poor Law, separating the 'deserving' from the 'unde-serving', thus mirroring the fate of the Australian 'stolen generation'.

Adoption as a Focus for Change

The shifting attitudes around adoption have been especially tense with commentators (Frost and Stein, 1989; Parton, 1985) highlighting how the policy of 'permanency planning' was strongly influenced by the tragic case of Maria Colwell. After being removed from foster parents she was returned to the natural family, where she in 1973, died of neglect. As such she became a powerful illustration of sentimental and incompetent social workers pandering to feckless families.

Although difficult in this climate, some professionals nevertheless sustained the argument for preventative measures to support children to stay in their own homes. Various strands of this radical campaigning included the advice giving and advocacy organization, the Family Rights Group, founded in the early 1970s and ABSWAP (The Association of Black Social Workers and Allied Professions) which argued that disproportionate numbers of black children were being adopted by white families. Because these families tended to live in rural or suburban areas these children were being lost to both their actual families and their communities, leaving the children without knowledge of their heritage and growing up with 'black skins, white masks' (Fanon, 1970). ABSWAP described this as a 'one-way traffic ... a new form of slave trade, but this time only black children are used' (cited in Kirton, 2000: 21). This new example of 'stolen generations' also exposed the racism of the wider society that seemed to leave so many black families vulnerable.

ABSWAP's impact was dramatic and led to concerted and successful efforts to recruit alternative parents from within the black communities and move towards the policy and practice of same race placements. The Children Act 1989 requires consideration of a child's religious persuasion, racial origin and cultural and linguistic background to be taken into consideration.

Subsequently the debate shifted again, towards how 'dual heritage' children can be helped to value both aspects of their parentage without losing either (see Dean, 1993; Kirton, 2000; Okitikpi, 2005) but what is remarkable is the way that the traditionally private arena of family breakdown became a collectivized and politically charged campaigning issue that made important gains.

Dorothy and John's story, see below, may seem of a different order but the changes in social attitude are no less dramatic. Where adoption was once viewed as a permanent separation, the process 'hermetically closed' (Nickman, 1996: 260), this gradually begun to change and section 26 of the Children Act 1975 gave children the opportunity to trace birth parents through access to original birth certificates. The implications of this is acted out in Mike Leigh's film *Secrets and Lies* (1996), where the death of her adoptive parents releases Hortense, a professional black woman, to search out her birth parents and which leads to repercussions based on distancing and deception, hence the title of the film, which have been maintained over 25 years. It shows the lives of those desperately wanting children they cannot have and others apparently not wanting the children they do have.

Adoption contains, then, many layers of loss and distancing, whether having to cope with 'retroactive losses' (Nickman, 1996) or the 'grieving for unrealised expectations of past relationships' (Romaine, 2002: 125). Adoption, for both children and birth parents, involves people 'at the edge of certain social boundaries' (Haimes and Timms, 1985: 11).

Case Scenario   Dorothy and Her Adopted Child John

Dorothy is 45, married to Max, and they have just celebrated their 25th wedding anniversary. There are two children, in late adolescence. If asked Dorothy describes herself as 'contented and conventional, at peace with myself after a difficult childhood'. Quite unexpectedly she receives a letter saying that the child she had placed for adoption is now wanting to meet her. It takes her back to a very difficult time when aged 15, and a virgin, she was raped at a party by an anonymous stranger who subsequently disappeared out of her life as dramatically as he had entered it. She was made to feel responsible for what had

(Continued)

(Continued)

happened and 'before I began to show I was spirited away from everyone I knew and loved and sent to relatives who were strangers to me'.

While having her baby Dorothy felt that she was treated differently from the other women on the ward; certainly there was no proud father or grandparents to visit and nurses were formally polite but awkward around her. Once the adoption papers were signed Dorothy returned to her home where her mother told her she was very lucky to now have 'a clean slate' and assured her that 'it' would never be spoken of again. And nor was it, not even with Max who Dorothy subsequently met and married.

The son, John, is now 30. He knew from an early age that he was adopted and says that he 'absorbed' the information without ever really taking it in as especially important. He loved those he knew as his parents and that was it. 'I'm not very psychologically minded, "what you see is what you get" is my motto.' Something shifted, however, when his girlfriend became pregnant and decided on an abortion which John went along with quite willingly, not feeling ready to be a father. Five years later, still with the same partner, they had a planned pregnancy and John is 'bowled over' about being a father, and provoked into wandering about his own father. He is also saddened by the earlier abortion, for that 'lost child', and realizing that he would not now exist if his birth mother had made a similar decision when he was conceived.

Dorothy's Story

There are many reasons why a woman loses a child to adoption, and how this resonates with many other losses, such as surrendering her power to professionals and/or family and losing her sense of self through shame. There are also the losses involved with being poor which can leave women and girls more vulnerable.

Mander draws on her own experience as a hospital based midwife to make a telling comparison of mothers planning to have their babies adopted and those whose children died at birth. In both cases, the babies were 'removed quickly and often unceremoniously' (1995: 2). With Dorothy, the professionals may have acted this way because they felt punitive towards her, or did not want her to attach to the child, or assumed that in choosing to give up a child she had no need to grieve.

Subsequently, her mother commits Dorothy to a code of silence so while she may still be living with shame and self-blame the grief is disenfranchised, the loss cannot be shown or shared and there are no accepted rituals or rites of passage to support the process and allow a 'letting go'. Mander cites research that describes the grieving characteristics in these situations as deep, triggered by anniversaries, marked by a search for meaning alongside a sense of aimlessness, with the stress of secrecy leading to disassociation. The yearning behaviour, which is so characteristic of the mourning process, here has a reality base since the child is still alive and so a physical meeting remains possible. Mander argues that all of this can delay or prolong grieving (1995: 191).

John's Story

The loss is felt also by the child who has been relinquished so that adults searching for their birth parent(s) may need a reality check on their fantasies about the parents and want to discover why they were placed for adoption (Haimes and Timms, 1985) while finding out more about their own identity can help them to find their own place and continuity within their two families and so enable them to 'come to a trust in their joint and separate futures' (Romaine, 2002: 125). We know that John had previously surrendered his curiosity because he had been happy in the family he knew and he may have felt for the losses experienced by the adoptive parents when they were unable to have their own biological children. Given this, he may feel disloyal for wanting to know about his birth parents.

Research suggests that individuals like John are being faced with many losses: of the biological parent(s), of the life they may have had, of the sense of themselves they had gained within the adopted family. In a parallel process with the birth mother, the loss is disenfranchised through secrecy, shame and a lack of societal support for their struggle. In the Haines and Timms research, there is surprise from one respondent that a parent was Polish since it challenged her taken for granted Britishness, another respondent found a new forename which she started using since it was her 'proper' name (emphasis in the original) (1985: 56). Adoption files may offer up letters, photos and other mementos: new pieces to be fitted into the puzzle, while some pieces will remain lost if a parent cannot be found, or died before being traced, or refuses to meet the child. Meetings can also prove anticlimatic, thus for John finding his mother may not be enough since he is still left knowing nothing about his father, and it was that that prompted his search. He may be angry with the young girl who conceived him so carelessly, and equally carelessly gave him away but not recognize that girl in the middle aged woman he now finds.

If adoption is a form of 'death' (Shawyer, cited by Haines and Timms, 1985: 63), with the adoptee having to mourn the lost past, then finding a natural parent entails a new birth alongside a new death of the adoptive family/self or it might be more an integration of the two aspects of one's life into a new narrative, 'a beginning, middle and end' (adoptive respondent cited in Haines and Timms, 1985: 81).

Nickman argues that even when adoptees have no knowledge or memory of their birth parent(s) there is still a relationship, 'a mental construction of the absent progenitors is a necessity' (1996: 257), and he goes on to argue the psychological impact of these various covert and overt losses. My interest here, however, is also in the social dimension. When adoptees actively trace the birth parent they are seeking what Haines and Timms describe as a social as opposed to an ego identity (1985: 11), they are wanting to 'correct their marginal status ... to ask, without censure, about one's story... to place themselves in a narrative' (1985: 50). Haines and Timms go on to argue that while it relates to the apparently private sphere of the family it is also a 'public' request since they are using a legally, socially sanctioned set of procedures (1985: 51) which also provides a new social being, someone with a family tree and history to share with loved ones, in the case of John's scenario, John's own son.

Points for practice

- Loss and how it is experienced differs across cultures.
- Individuals may seem to share a similar experience, such as 'a disability', but will understand this very differently depending on a whole range of factors, e.g. age, gender, religion, ethnicity.
- If you are working with someone very different from you, be sure to check out how the particular type of loss sustained is understood and addressed in that person's cultural context.
- Attitudes are not fixed but can change very rapidly, across and within generations.
- Take care to attend to the stories that individuals tell about themselves and the world they live in.

Further reading

Ariès, P. (1981) *The Hour of Our Death*.
Walter, T, (1999) *On Bereavement, The Culture of Grief*.

For child care:
Briskman, L. (2003) *The Black Grapevine, Aboriginal Activism and the Stolen Generations*.
Gordon, L. (1989) *Heroes of Their Own Lives: The Politics and History of Family Violence*.

For the debates about the 'Good Death':
De Hennezel, M.(1997) *Intimate Death, How the Dying Teach Us To Live*.
Lawton, J. (2000) *The Dying Process, Patients' Experiences of Palliative Care*.
Weinstein, J. (2005) *A Shoulder to Support Me, Not a Shoulder to Cry On* offers a fuller description of the research in which Sam featured.
See the journal *Morality*, promoting multidisciplinary study.

4 Social Work Values

Chapter contents

- Changing values in social work incorporating the GSCC Codes of Practice
- Identifying personal and professional value systems, both generally and in relationship to loss, death and bereavement
- The theme of 'support versus surveillance' as it emerges through the example of a death of a child at birth
- The theme of 'outcomes versus process' explored through life limiting and chronic illness

---

Introduction

This chapter focuses on social work values as they relate to loss, death and bereavement. On the surface, and as expressed in the GSCC (General Social Care Council) Codes of Practice (2002), these seem uncontroversial in their expectations. For example, we 'communicate in an appropriate, open and accurate and straightforward way' (2.2), 'work openly and co-operatively with colleagues' (6.5) or work with 'conflicts of interest' (2.6). Nonetheless our values systems, on personal, cultural and professional levels, may bring us into conflict situations, not just with our agencies and service users but within ourselves. This chapter explores these dilemmas, as linked to the changing value systems within the profession as they emerge within two case scenarios. The first is *Susan* and *her family*, and the death of a baby through a stillbirth where the theme is support versus surveillance. The second focuses in on outcomes versus process, seen in the context of life limiting and chronic illness, specifically *Wanda*, a child with Cystic Fibrosis.

Changing Ethical Dimensions of Social Work

In the preceding pages a certain set of values have underpinned the case scenarios, the choice of theories and the way the book has been organized. To summarize briefly:

- I emphasize *disenfranchised grief*, that myriad of often missed aspects of mourning.
- I explore *narrative* which is valued for the voice it gives to the service user's perspective.
- I look to the *collective and campaigning aspects* because this reflects how I see change can be achieved within the *wider social and political context.*

In privileging these ideas I reveal the ideas that collectively make up my overall value system and serve as a guide to action and my ethical practice, which has been described as a 'filter which defines the things we accept or reject' (Beckett and Maynard, 2005: 8). Commonly these ideas are so integral to us we take them for granted; their impact on how we see the world, and act on that understanding is insufficiently recognized. It is the purpose of this chapter to make the process explicit.

Social work has always worked within ethical frameworks, normally identified with Kant's 'respect for persons' or Bentham's 'Utilitarianism', the concept of the greatest good for the greatest number (see Beckett and Maynard, 2005, for a recent summary of debates as to whether values are core or relative, the legislative and policy implications, etc). These frameworks are not timeless and are continually being reworked, thus the early values of social work, associated with casework, were classically phrased by Biestek (1961) in terms of 'individualisation', 'client self-determination' and 'respect for persons' but these traditions were not easily sustained through the 1970s. They were caught between the sharper governmental agenda, with the emergence of the unified Seebohm departments and the reaction to the various child care scandals, and the challenge of 1960s influenced radicals who resisted the hierarchical power relationships between them and their clients as the term then was, between them and their managers. Subsequently the profession has sought to square this circle through the use of various terms to explain the relationship between social workers and the people with whom they work. There has been 'citizenship', 'partnership', 'empowerment', 'anti-discriminatory' and/or 'anti-oppressive' practice and the relatively new emphasis on 'cultural competence' (Raiff and Shore, 1993) when working with the black and ethnic minority communities.

In the midst of all this is the new imperative of social workers having to be formally registered and with this license to practice comes adherence to Codes of Practice developed by the General Social Care Council (2002).

GSCC Code of Practice for Social Care Workers

As a social care worker you must:

1. Protect the rights and promote the interests of service users and carers.
2. Strive to establish and maintain the trust and confidence of service users and carers.
3. Promote the independence of service users, while protecting them as far as possible from danger or harm.
4. Respect the rights of service users while seeking to ensure that their behaviour does not harm themselves or others.
5. Uphold public trust and confidence in social care services.
6. Be accountable for the quality of your work and take responsibility for maintaining and improving your knowledge and skills.

These seem clear even if it is too early to judge their effectiveness, whether in terms of the circumstances under which social workers might be struck off the register or the degree to which these statements have percolated down through the system and helped change the ethos of social work organisations and individual practitioners. It is not, however, a straightforward process and the fault of any Code, whatever the professional setting, is that they tend to sanitize the issues, fail to acknowledge the dynamics that might sabotage good, ethical practice. Thus, good practice now requires patients to know that they have a terminal illness but a Code cannot prescribe that 'the bad news' will be broken sensitively. The Code approach implies that unethical practice is the result of neglect or failures of individual professionals, a mixture of carelessness and callousness and while scandals can occur because of these factors problems in ethical practice often relate to something far deeper.

Throughout this debate we have to confront what happens when social workers seek to establish and maintain trusting relationships with service users while simultaneously holding a 'social control' role. If ignored we are faced with a situation, as identified by Jordan (1990), where as the world within which social work operates becomes more authoritarian so the professional language becomes more emancipatory. This writer subsequently (Jordan with Jordan, 2000) notes the impact of New Labour's policies on children and family work which leave social workers looking 'both ways', simultaneously acting as 'enforcement counsellors' of 'tough love' policies and wanting to resist such polices. Turning to mental health, Pilgrim refers to 'the care-control confusion' where the first phrase 'care' is an 'evasion of reality ... about the latent control function of psychiatry' (1999: 28). How this is felt from the rank and file of social workers is reflected in a recently convened conference, 'Social Work in the 21st Century; a Profession Worth Fighting For' (April 2006) whose theme was: '"We didn't come into social work for this". We didn't become social workers to be rationers of care and controllers of the poorest sections of the working class' (Lavalette et al., 2006). Wilks addresses these arguments within explicit ethical frameworks, tracing the tensions between 'rule-following technicist tendencies' of present day organizational practice and the social work profession's identity with 'the politics of identity and resistance' and the links to 'feminist ethics of care' (2005: 1250–1) and suggests some resolution through the use of narrative approaches, a point to which I will return.

Before relating this specifically to our work with loss, death and bereavement I suggest that you examine the tensions that exist for you, your fault lines and filters.

Exercise 4.1   Exploring your Personal Value Systems

(adapted from Beckett and Maynard, 2005)

1. List those basic beliefs that comprise your personal value system, the ideas you have about what is 'right' or 'wrong', particularly those you feel most strongly about.
2. Now make the following headings: 'societal values', 'agency values', 'social work values' and make a list below each of these.
3. Place a tick by those which are compatible with the values you identified in 1, a cross by those where there are tensions.

Exercise 4.2   Exploring your personal value systems, continued

You have had several meetings with Peter to help support him with his voices and the many disappointments of his life. He is often angry, with his family, his doctors, life in general. On this occasion he starts sounding off at God who has struck him down so cruelly when he has only tried to do good in his life. Then he pauses, says he is being tested like Job in the Bible and asks you to get down on your knees and pray with him for forgiveness, so that he can find the humility to accept his losses.

Douglas, the former lover of Mat, who is now dying of an AIDS-related illness, comes to see you. He is deeply distressed at being excluded from caring for Mat. The whole experience has really touched him, he had given up a well paid job and shifted from a very hedonistic life style to one committed to AIDS awareness work within the gay community. You feel very warm towards him and then he tells you how guilty he feels since he is also HIV+, and through practising unsafe sex had infected Mat.

Lou is getting more self-assured, ready to get out and about. She tells you one day that she has a real sense of George's presence around the house, she catches his smell, feels his hands fleetingly upon her, finds feathers in the most unusual places and knows that this is his way of trying to reach her. She wants you to find out about mediums so that she can follow this up.

Kuldip is talking about wanting to get back to work but she pauses, looks very upset and confides that she saw one of the London tube bomb victims being interviewed on the news. 'I almost envied her, she's got a proper reason for being in a wheelchair, mine is just some sort of virus. I can hear my work colleagues saying I'm just skiving, couldn't take the pressure, or saying I deserve it all, it was "my lot" that did the bombings'.

How do you react to each of these situations?

How are your feelings about each of the service users altered as a result of their comments?

Do you now need to revise the lists you drew up in the first part of the exercise?

These two exercises help identify how value systems may compete with and/or complement each other within the individual practitioner. Now read the following.

Changing Ethical Dimensions of Death, Dying and Bereavement

The previous chapter charted the developing ideas that allow new, even exciting, meanings to be found in the experience of loss: the innovative funeral rites which more carefully reflect the life of the deceased, the creation of positive spaces for people who are dying and their families and friends. Here is what Nuland described, when witnessing deaths from AIDS-related illnesses, as the 'caregiving surround', a chosen or 'affinitive' family that may complement the biological family (1994: 196).

These ideas are often directly related to the philosophy and practice of what has become known as the 'Good Death':

- A sense of someone living as fully as possible up to the point of death.
- Where the death is 'accepted' thus allowing for the saying of appropriate goodbyes to those close to them and the completing of unfinished business.
- For this to be facilitated there needs to be pain control, a degree of dignity and privacy, choice of where one wants to die and support for spiritual and emotional needs.

For many this does 'not appear as contentious' (Age Concern, 2005: 9) but it certainly was in its inception and has become accepted only because of the sustained campaign against the crudest interpretation of medical values, essentially identified as being about 'care' meaning 'cure' with resulting disinterest in those who are dying. Now, however, the 'Good Death' has become the dominant paradigm which needs questioning. As a concept it is fraught with difficulties, as illustrated in Sam's story in Chapter 2 and it is often very different from people's actual experience, indeed the problem may lie with the very term. A 'Good Death' can set too high an expectation, to the point of romanticizing death (Farber et al., 2004), while Nuland, an experienced doctor on the wards of general hospitals, challenges any 'mythical' term that detracts from the reality of the process that is 'a series of destructive events that involve by their very nature the disintegration of the dying person's humanity' (1994: xvii). Lawton (2000) takes the argument into the spiritual home of the 'Good Death', a hospice. Observing dying patients she is struck by their physical 'disintegration' and how this undermines the stated ideology that people can be helped to live right up to the moment they die.

The expectation that people can negotiate a 'Good Death', whether for themselves or their friends or family members, is also tested when so many have experienced life as harsh and ungiving.

Examples

Chronic, non-malignant conditions, like lung or heart disease, do not generally attract effective and sensitive palliative care. This is more readily available to illnesses such as cancer, AIDS or Motor Neurone Disease but best practice is located still within hospices whose provision across the country is very patchy (Hearn, 2005). In 2002 only 3% of all recorded deaths took place in hospices and as few as 1% of people with a non-cancer diagnosis gain access to specialist palliative care services in their last year of life (Age Concern, 2005).

CRUK (Cancer Research UK) reports that 'affluent people are surviving longer after a cancer diagnosis than deprived patients and the gap ... is widening'. Wealthier patients, having a better understanding of their health needs, notice worrying symptoms and demand more of the health service such as early diagnosis and the latest treatments. Poorer people take longer to recognize ill-health and have more difficulties accessing health care. Equality of access to treatment and diagnosis would save an estimated 3,000 lives a year (Hall, 2004).

A newspaper reporter in an Edinburgh city mortuary notes that many of the bodies are of suicides or the victims of car accidents or crime or who have died alone in their flats, often of alcohol or drug related causes. The pathologist reflects on how their stories are 'tinged with such despair' and that 'we are, without doubt, becoming less and less of a caring society'. He explains the few non-white bodies in terms of a continuing sense of community in the city's Asian and Chinese populations. what journalist comments that the deaths are largely 'invisible', the event that brought them to the mortuary 'owing nothing to either glamour or glory', these 'victims of loneliness' come from 'a class of people ... irritating, ignorant and incompetent' (Armstrong, 2006).

There are, then, gaps between society's aspirations and people's lived experience and when this touches on highly held values and events do not work out as planned, professionals, wedded to their belief system, can push the blame down, onto the individual or the family, rather than seeing it as 'more widely located within a society that constructed the social problem of the denial of death' (Hart et al., 1998: 70).

Changing Social Work Values Concerning Loss, Death and Bereavement

---

Case Scenario   Susan and the Death of a Baby

Susan, 37, is pregnant by Daniel and she has two daughters (Denise, 10 and Sarah, 8) from an earlier relationship. The pregnancy is difficult but Susan feels she has taken as much care of herself as she can given the demands of her family. The pregnancy has run its course and the family has prepared itself for the new arrival, which they know to be a boy. In hospital Susan has to have a Caesarean operation and the baby dies shortly after birth. At this point the social worker does her best to support the couple.

   Susan and Daniel are encouraged to hold the baby, photos and handprints are taken. There is a cremation but it is attended only by Susan and Daniel, Susan's parents are too upset to attend and Susan does not think it 'appropriate' for either Denise or Sarah to come.

   Five months later the family remains in some crisis: the ashes are at home, in a cupboard, until a decision is made about a permanent resting place. Daniel feels all the support has gone to his wife 'but I'm mourning too'. Susan has been to the GP, describing herself as 'very depressed'. The children are missing school. It emerges that between Susan's divorce and her meeting Daniel she had an abortion and she is now convinced that it was the medical aftermath of this that caused the stillbirth. The couple had married when Susan became pregnant.

- What is your emotional response to this situation and to the various participants?
- How does this link to your own professional and/or personal values?

The Values Confronted in the Loss of a Baby

Although this scenario refers to a stillbirth many of the issues explored below relate to all the various other ways that a pregnancy might not come to full term or a baby dies shortly after birth. These are potent losses, 'in every society, dead embryos or newborns are reminders of the fragile boundaries between life and death' (Bleyen, 2005: 8). Their loss will be felt on an *existential* and/or *spiritual level*. It is a *multiple loss*, of a significant individual, of a stage of life, the loss of creation and of potential (CPS: 2001), of potency where a parent, especially perhaps a mother, has apparently proved unable to bring a child to life.

There are *cultural values*, a child's death seems more untimely and shocking in modern western societies where successful child birth is a norm. This is not to deny the sadness captured by Currer's powerful image from Pakistan of a pregnant woman coming to hospital with a shoebox ready to serve as a coffin (2001).

Medical values are dominant for it is not long since hospital policy was to dispose of stillbirths as biological waste so the loss was *disenfranchised*. This changed, partly because of pressure by professionals heeding Bowlby's clarity about the emotional attachment that is made during a pregnancy. There was also campaigning by parent groups such as the British Stillbirth and Neonatal Death Society, or SANDS (www.uk-sands.org). Consequently parents are now offered memorabilia of the baby and there is a formal funeral, ways of honouring a real child who has lived. *Religious values* are evidenced in, for example, Judaism where if the stillbirth is that of a boy he is circumcized.

This text has already shown that there are times when it is social workers who are actively involved in parents 'losing' a child, either in the historical experience of the 'stolen generations' (Chapter 3) or as powerfully revealed in various iconic social dramas such as *Cathy Come Home* (Loach, 1966), *The Boys from the Blackstuff* (Bleasdale, 1982) and the film *Ladybird, Ladybird* (Loach, 1994), which all illustrate children being removed from parents for reasons of social conditions such as homelessness and unemployment. The 'Profession Worth Fighting For' Conferences, initiated in 2006 and ongoing, bring this right up to date in its workshops addressing, for example, the ways social workers can resist removing children from failed asylum seekers (www.socialworkfuture.org).

Support vs. Surveillance

Returning specifically to Susan's case the social worker balances both *support for* the family and a *surveillance* role (Krueger, 2005).

The parents may be genuinely distressed and questions need to be asked about the possible causes of the stillbirth, which may not be just medical. Sudden, unexpected deaths in infancy can be an indication of domestic violence and maltreatment (Stanton, 2003) although it is also argued that stillbirths and other forms of infant mortality may be more related to social factors such as deprivation and ethnicity than to deliberate neglect (www.barkinghavering.nhs.uk/pdf./ BirthWeightAug2004.pdf.

Drug dependency may also be an issue. An American study estimates that one in ten deaths in the womb is because of the mother's cocaine use (Sample, 2005) and an American woman is currently serving a life sentence because her addiction was found to have caused a stillbirth (www.lindesmith.org). A BBC documentary series, *Someone to Watch over Me* about social workers (Faulkner and Foster, 2004) shows the concerns about whether a pregnant heroin user should keep her child. So social workers are inevitably caught up in a surveillance model, the investigative spotlight being focused on a family like Susan and Daniel while they are simultaneously grieving an unexpected death.

Feminist Values

Feminist values and analysis have become an important element within social work, moving from being part of the 1960s, radical critique of social work to holding a more mainstream position, although not without some tensions. Core elements of feminist practice require an understanding of women's' experiences and the relationship between the intimacies of family life and the structural inequalities of employment, housing, etc. It is about how, reviving the old slogan, the personal is the professional is the political (see Dominelli, 2002).

Cline brings this debate to the arena of loss, death and bereavement, emphasizing the special significance for mothers whose children die which is partly shaped by society's expectations of 'motherhood' where the woman is assigned the primary role of bringing a child to full term and keeping it safe. There is also the biological element: carrying a child in the womb for nine months, feeling its first moves and fearing for its existence is likened to 'experiencing death from the inside' (1995: 164). *'Bereaved mothers do not "get over" their loss, they rebuild their lives around that loss'* (emphasis in the original) (1995: 164). For Susan there is the other loss of the aborted child and her now feeling punished for this, bearing all the responsibility for what happened in a way not dissimilar to Dorothy's experience of being raped and then having to place her child for adoption (see Chapter 3).

There is a powerful argument here for the social worker to give priority to Susan's experience of the loss, or even to make this the only focus as a way of redressing the experiences in the hospital, the family and in social work generally where 'the subordination and devaluing of woman (is) ... so strongly ingrained that even the wisest in the field had trouble broadening their vision' (Walters, 1990: 14). So there is a need to value Susan's experience in a way that informs the wider story rather than marginalizing her as may have happened in the past.

Family Narratives

Looking wider, there are also the competing and complementary values the different family members ascribed to the child while in the womb, the sense they have made of his death and what it says about the family within which they now live.

One can imagine the *family narrative,* Susan's pregnancy representing her new relationship with Daniel and this confirmed again and again as the family prepares the nursery and views the scans, with their intimate, humanizing images of a developing child. For Daniel there may be special significance in this son joining him in this family of women and now he is left with his own strong feelings. Recent research illustrates the degree to which men suffer from anxiety and PTSD after a stillbirth, symptoms that may not be resolved until a subsequent live birth. The research concludes that 'fathers need support in their own right' (Turton et al., 2006, see also the SANDS publication *Fathers Feel Too* by Don, 2005).

Susan and Daniel are nursing their own hurts. As we have seen, Susan is carrying not just the habitual feelings of guilt, blame and fears concerning the prospect of future pregnancies, but also her secret shame of her previous abortion while Daniel is nursing his grievance that his role as father is not being fully recognized. They may both be feeling that, having married because of the pregnancy, they are now trapped in a relationship which has lost its immediate purpose and value.

In Chapter 6 we return to this scenario to see how the social worker can specifically work with the family but it is enough now to comment that couples can become closer once they can 'acknowledge, understand and respect the uniqueness of their partner's process' (McLaren, 2005: 89).

In this scenario the two girls, aged 10 and 8, have slipped out of view which indicates the way that *children* can be devalued in this society, especially when it comes to loss and bereavement. Not all communities and cultures silence their children at such times. Kenny notes that in working-class Bolton they view the body, attend funerals, find it comfortable to talk about the deceased, '"speaking into being" a spiritual presence' (1998: 2) and she refers to similar attitudes in the religious beliefs and/or customs of various ethnic minority communities. Kenny also recognizes that children's understanding and acceptance of death will be dependent on their social and intellectual development while McCarthy and Jessop (2005) stress the importance of the context and nature of the loss and the meaning that it holds for the individual child. Children who experience a significant loss may need many years to fully process the impact it has had (see also Christie, 2005).

The support vs. surveillance dilemma might also emerge in that the children are missing school to the point that concerns are being raised. After a stillbirth mothers can turn away from their surviving children (Bowlby, 1991: 123) so it may be that the girls are not being sufficiently supervised or are looking after their mother to the extent that they are in danger of losing out on normal friendships, educational achievements or simply the sense of having a childhood (Carpentier, 2006). 'Children who care' can often drift into becoming 'children in care' (Dearden and Becker, 1997), indeed the category of 'parent's health' is the third most common reason given for children entering the child care system (and may be a contributory factor to far more cases than is recognized) and is often influenced by the belief that such children are at risk, whether from neglect, actual abuse or a fear of the role reversal inherent in having to look after rather than be looked after.

Social workers, if influenced by such concerns, can become inquiry wary, anticipating something going wrong and the anger of managers and accusatory newspaper headlines. Preoccupation with risk factors can leave parents who are ill or disabled feeling 'that confidence in their parental role is conditional, even begrudging' (Newman, 2003: v) but Newman's analysis of the available literature sees this caution as misplaced, arising from research that is based on limited studies, uncertain statistics and worst case scenarios, with little recognition of the resilience of children. He argues that 'encounters with illness and disablement are normative experiences ... especially in more disadvantaged communities' (2003: 107) or can be actually positive, the experience of caring leading to increased empathy. Where children are removed families experience this as deeply divisive and punitive, rather than helpful (see Stanley et al., 2003, for a useful summary of the evidence).

This discussion can help us see the narrow line between support and surveillance, how our picture of a mother can be turned from caring to careless, a family from supportive to dysfunctional and how these are influenced, at least in part, by the organizational and professional values we hold.

Outcomes vs. Process

In seeking to understand the 'rush to judgement', indicated in the above discussion, we need to be aware of the tensions within social work between outcomes and process. As one commentator puts it:

> Social workers now ask *what* clients do rather then *why* they do it – a switch from causation to counting, from explanation to audit. Depth explanations based on psychological and sociological theories are

superseded by surface considerations. It is the visible surface of social behaviour which concerns practitioners and not the internal workings of psychological and sociological entities. (emphasis in the original) (Howe, 1995: 88).

This suggests that we are allowing ourselves to be rushed in our work, not paying sufficient attention to, or directly undermining and ignoring the stories clients are trying to tell us. The other danger is that, in our enthusiasm for new theories, we use them to impose 'a new orthodoxy ... (but) all models, being a tidying up of untidy human experiences, run the risk of betraying that experience' (Kohner, 2000: 356).

Research evidences the degree to which professionals unconsciously shape clients' stories to fit our own perceptions. McCabe at al. (2002) document doctors choosing to smile, laugh and look away rather than address the uncomfortable questions and concerns of psychiatric patients while Hall et al., (2003a) follow case conferences where mothers request that their child comes into care and a line-by-line analysis of the meetings shows just how subtly but surely the mothers' comments are turned around until they are acceptable to the professionals' value system and theories of motherhood.

Pithouse identifies a number of contradictory themes within the story of 'the client' (the term used in his research): on the one hand they are valued 'as an abstract notion, revered', offering the hope of autonomy and self actualization where social workers maintain a position of being non-judgemental. In 'real life', however, clients 'are often a troublesome and morally deficient type of people' with 'practitioner-folklore' regarding them as 'venal and unappreciative and in need of careful management', (1987: 81), they are a 'problem-species' (1987:87). Pithouse observed workers, on occasion, mimicking and caricaturing clients and routinely lying, clients being told that their social worker is 'out of the office' when s/he simply wants to avoid them.

It is quite shocking to read examples of social workers acting unethically. Perhaps these incidents occur because we are now less well equipped, in terms of time, resources, skills or organizational support, to deal with difficulty and challenge and this is the fault of 'the audit society' within which contemporary social work operates, 'a culture of inspection and control ... and the underlying anxieties about dangerousness ... (and) the risks of corruption to moral and professional integrity' (Cooper and Lousada, 2005: 22).

Possibly structural and organizational changes have had a significant, perhaps even fundamental, impact on social work or have only served to exacerbate a tendency that has actually always been present within social work, and other health and social care professions. It is perhaps inevitable that those who are motivated to help and make things 'better' find it immeasurably hard to stay with difficulty and despair. As pointed out earlier, Philpot captured this in his comment, in relationship to palliative care, that social workers can be left feeling 'useless in the face of such remorseless finality', having to 'set aside' their normal, or preferred approach of 'activity and optimism' and focusing instead on 'pain and sorrow' (1989: 11–12). Grenier (2005) observes that social workers, when undertaking risk assessments of older people, endeavour to identify all the uncertainties, of health, frailty, family support, but avoid confronting the one thing that is certain, the service user's mortality.

It is these tensions between *outcomes* and *process* that I want to explore now. The following case scenario specifically addresses a family affected by Cystic Fibrosis but has implications for chronic illness and life limiting conditions in general.

Case Scenario Wanda and her Parents, Caring for a Child with Cystic Fibrosis

Lorraine and Michael are in their early forties and have an only child, Wanda, aged 12 who, two years ago, was diagnosed as having Cystic Fibrosis (CF). Lorraine describes how it was 'a relief' getting a diagnosis after a prolonged period of worry, 'we knew something was not right but had no way of naming it'. Wanda is doing well at school, taking full part in various sports activities which she loves. Until a recent hospitalization the illness had been, for the most part, mild and stable, just the occasional crisis and in-patient treatment but managed mainly by regular home based physiotherapy and medication. Wanda had the condition explained to her when it was first diagnosed and she was very cooperative with all the treatment until the most recent hospitalization after which she became withdrawn and rebellious, refusing her enzymes. At these points Lorraine starts battling with Wanda while Michael feels sorry for his daughter, tries to placate her and so the row ends up being between him and his wife.

Lorraine and Michael both know from other parents they have met the potent combination of a child hitting adolescence at the same time as the condition deteriorates. They try to be very

(Continued)

(Continued)

positive about Wanda, love her deeply but are becoming increasingly concerned about the future, the additional demands that CF will make on all of them. They wonder what life will hold for her and feel sad at what they fear she, and they, will miss out on.

- What is your emotional response to this situation and to the various participants?
- How does this link to your own professional and/or personal values?

The Competing Values Underlying Disability – Medical, Psychological and Social

Disability, as a generic terms, is very broad, incorporating experiences as diverse as Wanda and her parents and those described in other scenarios: Kuldip, the aspiring young Asian woman with the unexplained virus, Sam's wife disabled by cancer, Mat, facing death in the latter stages of AIDS, Peter, whose disabilities are linked with mental illness. What they all share is a condition that 'eventually becomes part of everyday life and the loss might be reinforced on a daily basis' (Katz, 2002: 152).

Certainly there are psychological depths to disability with these losses often likened to a bereavement, and the 'stages model' invoked, in the sense of the 'death' of normal expectations of the present and hopes for the future. It is, however, more complicated since the disability continues to cause new losses in both the private and public arenas so 'resolution' is difficult to reach and the pain is ongoing. Degenerative illnesses are notoriously capricious, thus CF has been described as 'a life's journey in the shadow of early death, in the presence of uncertainty and unpredictability, not to mention dedication to hard work and continuous therapy' (Markovitz, 2001: 380).

The reference to the need for 'continuous therapy' also indicates the importance of the medical model, its dominance in discussions about disability. Staying with CF, as a result of medical breakthroughs and careful clinical management the average age at death has increased, in the last 40 years from 3 to 32. Similar developments elsewhere, for example with AIDS, means that many conditions are now viewed as chronic rather than terminal illnesses. Emphasizing the medical model, however, implies a very specific value base, as indicated in the phrase 'being a patient' which is a fair representation of what is expected of people once they are 'under the doctor'.

'Under the Doctor': Examples of the Medical Model

Sealey, the partner of someone with kidney failure, comments on how 'the routine was unremitting ... we were becoming more and more deeply entrenched in a day-by-day existence centred on dialysis ... control of our lives was steadily passing from us' (1993: 204).

Young woman with a profound bodily paralysis in a rehabilitation unit: 'Your body is handled, but not touched' (Seymour, 1998: 76).

In CF the routine treatment is home-based physiotherapy, 'techniques ... that ... are time-consuming, intrusive and bitterly resented' (Bush: 2001: 11) turning the parent into 'the enforcer' (McLaughlin, 2001: 53).

The values underpinning the *social model of disability* are radically different with an emphasis not on the individual's 'impairment' as the problem but more *the disabling society* whose unease and ignorance of disability puts up the barriers thus leaving those with disabilities as 'enforced' members of one of the most discriminated against groups in society' (Morris: 1989: 9). The Disability Movement argues that this needs confronting collectively and politically and also contests the 'loss model', resented because it implies the mindset of 'tragedy' and 'impairment' and assumes a link between disability and emotional problems. The loss model also, so the critique goes, allows only for integration with or adjustment to the reality as defined by non disabled people. Consequently counselling is, for the most part, rejected since it 'cannot *fix* disability because disability is a problem created by society and not the individual' (emphasis in the original) (Reeve: 2000: 671).

Tensions Between Outcomes and Process for Social Workers

In the midst of these value led, philosophical debates, social workers working with disability have to respond to a plethora of working parties, laws and guidance notes. Oliver and Sapey (2006) summarize these well and highlight the tensions for social workers as they are caught between organizational changes, party political concerns about increasing costs and effectiveness and the demands of increasingly confident campaigning by people who are themselves disabled and fiercely resist what they see as the self interest, prejudice and power of the professional lobby, including social workers. On this shifting ground social workers have not always proved very sure-footed. If changes of practice can only follow from more positive attitudes '(I)t in this area of social work services specifically that the least progress has been made' (Oliver and Sapey, 2006: 18).

Part of the problem for social work is the continuing dominance of the medical model so it is important in this section to be clear about how social workers can value our own role as well as fully appreciating the contribution of health care professionals.

On the *outcome* side social workers can offer a great deal when drawing on their assessment skills, including an expert knowledge of resources and an ability to advocate so that they might better match client needs. All this falls clearly within the *case management role* and Oliver and Sapey (2006), coming from the social model of disability, particularly value those social workers who give priority to practical support to individuals and families rather than obsessing about possibly non-existent emotional needs.

The social model is also important in social work, especially given our commitment to the *anti-discriminatory dimension* but we need also to stay with the *process* element, remembering Crow's (1996: 58) argument that the emphasis on social barriers can mean little or no acknowledgement of the degree of physical pain, difficulty and unpleasantness which is part of the experience of disability. Reeve (2000), whose deeply felt criticisms of counselling were cited above, nevertheless does see the possibilities of *feminist* and *transcultural* approaches, in essence *a consciousness raising* which encompasses the personal and the political, the subjective and the objective experiences of disability. Lenny will only give the time of day (or 50 minutes in the counselling room) for person centred counselling since this, as compared to psychodynamic or behavioural approaches, 'does not impose its own meaning on situations, does not make judgements in advance or put labels on people. It is not about someone's impairment or their disability but about helping them to make sense of the relationship between the two' (1993: 239).

Outcomes and Process when Working
with Wanda and her Parents

As in this chapter's first scenario, Lorraine and Michael are facing *the loss of a child,* not a stillborn baby, but it is a *multiple loss* of a significant individual, of a stage of life, the loss of creation and of potential (CPS: 2001), of potency where the parents are apparently unequal to the task of protecting this their only child, indeed one parent will actually have inadvertently bequeathed the killer gene thus reinforcing feelings of *guilt* or *self-blame*. The parents must put on hold all expectations since they cannot be sure if their daughter will live into adulthood, or become a mother.

Lorraine and Michael can be offered the opportunity to step back from the busyness of the illness and get in touch with their feelings. For many parents 'grieving begun when they were first given the diagnosis' and remains so, even if not always within their awareness (Madge, 2001: 315). Certainly any situation where a child has a life limiting condition is awe-ful given the emphasis on 'preparing for uncertainty' with parents not knowing 'whether to prepare for life or for death' (Solnit 1993: 33). Understanding where they are in a disease trajectory can help normalize what is otherwise a strange and frightening series of events. However they do it the parents need to find some balance if they are to stop fighting each other and focus on providing appropriate support and home care for Wanda. 'The family unit is not only affected by the illness but the family also has an impact on the illness and its course over time' (McCubbin et al., 2001: 219) with high levels of criticism and hostility and low levels of warmth in family relationships generally correlating with poorer physical health of the child. Research (McCubbin et al., 2001) indicates that deterioration and dysfunction is not inevitable, instead there can be patterns of resilience with families actually strengthened by the way they respond in the face of a crisis.

Wanda is very aware of how her condition is becoming more intrusive, increasingly visible, both to herself and to her peers who may be curious about her condition. She is, then, acutely aware of her differences, marked as deficiencies, as compared to the exacting standards of approaching adolescence, the peer pressures about how girls 'ought' to look and behave which will be so at odds with the demands of her disability: the special diets, the symptoms such as coughing, delayed puberty, absences from school, etc. This is sharpened when she heard at her last hospital appointment that a contemporary, previously befriended at clinics, had died and she is suddenly faced with her own presumed fate.

Wanda might manage this crisis in a number of ways. Like many other life limiting, chronic conditions, CF has a 'dynamic process'. Some children can maintain a positive outlook by adopting an attitude of 'adaptive denial' or 'compartmentalisation' (Angst, 2001: 132), simply getting on with the daily demands of life and not talking or thinking about their condition unless faced with no other choice. Peek describes how she saw her condition as unremarkable, 'something I'd always known, something that was just about me, like my hand was always my hand' (2001: 29). This is less of an option for Wanda right now. Regarding her friend she needs to be allowed to mourn his death and express her own fears about her mortality, rather than simply refusing her medication because it seems so pointless. This theme is returned to in Chapter 6 where it is suggested how group work can help Wanda, and her parents, through this crisis.

Reviewing her illness can help Wanda to reality test, see that this is not necessarily her immediate future. Previously Wanda may have been too young to make the conceptual leap that allows her to submit to painful chest physiotherapy if she is not actually coughing (see discussion in Angst, 2001: 126). She may now be mature enough to be more involved in discussions and decisions about the illness and treatment options, managing the care tasks, learning to balance independence with interdependence. Giving all due importance to 'self care' or 'self-management', whether in CF or similar conditions such as diabetes or sickle cell, can generally enhance self-esteem. The review can incorporate her social life, current activities and how far she can sustain her sporting and academic achievements. Wanda can be helped to manage her adolescence and express her fears that, at a time when her peers are experimenting with increasing independence, she senses a growing reliance on her parents and the encroachments on her autonomy as her body lets her down.

Wanda might also be ready to see that disability need not be only a loss. Someone who has a disability comments: 'I suffer too much emotional conflict to come properly to terms with the situation, though despite this I seem to have survived and even more incredibly can still experience great joy and happiness' (Morris, 1989: 79). Seymour goes further, she suggests that disability can serve as a catalyst, with individuals developing new ways of using and thinking about their bodies, 'remaking' their bodies and so transcending their world, and that of the 'normal', able-bodied. This perspective fits with the restoration/loss model (see discussion in Chapter 2) and the oscillation between the two.

Staying with process can also help with managing the pressures of a situation, like Wanda's, where individuals and families confront the impact of life limiting conditions. This is not to minimize the struggle. A nurse notes how the 'the hard part about diagnosis [is] trying to balance hope with reality' while another nurse comments that there 'are ... kids that you get really close to and when you see those kids deteriorate and you experience their death, it is always a really hard time' (Woodgate and Chernick , 2001: 90).

Solnit, describing his work with the parents of children with severe disabilities, says that he draws on 'cautious reserved optimism' and 'restrained pessimism', he argues that 'hopes for and commitments to a life worth living can be sensibly given the weight of a feather on the side of optimism' (1993: 33).

And he then asks a crucial question:

> Is such an approach an either/or trap, one that comforts those who need it least (doctors and nurses) and deprives those who need it most (the child and its parents) of an uncertainty, an ambiguity that is painful and realistic? (1993: 33)

Conclusion

The GSCC Code of Practice for Social Workers lays down some useful markers but the above discussions indicate just how deeply complex and contradictory the application of values is in daily practice. This is played out between professional groups, such as the different values pertaining to medical, social and legal models around disability or child care, between service users and professionals and then within the profession. Social workers in such situations appear to be having to choose one voice over another which puts them in a win–lose situation. Narrative ethics, however, offers a different perspective allowing us to identify and work with:

> a series of intersecting stories ... juxtaposing different accounts ... looking for commonalities, points where the stories coincide, placing one story within another, the history and outcome for an immediate choice played out within the larger narrative of a service user's life ... the movie as well as the snapshot. (Wilks, 2005: 1257)

Points for practice

- Ethical issues underpin all aspects of social work practice.
- The GSCC Codes of Practice have been developed so as to support you in your work and they may sometimes present as contradictory in your direct practice with service users.

(Continued)

(Continued)

- Conflicts of interest can arise between your personal ethics and values and those that underpin the professional practice expected of you.
- The conflicts of interest can also be between your social work ethics and values and those of other professional groups with whom you are working.
- It is important for you to be able to talk about situations where your own ethical beliefs, personal or professional, clash with what is expected from you, so that you can be supported in any action that needs to be taken.

Further reading

A sound introduction to values in social work is provided by:
Becket, C, and Maynard, A. (2005) *Values and Ethics in Social Work.*
Jordan, B. (1990) *Social Work in an Unjust Society* offers a more critical account.
Explicit links are made with Narrative by Wilks, T. (2005) 'Social Work and Narrative Ethics', *British Journal of Social Work,* 35: 1249–64.

For more about stillbirths go to www.uk.sand.org

For children, www.childbereavement.org.uk

For disability, www.leeds.ac.uk/disability-studies

5 Social Work Skills, Methods and Theories in Work with Individuals

Chapter contents

- Further focus on assessment and understandings of loss
- Cognitive behavioural methods, how they can be used and the skills of social workers
- Bereavement counselling, aims and the skills of social workers
- Ideas of 'the self' as explained by psychodynamic concepts and the 'threatened identity'
- Links back to narrative, case examples linked to the social work skills
- Working with the spiritual dimensions of loss

Introduction

This chapter acknowledges the growing repertoire of theories and interventions open to social workers in working with individuals. How we decide on a particular approach will clearly rely on our *assessment skills* and the discussion here will build on the discussion in Chapters 1 and 2 concerning how *we understand the losses*. Ways of *working with loss* are explored through *cognitive behavioural approaches* and *working with the sense of the self*, drawing on *psychodynamic* ideas; and the idea of the *threatened identity*. This takes us back to *narrative* and how we address *the spiritual dimension*, in ourselves and our clients. The models will be applied to the case scenarios of *Lou*, whose deceased husband suffered from Alzheimer's Disease and *Peter* who has enduring mental health problems.

This chapter is a bridge between the previous chapter, showing how social work values can be applied in practice, and the next which looks to working with individuals within a wider context: family, groups and community.

Case Scenario   Lou, a Widow Whose Husband, George, had Alzheimer's Disease

Lou, 77, and George (also 77) had been married for 59 years. Shortly after his retirement at 65 George developed the symptoms of Alzheimer's Disease and his condition deteriorated from the initial forgetfulness and low-level confusion to the point where he could not be left alone and became physically and verbally abusive. Nevertheless, despite her poor health, due to angina and arthritis, Lou insisted on managing without any outside support until her children eventually persuaded her that George should go to hospital for an assessment, 'so we know what's happening mum, and to give you a break'. George died very shortly after being admitted to hospital.

Six months later Lou is living alone, sleeping badly and is in a lot of physical pain. She sees little of her children and has no contact with neighbours, friends, etc. 'George always said if you've got family, you don't need no-one else.'

Looking back on her marriage Lou comments, almost defiantly, 'we had an old fashioned marriage, it suited us. We did that promise, "in sickness and in health" and then I put him away and he just turned his face to the wall and died. If we'd not been so loving, the two of us, perhaps I wouldn't be missing him so badly now. Or the children wouldn't be turning their back on me. Or I'd have more friends. We must have done summat wrong.'

The oldest son has contacted social services, concerned about Lou's physical and mental frailty, and that she is still distressed by the bereavement, 'she should be over it by now, the dad we all knew and loved died a long time ago.'

Case Scenario   Peter, Living Alone with his Voices

Peter is 28, African-Caribbean, and unemployed apart from very occasional casual work. He lives alone in an inner city area, and presents as very isolated with no friends.

When Peter was 18 his father died in a car crash; shortly afterwards Peter had his first breakdown, was detained in hospital and diagnosed with schizophrenia and he was compulsorily

(Continued)

(Continued)

detained once more, six years ago. Peter has no contact with his extensive family of origin and while he does have a three-year-old child by an ex-girlfriend, whom he sometimes spots in the local market, he avoids approaching them.

Peter attends a mental health centre run by a voluntary group where he enjoys learning some basic IT skills. When asked, Peter says 'I'm ok, I'm fine, I'm getting by' but he does admit to feeling bitter that his life has 'just been a waste'. He dislikes taking his medication and is threatering to stop taking it: 'all those pills can't be good for me, they are doing my head in.' He says he feels 'at peace with my God and my music' but unfortunately his neighbours are less at peace; they complain to the landlord who contacts social services about his playing his music too loud and too late. They are also concerned that he neglects the flat, which is attracting vermin, and are disturbed by his shouting. Although he is reluctant to admit this Peter is actually trying to drown out his voices, 'they give me nothing but grief, they're evil, man'.

Peter and Lou could well live in the same geographical community, just a short distance from each other, but their stories suggest that they live in different worlds, divided by age, gender, race and their general life experiences. What they share, however, is a sense of their losses, both specific and cumulative.

Like many, perhaps most, service users Lou and Peter have not independently sought out social workers, but have instead been referred by others who are identifying problems and risk factors. This returns us to the themes discussed in the previous chapter about *social work values.* The professionals will be holding in their work the tensions between *surveillance,* the degree to which service users may need protecting from themselves, and their wish to *support* them to stay in the community. In the possible urgency of the situation they need to identify and work towards *outcomes* while also attending to *process,* ensuring that the stories the service users have to tell can emerge and be valued.

Ideas of 'The Self'

This chapter explores the specific interventions that social workers can apply and while the focus remains on Lou and Peter the discussion will be relevant to other groups of service users. There will be a discussion of the potential of Cognitive Behavioural approaches which are increasingly popular in social work given their strong evidence base and support for short-term interventions. CBT is based on a very particular understanding of the self and, as a way of contrasting this with other approaches, Barker (1999) describes it as 'fixing the function' whereas psychoanalysis is about 'healing the soul' and humanistic therapies are 'in search of the person': quick phrases but containing a core of truth.

Staying with the humanistic therapies, there is an emphasis on the *real* as opposed to a *false self*, that combination of the descriptions that have been given to someone who then takes them on board uncritically. The assumption is that all of us can take full response-ability for our thoughts, feelings and actions, can be congruent and authentic and thus live more fully and 'self actualize' (Maslow, 1968), become a fully functioning being (Rogers, see Mearns and Thorne, 2000), achieving organismic self-regulation (gestalt, see Clarkson, 1989). But we stop ourselves from reaching that place, retreat to the creative adjustments (gestalt) that kept us safe in the past but may not be serving us well now.

Breakwell (1986) provides another way of understanding the self and the dynamics, she terms it a threatened identity and this lends itself well to the impact of loss and bereavement. In this model one person is marked out from another through a set of social, psychological and behavioural characteristics, and there are concentric circles of the *spiritual*, entailing thinking and feeling, the *material*, what one owns, the *social*, how one relates to significant individuals and groups, and the *bodily*, the physical organism.

When our sense of how we see ourselves is threatened, our response is to go through a process of *assimilation-accommodation* as we acknowledge and grow into our 'newness'. By *evaluating* that new aspect we come to give it some sort of meaning and make it *authentic*.

Integral to the success of this process is (not necessarily in this order) the need for:

- *continuity* in self-definition
- *distinctiveness* which is vitalizing, and
- *a sense of self-esteem*.

These attributes, the promise of self-actualization, can seem a challenge for the best of us but even more for Lou, whose life changes have been so dramatic and then again for Peter, who has apparently been so damaged by life over such a long period of time. Rogers, however, developed his ideas about the effectiveness of 'the core conditions', the healing power available to the client when offered empathy, congruence and acceptance, as a result of his work with highly disturbed, schizophrenic patients (see discussion in McLeod, 2003).

Assessment

What we need to start with, however, is an *assessment* to allow the opportunity to see if what is required is *a crisis intervention* and/or an *appropriate care plan* and what *theories* and *models* can be drawn upon.

There have been many debates within social work about the way to approach assessments with Smale et al. (1993) offering *the exchange model* as a challenge to other bureaucratic and procedural, top down, information giving, one-off acts of assessment. Assessment should, instead, be a shared practice, based on partnership with a fully involved service user at the very centre of the process. This follows the guidance of the various National Service Frameworks, for example the NSF for Older People (Department of Health, 2001) makes the needs of older people central to the reform programme for health and social services demanding the rooting out of discrimination, providing person centred care, promoting health and independence and fitting services around older peoples' needs.

The Single Assessment Process for older people (Department of Health, 2002) and its *interdisciplinary* approach should prevent a situation whereby Lou, having been left outside the professional loop for so long, would be confronted by a range of officials seeking similar, but not identical, sets of information. A full assessment at this point should allow the emergence of the best possible picture of practical, social, psychological and medical needs, fully incorporating Lou's perspective of the situation.

Working with Lou

The social worker needs to start by asking Lou how she sees her current situation and what she feels would help to make things better. Has Lou received any support with bereavement? Are there any immediate practical or financial issues that she is concerned about? A *full medical check* would help clarify what in her physical deterioration might be an inevitable part of the ageing process and what can be addressed, such as medication for the depressive feelings and sleeplessness. Home support might be available and links made with outside community resources, whether age specific or faith based. This is shifting the focus from 'the problem' to 'the individual' and further to 'the community' as seen in the *networking model* (Trevillion, 1999). This community dimension will be explored more fully in Chapter 6.

The care management model is clearly important and it can prioritize practical issues to the detriment of other concerns, leaving 'a number of emotional and psychological needs unaddressed' (Lymbery, 2005: 31) and this relates to my own observations of a care manager on home assessment interviews and meeting women who tell him of their recent losses. One needs an assessment because the sudden death of her daughter leaves her without a carer, the other had once served as a councillor on the Social Services Committee and now she shows her ruefulness in shifting her role from providing services to needing them. In neither case did the care manager acknowledge let alone address their feelings (Weinstein, 1998a).

Lloyd (2006) usefully rehearses the contemporary concerns about social work practice with older people, specifically the agency driven, outcome focused interventions which have come to dominate the care management and assessment process. Within this model 'loss' is not on the agenda, as an example one very recent text entitled *Social Work with Older People* (Crawford and Walker, 2004) has no reference in the index to 'loss', 'death' or 'bereavement'.

> ### Exercise 5.1 Assessing Lou's Losses
>
> Referring back to Chapter 2 if necessary make a list of:
>
> * Lou's losses and what they might mean for her.
> * Where she might be in the mourning process.

If loss is generally neglected in the texts and in practice it is all the more important that we keep it firmly in mind. Certainly Lou's family are in no doubt about what they think is happening and they turn to the widely recognized *stages model* whereby Lou, six months on from the death, is expected to have 'got over' the loss and be ready to move on, especially as the *physical* death has been preceded by a prolonged *social* death with George first becoming lost to them through his dementia and then his hospitalization. It may be that they have gone through their *anticipatory grieving* and cannot understand that their mother is in a different place. This is an example of *disenfranchised grief,* her own experience is trivialized by her family in the assumption that she should be less affected by the loss (Thompson, S., 2002).

For Lou, hers is not just an individual loss but something that resonates with *the wider experience of ageing,* often felt as a difficult and negative period. Thus Blythe describes the older people he interviewed as living in 'deprived time. They are aware of ceaseless depredation and of everything being snatched from them or placed out of reach, and of being narrowed and lessened and ground-out of their very personality' (1979: 15). Orbach describes the ageing process as 'not so much growing up but growing down' (1999: 153) and Viorst comments that 'it's hard for the soul to sing as it gets older' (1987: 318).

Alternatively Erikson's (1965) classic study of *the ages of man* sees old age as having many potential satisfactions and allows a place of wisdom once the tensions between integrity and despair can be resolved. Grandchildren can bring pleasures without responsibility while *disengagement theory* (Cummings and Henry, 1961) suggests that as older people gradually relinquish the roles that they carry in society this allows for their depleted levels of energy to be usefully transferred to less demanding areas. This presupposes, of course, that the choice is consciously taken by individuals rather than a forced response to patterns of exclusion and discrimination.

Throughout this scenario there are connections between the *social/structural* and the *individual/ psychological.* Older people are, as a group, generally dismissed and discriminated against in this society and suffer disproportionately from poverty, thus Age Concern's estimate that in the UK, one in five pensioners live in poverty (2005).

For Lou there are losses linked to the *physical:* her health is deteriorating but some of her symptoms could be mitigated if diagnosed. There may be accompanying *psychological problems,* including depression which is often under reported among older people, leaving individuals experiencing loss of energy, appetite, etc. Sleeping badly may be partly a result of the depression, and also her constant pain which, in turn, feeds the depression. Perhaps, also, it is caused by the disruption of the physical closeness she has taken for granted for so many years. Lou and George had shared a double bed until the day he left but she feels embarrassed admitting to her children how much she misses their 'cuddles'. For a fuller discussion see Manthorpe and Iliffe (2005).

The losses inherent in these situations may be exacerbated if she shares her generation's reticence about talking about death and other losses in the 'modern' way and she may yearn for the more traditional approaches that are no more. But even if Lou has the words it appears that her family does not want to hear them.

The bereavement is a hard one. Lou may not be religious as such but there is a *spiritual or existential dimension* as she confronts her own mortality. After a long and intimate marriage Lou experienced the loss of communication, companionship and reciprocity and the loss of her own independence and interests. As an informal carer, in the immediacy and intensity of looking after George, many of her feelings had been put on hold but what is now surfacing is a mix of confusion and resentment and she is probably not helped by her family's apparent reliance on a *coping style of denial and avoidance* which can add to the sense of the burden. Kitwood presents a case study, which seems to reflect Lou's issues, where the carer needs help with 'feelings of anger, inadequacy and guilt ... to come to terms with his own tragic predicament' (1997: 41).

So what we return to again and again is Lou's sense of self. Her *narrative* about herself as part of a large and loving family has been spoilt. She is now a widow, and the reciprocal nature of her role of 'wife' had, in any event, changed significantly over the length of George's illness. Her relationship with her children is being renegotiated, and not in her favour. Having seen how her children so easily persuaded her to put George 'away' she may be wondering if this is her future too.

The Possibilities for Good Practice
Working with Lou

Cognitive behavioural therapy approaches have a very strong evidence base for working with anxiety, depression and low self-esteem and is seen as effective with older as with younger populations (Hill and Brettle, 2006).

Cognitive Behavioural Therapy (CBT) Approaches

Beck (1989) sees CBT working on three levels:

1. *Intellectual,* identifying the key *negative automatic thoughts* and/or *behaviour,* assessing how these are unhelpful and false and can be replaced.
2. *Experiential,* helping the individual to experience situations which could challenge and change these false assumptions.
3. *Behavioural,* developing new coping techniques.

The Social Work Skills in CBT

- *Working short term,* usually 12–20 sessions over a three-month period.
- *Active experiments:* diagrams, blackboards, role play, practising thought stopping or taking time out, reframing internal emotional states, to encourage 'excitement' in place of 'fear'.
- *Setting homework,* e.g. the individual keeping a daily diary recording emotional upsets, negative automatic thoughts and the alternative rational responses that might emerge instead. The worker assesses what are facts, what are beliefs, how often the service user has them, how intense (rated on a scale of 1 to 10), how long they last and their context.

(Continued)

(Continued)

- Helping the service user *gain confidence through increased mastery and achievement,* identifying and modifying the unhelpful assumptions they have about the world.
- The social worker is essentially a *teacher*, sharing the work with the service user and being active, directive and challenging.

Cognitive theory recognizes the way we can often have conflicting ways of thinking about ourselves even when describing the same set of circumstances – 'activating two different schemas' in the terminology. This can actually be helpful, just as Piaget (1952) notes that children's cognitive development relies on their needing to integrate competing schema so adults can benefit from reflecting on how they can use their contradictory thoughts as a way of moving on. Thus an individual can report generalized and extreme feelings of stress at work and also acknowledge those few times when s/he can manage a crisis at work without getting immobilized by stress. The service user can then be helped to explore these more fully, incorporating the otherwise competing 'stressed at work' and the 'not stressed at work' stories and constructing a 'higher order' story. This might be 'when I make sure I ask for the support and help I need, I can avoid becoming too stressed'.

Exercise 5.2

Lou: her negative automatic thoughts

Identify the various negative automatic thoughts that Lou has about her life and do not seem to be serving her well.

- *Her role as a carer: 'I put George away.'* Lou can be helped to recognize how hard so many people find it to care for someone, especially a long term partner with Alzheimer's Disease. This opens up the opportunity for her to judge herself less harshly, to see how well she did to keep George at home for so long rather than how fast she surrendered him to the hospital.
- *Her marriage: 'We must have done summat wrong.'* She can reflect on what she and George achieved together, the value in the choices they made about how to live their life.

- *Her children: 'They are turning their back on me.'* Lou can be helped to hold the possibility that their getting George into hospital arose not from callousness but from their love and concern for him and for her. Their behaviour now, not visiting Lou, is painful for her but may be the only way they know of managing their grief.
- *Her depression:* Lou might be helped to see that her mood is not an all encompassing bleakness. Keeping a diary, noting good moments and memories, sharing these with the social worker, can give some perspective to her life.
- *Loneliness: 'We don't need no-one.'* After such a long period of isolation within her marriage, Lou can be encouraged to make moves out into the wider world. One such foray is not successful: she goes shopping and gets distressed when, ordering a cup of coffee in a café, her arthritic fingers cannot open the plastic milk container. More successful is her trip to the club linked to the church where she plays bingo followed by a fish and chips dinner, both of which George would have dismissed as 'common' but she thoroughly enjoys.
- Social workers are not trained as counsellors, let alone as specialists in bereavement, but we do draw on counselling skills to help vulnerable individuals like Lou find some meaning in their recent difficulties (Seden, 1999; Miller, 2006) and her anger and distress can be heard and explored further but in a contained and safe environment. All of this is the established or traditional way of working with bereavement while Walter's (1999) concerns with the biographical model fits with Lou sharing her memories of George, especially when the social worker is on home visits where photos are readily available. Through such means Lou can get to know George again, more fully even, leading to time for personal reflection, reviewing her past life and looking forward and acknowledging her own mortality. This is all especially potent for Lou since it is argued that prolonged contact with someone with Alzheimer's Disease, whose memory becomes so fragmented, can leave the carer similarly fragmented and needing to bring back together the scattered pieces of their existence (Balfour, 2006).

Bereavement Counselling

The aims of counselling:

- Support the grieving and mourning processes.
- Encouragement of the expression of grief, sadness, anger, anxiety, hopelessness, helplessness, despair.

(Continued)

(Continued)

- Review the positive and negative aspects of the lost relationship.
- Work through old unresolved losses (Raphael, 1977).
- Reassurances about the normality of the psychological accompaniment of grief.
- 'Chance to take stock ... and to start discovering new directions' (Parkes, 1980: 6).
- Allow the mourner to gain a fuller and enduring sense of the deceased (Walter, 1999).

The skills of bereavement counselling:

- Qualities of empathy, sensitivity, honesty, gentleness (Lazarus, 1971).
- Individuals able to see the gains they make as a consequence of their own work (Lambert and Cattani-Thompson, 1996).
- A safe place where individuals are taken seriously and shown respect (Weinstein, 1998b).
- 'Stay with the process and listen, not push for outcomes, show respect for what is there, see the usefulness and even the beauty of the way others express their mourning and sense of loss and allow oneself to be the firm ground on which the other stands' (Zinker, 1994: 262).

Reminiscence Work

Jung, when an older man, describes his attempt 'to see the line which leads through my life into the world, and out of the world again' (1967, cited in Orbach, 1999: 153). *Reminiscence work,* or *life review,* is a well evidenced technique where practitioners work therapeutically with what older people often most enjoy, telling their stories and the process is honoured and structured through the sharing of letters, photographs and/or diaries. As with any approach it will not be appropriate with all service users or it may be used carelessly by the worker (see useful discussion in Biggs, 1993: 61–76). Research suggests that for some it seems at best an irrelevancy, at worst distressing but a significant proportion do find it a therapeutic process (Coleman, 1986). Gibson's research into small, time-limited groups in residential and day care settings, reports positive responses overall. Grief for inevitable losses, of homes and gardens, pets, health and strength, is a constant theme and when these 'losses, and difficulties courageously surmounted' are 'vividly recalled', members 'spoke warmly about the sense of strength and support they derived from sharing some of their pain, often for the first time' (1992: 33–4). Gibson goes on to say that members gained in self-esteem. 'It was as if by having their past publicly affirmed as important by other people they could feel better about themselves in the present' (1992: 34).

Case Example   Reminiscence Work with Lou

On one visit the social worker notices that the photo of Lou and George's wedding day, normally clearly on display on the mantelpiece, has been laid flat on its face. Lou comments, 'I couldn't bear looking at it any more, it's too upsetting, too many bad memories.' She repeats her familiar phrase: 'we must have done summat wrong' but this time she sounds angry, not resigned. The social worker picks the photo up, says what a handsome couple they are and Lou also looks.

Lou is asked to imagine herself back to when she was 'the blushing bride' and what that day had been like for her and what her hopes had been. Lou hesitates and then warms to the subject, her voice softening as she remembers the specialness of that occasion. The social worker then asks Lou how the marriage had been, not just 'the sickness' of the last period, which has been understandably uppermost in Lou's mind, but also the 'health'. Lou is able to admit that most of their life together had been really good and happy and that even during the period of the Alzheimer's' Disease there had been moments when a smile or some other recognition compensated for the more difficult times and she recognized the George she had loved for so long. Asked what she wants to do with the photo now Lou places it back in its place of honour.

By constant reminiscing, individuals will maintain a sense of self through all their bodily changes and feel less diminished as their faculties fail ... [it can be] compared to the remembering and working-through that features in psychoanalysis ... [and] facilitates mourning for the many losses they have inevitably had to suffer. (Orbach, 1999: 173)

Working with Peter

With Peter there is some urgency in how the case has been reported and social workers might well find themselves looking to medical models and preoccupied with a need for surveillance. Surveying the current mood within societal and professional circles Laurence has commented that fear drives the mental health system (2003), especially when it involves disturbed young black men as symbolized by Christopher Clunis, who stabbed a stranger to death in 1992. Consequently Peter's *race* and *gender* has an impact with 'black people and the mentally ill occupy(ing) a similar position as outsiders' (Wilkinson, 1998: 209).

The Possibilities for Good Practice Working with Peter

Given the above, a careful assessment is imperative and, as with Lou, it needs to be service user led and underpinned by a multidisciplinary perspective. The Care Programme Approach (Department of Health, 1990), first implemented in 1991 and subsequently revised and integrated with Care Management to form a single co-ordinated approach, focuses on multi-professional assessment. The emphasis on the service users, and carers, was reinforced in the National Service Framework for Mental Health (Department of Health, 1999) and then 'Our health, our care, our say' (Department of Health, 2006), the first White Paper to prioritize the need to be 'person centred' over purely professional concerns. Stanley et al. (2003) stress the importance of collaboration, between social workers and health practitioners such as CPNs and GPs.

As with Lou there is a need for an urgent *medical assessment*, to confirm Peter's general health, possibly neglected as a result of his illness and exacerbated by the poverty of his living conditions. Also his *medication* needs reviewing following a clarification as to why he is wanting to stop taking his pills.

We also need to have some understanding of the losses he has experienced and what these may mean for him.

Exercise 5.3

Peter: understanding his losses

Referring back to Chapter 2 if necessary make a list of:

- Peter's losses and what they might mean for him.
- Where he might be in the mourning process.

Adults with severe and enduring mental health problems have been described as 'one of the most excluded groups in society' (Social

Exclusion Unit, 2004: 3) and Peter's losses are certainly *societal/structural*. Whatever his social origins he is now part of the underclass locked into the structural inequalities of bad housing, unemployment and poverty which further reinforce the loneliness of his existence, the lack of family, friends, neighbours: all that is valued by society. He is part of 'care in the community' but his community is a 'fragmented' one and he is a member of what Hoggett calls the 'psychological proletariat, living and (rarely) working in a social universe noticeably short on sympathy and empathy' (1993: 206).

His situation has an *existential* dimension. In the radical 1960s and its aftermath there was a widespread 'madness as sanity' movement, expressed in films like *One Flew Over The Cuckoo's Nest* (Foreman, 1975) and writers like Laing (1959), Fanon (1970) focusing on how racism and colonialism drive black people insane, Laing and Esterson (1964) critiquing the family with Orbach (1979) locating madness in the myriad ways that women are oppressed. Such perspectives are muted today so Peter's is a lone struggle with the discrepancy between how he understands the world and how it is understood by those around him.

There have been a series of *family losses* and it is not clear how far his original breakdown was linked to the sudden death of his father. Certainly he has lost contact with his remaining family of origin and subsequently his partner and his child. How much this is his rejection of them or theirs of him, or a combination of the two, is not clear.

Peter *lost his freedom* when, as an adolescent, he was sectioned and now he secrets himself away from the social care professionals who should be there to support him, fearing that the things he does possess, his voices, are turned against him.

With all of these losses swirling around and not being clear as yet about what has precipitated the current crisis it is not possible to decide where he is in the grieving process.

Cognitive Behaviour Approaches

Exercise 5.4

Peter: his negative automatic thoughts

Identify the various negative automatic thoughts that Peter has about his life.

Spiritual aspects: 'I'm at peace with my God.' It may seem paradoxical to start with a statement that Peter puts forward as a positive but

Peter's faith seems to be a further way of isolating himself. There are many black churches thriving in inner city areas and their potential for psychological healing and support is cited by one former mental health service user. If, in the black African and Caribbean communities, 'Faith in God is almost the norm ... God goes to the very core of who they are', it follows that these congregations offer 'an important and *unacknowledged* role in the support of black people with mental health problems' (my emphasis) (MacAttram, 2006: 10).

Isolation: The problems with his neighbours present an immediate practical problem given their concerns and ability to make life difficult for Peter. It transpires that previously they had a relatively good relationship but this changed when, in his last cash in hand job, Peter was underpaid and, on challenging the employer, Peter was racially abused and threatened with being reported 'to the social'. Peter now sees all white people, including his neighbours, in the same light. He might now be encouraged to recall and record the examples of support and friendliness he has experienced from his neighbours. He can be helped to recognize that while he may see himself as a victim that is not the case in the present scenario, his neighbours are not the rogue employer, and he can take responsibility for his present behaviour. The social worker could broker an agreement with the neighbours about how late and how loud Peter can play music so that he can see how his changed thoughts and behaviour has an immediate effect.

His voices: *'They give me nothing but grief, they're evil, man.'* This in an important fear and it is not clear if it is the voices themselves that are giving him 'grief' or how people perceive them: reporting his voices contributed to his previous compulsory admissions. Neither is it clear how many voices he has, whether they are all 'evil' and what does that mean for him. There is a passivity in how Peter responds to his voices but if he was to be introduced to a Hearing Voices group (www.hearing-voices.org.uk) he might learn that an estimated 10% of the population report hearing voices, not all of whom have a mental illness diagnosis or regard their voices as a problem (Meddings et al., 2006). Thus 'the voices' are normalized becoming just *one* aspect of a person's life, not the sole obsessive confirmation of madness or 'a delusion, to be dismissed and drowned out'. Techniques can be taught which may not effect the frequency of the voices but do change the way they are heard, the listener taking responsibility for whether the voices are accepted, rejected or explored (Laurence, 2003: 134–5). Interestingly the best-selling novel, *Human Traces* (Faulks, 2005) returns us to the nineteenth century and the earliest days of psychiatry to hear an argument that voices can be seen as a gift, a sign of the ability of some individuals to stay in direct contact with the gods. The loss is with those who are so cut off from their spirituality that they can no longer hear voices.

His medication: 'All those pills can't be good for me.' Peter is also vulnerable if he does stop taking his pills and the professionals respond negatively to this. We need clarification as to why he has problems with his pills and we might need to accept Peter's statements at face value and check whether a change of medication might help with the side effects that are keeping him awake and disorientated hence the music playing.

Peter has an enduring mental illness: This a powerful label for Peter and the professionals who hold his case files. After so many years Peter may be resigned to his fate as a patient. The *recovery model,* however, challenges the idea that mental health problems can only be seen as lifelong and debilitating. Peter may, in fact, never be totally symptom free but the suggestion is that he can re-define his experiences, allow them to mean something quite different and so 'grow beyond' the mental illness. The recovery model offers the potential for moving on through the process of 'hope, strength, potential for growth and personal empowerment' (Warren, 2003: 2) and the recognition that 'chronic illness has less to do with the disorder itself and more to do with complex interactions between the person and their social environment' (Wallcraft, 2005: 201). Within the model is a clear recognition of loss, and the importance of 'consciously grieving mental illness' as a way of bringing 'healing to many, even all, aspects of our lives' (Lafond, 2002: xix, cited in Wallcraft, 2005: 203. See also Allot, 2004).

Narrative Approaches

At the initial point of meeting with the social worker Peter may not be strong enough mentally to manage more than Rogers' (1951, 1961) core conditions and some careful challenging as illustrated above but, as time unfolds, the social worker can stay alert to the defences being presented and, just as Lou's turned down wedding photo opened up opportunities for the social worker so the case example that follows shows what can come from a chance comment by Peter.

Case Example   Working with Imagery

Peter is talking about the verminous state of the flat and actually says how much like a mouse he feels: smelly, parasitic, furtive, dodging round avoiding the traps and poison, leaving his droppings as defiant evidence that he is still alive. It is a striking image and Peter is very animated as he talks in a way quite different from his normal dull and lethargic tone. After a pause the social worker reminds Peter of something new in his life that he

(Continued)

(Continued)

is enjoying: the IT work at the day centre. There a 'mouse' represents something quite different, it is important because without it the computer cannot work, it manages and controls, can delete what is no longer necessary. Perhaps Peter can identify with that mouse. Peter plays with this image, likes the idea of scrolling up and down his list of pressures and deciding which to put in order, which to delete. 'I can open a shiny new folder, I don't know what to put in it yet but it's there on the screen just waiting for me.' He says he now feels quite different, 'empowered', and this is evident in his appearance.

In this example Peter is developing a different story of himself through the metaphor of a mouse, and the different meanings that the mouse can hold for him, and this links us back to the earlier emphasis on narrative approaches. To remind ourselves of the theory, as individuals we construct a personal history by choosing some stories, discarding others so that we can get to the point of 'dwelling within' them. This is a continually dynamic process and narrative is the way this is told to the outside world, and ourselves. Narrative is, then:

> affirmative and reflective, and focuses on dialogue, listening to and talking with the other. It aims to reveal by paradox, myth and enigma and persuades by showing, reminding, hinting and evoking rather than applying knowledge and approximating truth. The focus is narrative and different stories, so that social work at times may take on the guise of persuasive fiction or poetry. (Parton and O'Byrne, 2000: 3)

Parton and O'Byrne go on to link narrative to other approaches, such as *solution focused counselling* (de Shazer, 1985) and *possibility work* (O'Hanlon and Beadle, 1994) which owe their origins to *social constructivism* (Berger and Luckman, 1967). All this work is with the view that no event, problem or institution is a fixed truth, obvious, taken for granted. Instead we confront multiple realities which are open to many interpretations, constructed from a wealth of personal experiences and understandings and open to constant renegotiation in the process of interactions. In any possible response an individual will draw on categories and concepts which are historically and culturally specific, comprising myths and legends that have been passed down through the family and community. The idea of 'identity' not being a fixed concept but rather 'changing, complex and contingent' (Aymer, 2000: 126) can be especially liberating for those who are otherwise silenced or marginalized, it counters hierarchies of oppression or the polarities of right-wrong (black-white, male-female, gay/lesbian-straight, disabled-abled, religious-secular, etc.). Instead people are enabled to hear each other's truths, 'creating equivalent rather than dominant voices' and recognizing we all live in a 'socially complex and multi layered environment' (Aymer, 2000: 123). This is unsettling, but recognizing that uncertainty is the nature of the world that social workers and service users face can also be liberating.

Narrative and the related approaches are, then, powerful tools for individuals confronting a crisis in their lives and also serve to allow social workers to reclaim their practice skills, engaging directly with service users, being sensitive to the language they use and the stories they tell in an effort to help understand their experiences and their search for meaning.

The Skills of Working with Narrative

In terms of the actual practice it is important to attend to the *emotional*, *social* and *spiritual* dimensions of what is shared in the story and the *feelings* that go with them are expressed *in the present*.

Notice when:

- the service user is 'talking about' a situation, where the voice is flat and the tale is a sort of report or chronicle or has been repeated many times;
- the story is told through another voice, of angry parent or stern official or a little helpless child;
- persistent themes emerge, so that the individual story is also part of a general picture that the service user seems to have about the world, and their place in it.

The way of working will be to:

- listen for how the story is told and to encourage the feelings that go with them to be expressed in the present;
- look for suggestions of unfinished business;
- use metaphors and imagery and to bring the story alive;
- in Polster's striking phrase (1990) *mine* for the stories which service users might bury away as unimportant or unexciting;
- enable the individual to see other aspects of the same story, what can, drawing on gestalt terminology, emerge from the ground and become figure;

(Continued)

(Continued)

- help the service user see how they can take responsibility for their story and *reauthor* the story;
- help the service user choose other, more satisfactory, ways of living their life.

Gestalt counsellors/therapists, O'Leary and Barry, 1998; Polster, 1990, 1995.

Working with the Spiritual

Before concluding this chapter I want to return to Breakwell's concept of the 'Threatened Identity', of which one important aspect is *the spiritual*. Although this dimension has been an important part of social work, our profession's origins lie in a 'mixture of Christian love and practical advice' (Jordan, 1983: 32), it does not sit as easily within the essentially secular nature of today's social work. Nonetheless it cannot be ignored, certainly not when working with loss, death and bereavement. Staying with death, 'funerals press the noses of the faithful against the windows of their faith' (Lynch, 1998: 91) and religious belief offers the chance for celebration and joy in a life well lived and a future together in a next world. Some religions have rituals that match the mourning process, from the initial intensity (several days of intense mourning and prayer in the family home) through to an easing where the deceased is still remembered but on special anniversaries and during religious services. 'This multifaceted work is typically seen ... not only as grief work but as spiritual ... assisting the deceased soul in its passage away from this world and into the next ... the religious perspective offers a "really real" reality beyond the objective reality of everyday life' (Walter, 1999: 25).

Spirituality is generally defined as a connectedness to others and the universe (Jacobs, 2004), an awareness of a higher purpose or order (Klass, 1996), providing 'meaning, purpose and power' (Aldridge, 2000). This chapter's two scenarios reflect the way that the spiritual relates to death and bereavement, and the wider experience of loss, and its complexities. Peter's spiritual beliefs are very much around for him but privately expressed and, as we have seen, the social worker is thinking on the possibilities of involving him in one of the area's religious communities. Lou turned to a faith based group to help break down her isolation and she did not need to be 'a believer' to derive comfort from a ready made community with customs familiar from her childhood and then reinforced at key moments in family life: baptisms, confirmations, marriages and funerals. Sadler and Biggs' review of the literature is useful in exploring the links between spirituality and 'successful' ageing (2006). While Moss (2007) brings spirituality into the exploration of values for 'people-work professionals'.

Exercise 5.5   Confronted with a Service User's Beliefs

You have had several meetings with Peter to help support him with his voices and the many disappointments of his life. He is often angry, with his family, his doctors, life in general. On this occasion he starts sounding off at God who has struck him down so cruelly when he has only tried to do good in his life. Then he pauses, says he is being tested like Job in the Bible and asks you to get down on your knees and pray with him for forgiveness, so that he can find the space to accept his losses.

How would you react?

It is always difficult to respond to a direct question or challenge from a service user, and this example is perhaps especially problematic. If the social worker is Christian it may seem natural, even a relief, to enter so fully into Peter's life and it demands a level of personal disclosure that the social worker may not have been prepared for. If the social worker is religious but not a Christian, the invitation to prayer may offend their own way of practice while an atheist may view the belief in prayer as a defence mechanism and escape from reality. Both will want to avoid sinking to their knees but not know how to refuse such a heartfelt request.

Jacobs helpfully reminds us that, as with other areas of our work, it is:

> not the social worker's role to solve spiritual or religious problems, but rather to create an environment that enables clients to explore their concerns and to find meanings that move them towards a healthy resolution or a comfort with their questioning. (2004: 191)

In response to Peter the social worker might say 'I can see how important this is for you. I won't pray but I will stay with you and witness your prayer and then we can talk.' This will offer Peter the Rogerian unconditional positive regard and leave space for him to process what the prayer and his relationship with his God means for him. The exploration can be based on the Puchalski (2000) model cited by Jacobs (2004) which is slightly adapted here:

F: What is your *faith*? Do you consider yourself spiritual or religious? What things do you believe in that give meaning to your life?

I: *Importance* and *influence*. Is your belief important in your life? Does it influence how you take care of yourself? Does it influence your behaviour during this period of loss and how you might recover?

C: Are you part of a spiritual or religious *community?* Does this support you and how? Is there a person or group of people you really love or who are really important to you?

A: As your social worker how would you like me to *address* these issues?

As a social worker, then, you need to be open to the way that religious beliefs and rituals can be used both to deflect our emotions and thoughts, and to heighten them, and not to be afraid of keeping yourself open to the service user's experience. It is also important to keep in touch with what this may bring up for you, that melee of feelings that emerged following Peter's request that you pray with him. Jacobs describes a similar situation in her own practice with a service user whom she 'really felt that God had left ... in the desert long enough'. She had to 'get in touch with my own struggles with God and my issues of countertransference ... my own experience of being abandoned' (Jacobs, 2004: 202; see also Swinton, 1986).

Points for practice

- Deciding between the many different social work methods and approaches may seem daunting in practice.
- Undertaking a careful, person-centred assessment, in partnership with the service user and those closest to him or her, is the first point of understanding how to proceed.
- The various methods then available to you, whether drawing on CBT, psychodynamic or narrative, all have at their heart an understanding of what constitutes 'the self'.
- 'The self' consists of what we think and what we do and is shaped by the social, the psychological and the spiritual.
- It is important for you to keep up-to-date with the availability of different resources and services within your area – social, health, psychological and voluntary sector so that your service users can find the best 'match' to their needs.

Further reading

The experience of living with Alzheimer's Disease and dementia is powerfully expressed through memoirs, such as:

Bayley, J. (1999) *Iris, A Memoir of Iris Murdoch*

Grant, L. (1998) *Remind Me Who I Am Again.*

Balfour, A. (2006) writes a powerful paper on 'Thinking about the experience of dementia: the importance of the unconscious'.

Mental health is also well covered in literature.

The novel by Kesey, K. (2003) *One Flew Over the Cuckoo's Nest* is a classic. *Poppy Shakespeare* by Allan, C. (2007) provides a very contemporary note.

Laurence, J. (2003) *Pure Madness, How Fear Drives the Mental Health System* sets the scene well while various websites keep one informed in a rapidly moving territory.

For theories covering CBT see the classic study by Beck, A.T. (1989) *Cognitive Therapy and the Emotional Disorders.*

Bereavement Counselling has many core texts but Lendrum, S. and Syme. G. (2004) *Gift of Tears* is well established.

Narrative is well explained by Payne, M. (2000) *Narrative Therapy.*

Social work theories are well introduced by Payne, M. (2005) *Modern Social Work Theory.*

For older people see:
www.ageconcern.org.uk
www.rcpsych.ac.uk/mentalhealthinformation/older_people.aspx

For mental health see:
www.mind.org.uk
www.blackmental health.org.uk
www.hearing-voices.org.uk

6 Social Work Skills, Methods and Theories in Work with Families, Groups and the Wider Community

---

Chapter contents

- Working with individuals as part of their wider world
- The skills of direct work with families in terms of seeing the whole family, and indirectly by helping the individual bring family dynamics into the room with the social worker
- The skills of working in groups
- The skills of working with communities

Introduction

This chapter continues the emphasis on social work skills and consolidates the learning from previous chapters. The discussion moves from the focus on the individual per se to the wider world they inhabit: family, groups and the wider communities. These dynamics are illustrated through previously presented scenarios. The tasks and skills of *working with families* are explored both through the direct work with the whole family where there has been a stillbirth (*Susan, Daniel and the daughters*) and the indirect work where an individual service user (*Marcia*) brings to the social worker's office her experience of her family. The potential of *group work* is explored through Wanda and her parents as they struggle with *a life limiting illness*. Working with communities is understood through the experiences of Lou, an older woman who is widowed and is now finding a new place for herself in the wider world.

Systems: Family, Groups, Communities

Understanding that we all have a place in a wider world is hardly a social work discovery. Hippocrates wrote of how 'All parts of an organism form a circle. Therefore every part is both beginning and end' (cited in Manor 1984: 15), John Donne is famous for his line, 'no man is an island' (1994) while Bill Clinton introduced the 2006 Labour Party Conference to the Zulu phrase 'Umumtu ngumumtu ngabantu' which translates as 'I am because you are', or a person is a person only through other people. Social work seeks to make use of these truths by means of systems theory.

Systems theory has had various forms within social work. As the *unitary approach* (Pincus and Minahan, 1973) it was developed in the 1970s as a critique of both casework and community work, the one for identifying the individual as the problem, the latter for focusing on the wider society. Systems theory sees neither as 'the problem', it is instead the interaction between the two. Some elements of this thinking were reactivated in the 1980s in *community social work* and now, arguably, in *care management* with its emphasis on 'social networking', 'partnership' et al. (see Evans and Kearney, 1996) and subsequently an emphasis on regenerating communities and issues around inclusion and exclusion.

Systems thinking is also influential when considering the *psychology of organizations,* allowing, for example, Dale et al. (1986) to see social work teams under pressure as defensive, closed systems, characterized by conformity to given guidelines and procedures rather than able to adapt to and develop practice issues. The energy goes into minimizing error rather than accepting the inevitability of risk, leaving children as much at risk from these 'dangerous organisations' as 'dangerous families'. The advantages of taking a systemic approach are shown by Cornish's (1998) account of a school coping with the death of a pupil, an aspect touched on in Chapter 7.

Evans and Kearney (1996: 26) usefully tabulate the contrasts between 'traditional' and 'systemic' paradigms as follows:

Traditional Thinking is Interested in	Systemic Thinking is Interested in
Action	Interaction
Individual	Relationship
Isolated	In context
One-person unit	More than one-person unit
Unidirectional influence	Reciprocal influence
Content	Process
Event	Pattern
Random	Structure
Reductionist	Integrative/holistic

Any consideration of systems theory incorporates the belief that:

- No one part of a system can be seen in isolation from the wider system.
- The whole is greater than the sum of its parts.
- Systems are highly organized and relationships within them remain consistent over time.
- Systems are conservative, they seek to absorb what is new and render them coherent and characteristic with the established patterns.
- Behaviour is best understood when seen as a circular process, not linear.
- All the elements in the network are interdependent, interrelated and co-ordinated thus you cannot change one part of the system without this impacting upon the whole, and vice versa.

Working with the Family

One of the most obvious and immediate examples of systems is *the family* and this has been a constant theme throughout the scenarios. Within social work it is usual to work with a named individual but it is difficult to ignore the wider family. Susan, for example, is the bereaved mother but her house is crowded with others seeking support. Wanda is the patient with CF but no help can be offered without considering the parents. In these situations nothing can change for the individual if nothing in the wider family changes but 'If appropriately mobilized, family relationships can also be a potent therapeutic agent' (Diamond et al., 1996: 2).

Sometimes the family is a little more distant, not an immediate part of the social worker's intervention, for example, the children of Lou or Sam, Kuldip has brothers as well as a puzzled father, Peter has an ex-partner and a child that he sees from afar in the market. It seems, then, that the family is always present in the lives of those with whom we work. While we are not family therapists we are applying the skills of *family work* when we consciously acknowledge and explore the ruptures within the family caused by the loss. The focus is on:

> helping distressed individuals who are showing symptoms or self-defeating behaviour within the context of the family. The means of doing this is by helping the family as a system to deal with whatever change of family relationships is required to promote a more satisfactory fit, thus affording the chance of development for its individual members. (Manor, 1984: 11)

We need to see a family as a system, a combination of individuals who have come together with a commitment to create something collective. So, a total family system consists of:

- its *components* – the individual family members,
- their *attributes* – personal characteristics,
- and the *interaction* between them.

And is characterized by:

- *Joint tasks:* in such basics as providing shelter, food, comfort, supporting individuals through their life stages such as bereavement and other losses.
- *A set of rules and roles:* not normally written down so these are implicit rather than explicit, which allow a family to live relatively harmoniously, maintaining and perpetuating the family system. Actions of individuals within the family are continually reinforced, positively or negatively through *patterned transactions* which are often self-preservationist and conservative.
- *Boundaries:* families are specific, distinct entities, social, cultural and economic units which, to varying degrees, are at once apart from and a part of the wider community. Families have a sense of their own identity, often relating to a *sustained period of time.* This continuity provides a family with some sense of past and future generations so that new members can be accepted in, and some excluded, but the essential identity remains constant.

If the family system is *closed* all the energy is firmly contained and there is a sense of being stuck, static, rigid as opposed to being *open* with boundaries that are clear and permeable and energy can cross over.

All of the above will determine the *equilibrium*, or the *homeostasis* of the family, the degree to which it can maintain its natural harmony and balance in the face of changes, whether to do with war and exile, or more normal occurrences such as death, divorce, a physical move, new members joining, life stages such as adolescence or ageing, etc. The question is the degree to which the system can adapt to the re-assignment of roles and changes in the meaning of relationships.

From a systems perspectives the interest lies not in *linear behaviour* but rather the *circular system,* the relationship between people, the *roles* that people get stuck in and the feelings they carry for others in the family. Thus rather than an individual being the 'ill one' the question is how were they chosen for this role and how are the individual's symptoms serving a psychological function for the family as a whole, holding the issue that others are avoiding.

Essentially the systems approach encourages curiosity: nothing is fixed, there are no big truths and this is especially relevant for this present period when we have within society such a range of family formations, belonging to different cultural and/or religious communities, which are busy being continually recreated as individuals try to make sense of the need for intimacy.

> The notion of systems is attractive ... because we have learned that no one member (molecule, particle, part, star) is solely responsible for the struggle of the family... . The concept of systems allows us to honor the complex aesthetic quality of the couple or family. (Zinker, 1994: 57)

Exercise 6.1   Tasks, Roles/Rules and Boundaries in Families Related Back to Susan and the Stillborn Child

First consider either your family of origin and/or your current family. Reflect on it in terms of the tasks, roles and rules and boundaries.

Now refer back to the scenario of Susan's family in Chapter 4. Using the same headings list a 'before' and 'after' to see how these help your understanding of the impact of the loss of the stillbirth.

Working directly with the family: Susan, Daniel, Denise, Sarah and the stillborn child.

Tasks

Before the stillbirth   From the first suspicions of a pregnancy, then the confirmation and the subsequent scans which give a gendered identity to the developing child, to the choice of decorations, colours and furnishings for the nursery, the pregnancy has established a set of tasks, and a rhythm and time scale. Although Susan is the one carrying the baby, other tasks can be shared with Daniel, Denise and Sarah. The rhythm is sustained right through to the routine of the hospital and, given that Susan is already a mother, we can expect that the familiarity of the procedures will reassure Susan even if, as an older mother, she has some worries. Another task that Susan and Daniel undertake is to get married thus reinforcing the sense of legitimizing the baby, and the relationship.

After the stillbirth   With this unexpected event all the family's expectations are disrupted. The hospital system can shift gear, provide tasks established by protocol to ensure that it did nothing medically wrong and they provide the photos, handprints and cremation that provide tasks they believe are useful rituals for the grieving family. Once at home, however, the ashes in the cupboard are a powerful metaphor for the family's struggles to find new tasks that are as meaningful as the anticipated ones. Susan is not the mother of a new baby and seems less able to mother the children she does have. The girls are missing school, an important task that is an investment in their future and Daniel is also mourning but has no task that can make sense of that.

Rules and roles

Before the stillbirth   In essence, Susan and Daniel have been seeking out the tasks that reflect and reinforce the traditional rules and roles of family life. The mother is there to carry and nurture the child in the womb, the father, to support in practical and emotional ways, as represented by the wedding which formalizes the relationship and makes them 'man and wife'. The children learn what it means to be older siblings and adjust to the firmer status of this new father figure. All of these rules and roles have nine months in which to be rehearsed and grown into.

After the stillbirth   The rules and roles of 'grieving family' are sprung on them all too quickly. Neither prepared nor trained for this situation they adapt to what is offered by the hospital but with no real ownership of, and comfort in them and the family returns to something of a void, people retreat into themselves and there is little energy to negotiate new ways of being. Susan takes on, it seems, the role of 'bad mother', blaming the current stillbirth on her previous abortion.

Boundaries

Before the stillbirth   The pregnancy was reinforcing the redrawn boundaries of this unit. What was a family of women had opened up to allow a new man in, Daniel, who then fathers a male child just to emphasize the point. The girls' father, if he is still in contact, will also be renegotiating his place in the system.

After the stillbirth the family has gone into reverse gear and become a number of elements sharing the same physical but not psychological space. The children, having been caught up in preparing for the baby, are excluded from the cremation, where they could say a goodbye to him. Susan's parents seem to have cut themselves off. The boundaries of the family are about to be opened up further by the appearance of the social worker.

Working with the family

Hellinger refers to 'the greatness of parenthood' lying in 'having children and losing children, and still holding to each other' (2003: 219) so this poses the challenge to the social worker to work with the clear, continuing tensions at every level and allow a new balance to emerge.

This scenario was explored in some detail in Chapter 4 in relationship to *social work values*, here the issues are put more firmly into the perspective of family work. Given that a child's death entails 'an intimate loneliness', a challenge to the 'parental self-narrative' (Riches and Dawson, 1996), it may be necessary to work with the individual family members first, to stay with that reality, before moving on to challenge and change it.

Alongside the usual feelings of guilt, blame and fears concerning the prospect of future pregnancies there is Susan's secret of her previous abortion while Daniel is nursing his grievance that his role as father is not being fully recognized. They may both be feeling that, having married because of the pregnancy, they are now trapped in a relationship which has lost its immediate purpose.

For Susan *feminist* perspectives allow an exploration of her role as a woman in this whole process, the feelings of shame or guilt she may feel at having the abortion and now failing to produce a 'perfect' child. *Gender* impacts on Daniel in terms of his *masculine* self image.

The children may need their own space, as individuals and/or sisters, to work out their feelings about this sibling who came back from the hospital as ashes. The impact may be huge and long lasting, especially if not discussed, and it may be seen as just one of many other changes in their life, and not necessarily the most meaningful. In the UK, up to 92% of those aged under 16 will have faced what they term a 'significant' bereavement (Harrison and Harrington, 2001) and McCarthy and Jessop (2005) remind us that children are resilient, usually surviving such events.

The *grandparents* have needs which may be neglected because they, like other members of the extended family, are not seen as the primary mourners, But theirs is 'a double blow', not just of the death of the child but also 'the pain of seeing their own children suffering' (Borg and Lasker, 1982: 107) and it may be this that kept them from the funeral. Guilt feelings, however irrational, may also have an impact as seen in the following words from a research respondent: 'It should have been me in that grave ... children and grandchildren are supposed to bury the old people, not the other way round' (1982: 108).

Once the individuals can identify and speak out their internal narratives, witnessed and developed as appropriate by the social worker, they will be more equipped to share these with each other. This can be approached in a number of ways.

The family can look at its history in terms of a *family tree* or *lifeline* (Lendrum and Syme, 2004); both illustrate the range of losses which have been experienced thus reminding the family of what they have faced, and survived, as individuals and as a collective. They can be encouraged to start communicating and making decisions, starting strategically with Susan and Daniel to enable them to get back into their parenting role. This may begin with immediate concerns, ensuring the children get back into the rhythm of school as well as focusing on the baby, what to do with the ashes and how, in the future, to mark the anniversaries and ensure his lasting place in the family. The siblings' involvement is important, to gauge their own needs and ensure that these are heard by the parents.

Wider issues might touch on the marital relationship and the impact of the pregnancy, 'their fantasies about the child they have lost' (Worden, 1991:105). McLaren draws on her clinical experience to comment that couples can become closer once they can 'acknowledge, understand and respect the uniqueness of their partner's process' (2005: 89) but she warns that this needs time. The family that can sit and talk with each other have a better chance in being able to turn outwards and face the world and devising a ceremony to scatter the ashes, and who they want to invite to that, is one sign of this engagement.

Social Work Skills in Family Work

- To 'retain a clear head and not to become confused, enmeshed or inappropriately confrontative'. (Gorrell Barnes, 1998: 13–14)
- To be aware of 'the meaning making' (Gorrell Barnes, 1998: 13) particular to each family and bring it into the awareness of the family members.
- To listen and look out for the patterns of communication in the family and bring this into their awareness.
- To encourage the individual members to communicate directly to each other.
- To help the family understand the power dynamics within the family based on gender, age, etc.

Marcia, bringing the family into the room
In the above scenario of the stillborn child the social worker has a clear mandate to meet and work with the family which will not be true in other situations. In the scenario in Chapter 2 it is Marcia who is in trouble with the law, not her brother or mother and her father is dead but

clearly they carry huge importance in terms of the caring role she played and her continuing grief for her father, indicated in her constant referring back to 'when my dad died'. The question, then, is how to bring them more fully into the room so as to help resolve issues for Marcia.

As the work progresses one theme that seems important is her mother's many anxieties, how she texts Marcia whenever she is out of the house, bombarding her with urgent messages: 'where are you?', 'what are you doing?' Marcia admits also texting her mother incessantly. 'If I don't, I don't know what might be happening.' She describes how she advises her mother all the time, about whether to sell the house, get a better job, how to manage Carl, etc. 'Now that dad's gone I have to sort her out, I always will.'

There are Marcia's complicated feelings about her father but her mother is so preoccupied with how awful she found his illness that she does not hear Marcia's upset. She simply repeats how 'very special' Marcia had been to her father, but that frustrates Marcia since she has no memories of being 'a daddy's girl'. Her sense of it was that she had no purpose or place in her father's life until he became ill. All her memories are of him being abusive, drunk or hung-over. Asked to reflect further she surprises herself by recalling two memories:

- The first is of playing snowballs in the garden with her brother, her father is building them an igloo and her mother is looking out the window from the kitchen where she is cooking supper.
- The second is watching her father carefully building a tree house for her and her brother.

She is very moved by these images but then quickly returns to the familiar story of the funeral: a huge event, attended by 400 people, a confusing whirr of uniforms and speeches which eulogized her father as 'the lad': always the first into the burning house, refusing promotions so as to stay with his mates, always ready for 'a good jaw and jar' but Marcia can only associate the 'jaw and jar' with rows at home.

The funeral, with all its competing images, is a dominant, persistent and disturbing image for Marcia. At one session she brings the memorial book from the funeral which contains photos of her father, and some other family photos. The social worker asks her to choose one photo for each of her family members and then lay them on the floor to represent how she sees her family.

Photos and Family Constellation Work

Choosing the photos
Father. Marcia chooses not one but a cluster: father smart in his uniform, relaxed in the garden, at the wheel of a favourite car. One print is larger, showing him ill in bed.
Mother. This is a smudged image, her mother turning away from the camera just as the photo is being taken.
Brother. Carl is very young, on a beach next to a sand castle.
Herself. She chooses two for herself: one, a large studio portrait showing her looking very adult. The other is smaller, she is perched nervously on a cycle that is too big for her.

Laying the photos down to represent the family
Father. Marcia starts with her father, puts all of the photos of him into a pile with the ill and angry photo on top, hiding the others from view.
Mother. She puts this photo down next to, but at a distance from, her father's.
Brother. This is placed just below her mother's and equidistant from her father's.
Herself. Marcia ignores the smaller photo, choosing instead the studio photo. She puts it directly next to her father so that it is now between the photos of her mother and brother.

Marcia: My photo and dad's are the biggest. And I've only gone and stuck myself in the middle ... Carl and mum's pictures are so little ... It's as if I'm shielding them from my dad ... dad looks so defiant, angry .... That's the look I get when I'm in a mood ... people always said we were like two peas in the pod ... I don't like it there.
Social worker: Notice also what you've done with your dad's photos.
Marcia: You can only see the angry one. All the others are blocked out.
Social worker: What about your other photo?
Marcia: This one here (she picks up the one that shows her on the bicycle) I'd forgotten all about that.
Social worker: You don't have to stay with the pattern you've made. You can change it around.

(Continued)

(Continued)

Marcia spreads out the father's photos so that now they can all be seen: the relaxed father, the fire fighter and the dying patient. Then she removes her portrait, breaths a sigh of relief but is still not sure what to do with the other one.

Social worker: I suggest you put your mum and your dad next to each other. Now put your cycling photo next to your brother's so you're facing your parents. You're together, brother and sister. And you can see your parents together. When you put yourself next to your dad you were too big, you ended up holding all his anger but it doesn't have to be yours. You can give it back to him. You can let yourself concentrate on being a child and let your parents get on with being parents.

Over the next few sessions Marcia reports changes in her life, she is managing her anger and anxiety better, is making time with Carl and her being different is allowing her family to change around her. She is trying to catch up on school work, aiming for university but she likes the image of her wobbling on a bike that is a bit too big for her so she is just going to see where it takes her.

She explains her anger when she was 'sent' to counselling, 'When they said they wanted me to "get over" my dad's death I thought that meant "forget him" and I wasn't going to do that. Now I see I can still think of him, feel him around me but not be anxious. I can find my distance. Like my mum with the texting, I don't have to do it all the time now, just in emergencies.'

Marcia seems to have really engaged with this creative way of exploring her stuckness in her family, her grieving and her way of seeing the world which was proving so difficult and dangerous for her. Traditional talking was limited in what it could offer, no sooner does she find new, happier images of her childhood than she flashes back to the painful ones that reinforce her fixed view of the world. What the social worker then does is to unsettle Marcia, help free her into other ways to see the family, and herself within the family. Bringing out the patterns of *invisible loyalties* within the family through the visual aids of photos allows her to take responsibility for changing what she sees and then acting on the insights back in own life.

The work with Marcia draws on Satir's *family sculptures* (1978), intended to provoke 'the client's intense confrontation with his or her family history' (Franke, 2003: 18), also Hellinger's *family constellation work* (2002, 2003, Hellinger et al., 1998) where individuals can identify and reject the often inappropriate roles they have taken on from their wider family. We are not sure what happened in Marcia's family history but what does emerge are the ways that Marcia had been entangled in the family dynamics, thrust into a too knowing and parental role which made grandiose demands of her. Relief came when she was helped to become a child again.

Working with Groups

Group work is a long established social work method although, as in other aspects of our work, subject to change. It is suggested that it has effectively disappeared within social services and survives only in probation because it has shifted emphasis to 'social control rather than social support or empowerment' (Doel and Sawdon 2001: 438). Nonetheless it does seem to have a continuing and growing influence within the self-help and voluntary movement and various, published case examples attest to its success in hospital settings. This text has consistently touched on the role of groups, formal and informal, ongoing, open or one-off, or even as Sutton and Liechty (2004) and Colōn (2004) point out, online, thus embracing new technologies. All of these are ways of reaching people, part of the 'support surround' referred to by Nuland (1994).

Groups seem to be a particularly rich resource for working with loss and bereavement, offering, in the words of one group member:

> an opportunity to share their pain with others ... the freedom to express feelings, regardless of how unusual they may seem to the mourner. The commonality of feelings and experiences provides support and normalisation in the safety of the group context. (Thompson, 1996: 7)

In the scenarios, Sam found a new relationship at the group which was the Hospice's Evening of Remembering, Susan and Daniel could join a self-help group, Compassionate Friends or SANDS. Lou found friends at a faith based activity centre for older people and Peter is a member of a MIND day centre and we anticipate the help he might get from a user-led Hearing Voices group. Professionally led groups for people with schizophrenia are also a potent form of support for those whose condition leaves them with 'an inability to handle the demands of daily living ... (whose) personalities are marked by limited, emotional responses and minimal ego strength'. Groups can provide 'social interaction ... to learn about himself or herself ... and an opportunity to learn more functional modes of behaviour' with reductions in anti-psychotic drugs and subsequent hospitalizations (Cwikel and Oron 1991: 164/5). Randall and Walker opt for a task-centred, problem solving focus since they were concerned that group members could not cope with more insight-orientated approaches. The group was able to facilitate the feelings linked to how they 'mourned the loss of previous life styles and were saddened by their diminishing prospects' (1988: 60).

Some Definitions of Groups

Papell and Rothman's (1966) classic three *models of group work:*

- *Remedial,* focus is essentially on the individual 'casualty'.
- *Reciprocal,* the group creates a mutual aid, problem solving system.
- *Social goals,* the group works to achieving social action and change.

Brown (1992) usefully adds:

- *Mediation,* individuals find a supportive and challenging space in which to examine and establish their social roles.

Groups in social work

'A context in which individuals help each other; it is a method of helping groups as well as individuals, and it can enable individuals and groups to influence and change personal, group, organisational and community problems'. (Brown, 1992: 8)

Yalom's (1985) therapeutic factors in groups

- The installation of hope
- Universality
- Altruism
- Imparting information
- Development of socializing techniques
- Imitative behaviour
- The corrective recapitulation of the primary family group

Zinker's gestalt therapist

'Growth takes place at the boundary between the individual and the environment. The encounter between what is me and what is not me which forces me to invent new responses ... moves me towards change' (1978: 163) and 'the group is a humanistic laboratory in which you can test the influence of behaviours you have found hitherto unacceptable' (1978: 166).

As a particular illustration of the role of groups this next section returns to Wanda and her family, introduced in Chapter 4.

Exercise 6.2 Using Groups

Think of a group to which you belong, whether formal or informal, based in work or at college or part of a social activity.

- Do you recognize the group in any of the above descriptions and definitions?
- If you were facing a problem in your life what would be the advantages and disadvantages of sharing it in a group?
- Now refer back to the scenario of Wanda and her family. How might a group or groups help this family manage Wanda's chronic illness?

Madge (2001) writes specifically about groups for those facing CF while Engebrigsten and Heap (1988) describe short-term group work with the parents of children and young adults with a similar congenital, progressive terminal illness. In these discussions you see reflected the struggles faced by Wanda and her family.

The Potential of Parents' Groups – Allowing Disallowed Feelings

Groups can be used for *education* and *networking,* and it can be easier to take in the *practical information* about the medical condition when this is shared and mulled over with people who are 'like-minded and like-suffering' (Madge, 2001: 311) and problems can be turned into coping strategies. Further, 'Peer-initiated challenges, support and encouragement are better accepted than those offered by a professional' (2001: 311). This takes us to the *psychological depths* allowed for in groups. Parents often experience what has been termed 'chronic sorrow' and 'protracted grief' resulting from continual readjustment to the progress of the condition, 'physical exhaustion and intense, painful and often conflicting feelings' (Engebrigsten and Heap, 1988: 199). These feelings can be experienced as 'sometimes eroding intradependence of each damaged family' (1988: 200). In the group it can be very healing for parents to experience being able to express their anger about, and rejection of, the sick child and seeing that they are not alone with these feelings. The group offers 'relief from emotional pressure and ... group recognition of both sacrifice and achievement and a rare opportunity to think aloud and exchange ideas' (1988: 200–1).

When this scenario was explored earlier we saw the degree to which Lorraine and Michael are falling out over their treatment of Wanda. Engebrigsten and Heap (1988) provide an example of this in their group (shown in the box below), how it provides ideal opportunities to air divergent views and for these to be understood and mediated.

Using Group Work to Manage Conflict Between Parents

Members are busy with stories about the rows that are sparked between parents.

'Worker: I don't think anyone is going to find the *right* way to be a family ... Perhaps the most important thing is to keep the issue open as something which can always be discussed, where one is always learning, and where changes with the children will in any case compel changes in the way you cope ... I feel I want to say how impressive it is to hear how each of you, whether in agreement or not, does the things you can do and complement each other in the overall care of your children ... what I hear in the group indicates impressively that you do share'. (emphasis in the original) (Engebrigsten and Heap, 1988: 203–4)

The Potential of Children's Groups – Coping with a Death

The balance of *information sharing* and *socializing* will be the same for the children's groups, and the opportunity to share the *psychological* pressures. Certainly in hospital based groups members frequently share their fierce resentment of the increasing demands of treatment and admit to their non-compliance being a way to assert their independence and challenge authority. Another theme is the 'awareness of mortality and a disinclination to look at the future' (Madge, 2001).

This is very central for Wanda. It is the death of a contemporary which provokes her dramatic change of attitude, although she has not been able to tell her parents how distressed and scared this has left her. Sutton and Liechty (2004) illustrate how Wanda, if she was a member of a support group, could be helped to manage hearing of or witnessing such a deterioration and death. The case study identifies the factors that belong both to group process theory and to our knowledge of dealing with death, loss and bereavement. In terms of group work it depends on the intended purpose of the group, how well established it is and the part the deceased played, whether as a role model or a more challenging and conflictual person. The loss aspect relates to how sudden or unanticipated the death was. The group leader needs to know how to manage the 'breaking of the bad news' and then allow the silence and to stay with it and to 'witness' the feelings. Concerning the funeral, the group may want to attend en masse or delegate individuals to represent them and/or find their own rituals to mark the loss of a member and to retain some sense of him. What will also have to be acknowledged is the transient nature of their own lives.

> The death is a reminder that extending oneself in trust and emotional intimacy entails the risks of pain and sorrow, and members may draw back from one another in the wake of the death. Having to acknowledge and accept death and mortality in a public place accelerates the intimacy felt between members. Similar to conflict, the death of a member can be a catalyzing event in the life of a group. (Sutton and Liechty, 2004: 529)

Social Work Skills in Group Work

- Be clear about the purpose the group and the accompanying leadership style
- Be aware, and challenge, individuals taking on fixed roles
- 'Create opportunities and "space" for each person to feel sustained, valued and observed' (Brown, 1992: 90).
- Convey 'therapeutic optimism', 'a realistic conviction that the group has the potential to achieve certain things for each member, and that membership can be satisfying and rewarding' (Brown, 1992: 90).
- Have skills in group-creation, group-maintenance and task achievement:
- *Group creation:* setting up a group requires careful planning and preparation. You need to think carefully about membership, purpose, time frame, venue and potential resources
- *Group maintenance:* at the beginning, the professional who sets up the group has to take a leadership role. However, maintenance involves ensuring that leadership is transferred to a large extent to the members so that all their different contributions are valued and they each become a valued member. Maintenance also requires helping groups through

(Continued)

(Continued)

difficult patches that might involve conflict or demoralization. Overcoming such problems strengthens the group in the longer term. If the group is time limited, it is important to celebrate achievement and end successfully. If the group has focused on loss and bereavement it is important that to be aware that the ending of the group may be experienced as a further loss.

Working with Communities

As with the discussion about 'the family', service users are inevitably a part of wider communities and these are the source of some important feelings since the more we experience life as privatized and atomized the more we try to fulfil that key psychological need which is to belong and accept and be accepted. But communities are complex entities and not easy even for the strongest of us to negotiate.

Exercise 6.3 Definitions of Communities

'Community' has been variously defined as:

- *a social system,* a set of social relationships,
- *a fixed locality,* a geographical area,
- *a quality of relationship,* a spirit of community.

(Popple, 2002: 151)

- How might this make sense for you in your own lives?
- How might it make sense for some of the service users we have met in the previous scenarios?

From the scenarios we have discussed we have seen how communities can be experienced in both negative and positive ways.

Some of the individuals whose struggles with loss we have witnessed have actively sought out communities, if not within a fixed locality then in terms of sets of social relationships and in seeking a spirit of community. Douglas seeks to make sense of his experiences by becoming involved in AIDS awareness campaigns. In Australia, Aboriginal activists establish *a black grapevine* to redress the injustices meted out to 'the stolen generations' while in the UK members of the black and ethnic minority communities campaigned both in their communities and their various professional bodies to change policy and practice relating to *same-race placements*. Similarly the *disability movement* has challenged and changed prevailing ideas as have, within the medical field, groups like SANDS and the Hospice movement. The 2006 'Profession Worth Fighting For' conference links social workers and service users and pressure groups to campaign together, against, for example, the threat to take the children of failed asylum seekers into care (www.socialworkfuture.org).

And the other side of the coin is in the journalist's (Chapter 4) account of the Edinburgh mortuary: all those who had died alone as 'the victims of loneliness' coming from a 'class of people ... irritating, ignorant and incompetent'. This is the community which lacks coherence and supportive networks, the *fragmented community* where service users survive as part of a 'psychological proletariat, living and (rarely) working in a social universe noticeably short on sympathy and empathy' (Hoggett, 1993: 203).

Silverman argues that 'It is important when we speak of grief not to talk about "them" but about "us"' (2005: 37) but, for now at least, it remains true that death increasingly takes place behind closed doors, or in liminal space such as residential homes, hospitals and hospices. Consequently the grief is expressed primarily through families and is 'limited to those in recognized kin roles' (Doka, 2002: xiii) with any problems in grieving interpreted primarily in terms of illness or intrapersonal dilemmas, belonging in the doctor's office or the counselling room and away from public scrutiny. Our complex contemporary societies involve many crisscrossed lives and networks so one individual's loss will often be neither known nor noticed. There is 'empathic failure' (Neimeyer and Jordan, 2002) which is only marginally influenced by the placing of flowers and other markers by roadsides for the victims of motor accidents.

Social Work and Communities

As with many other issues, the social work profession echoes the wider debates about 'the community'. Radical social workers in the 1970s were busy supporting community groups such as tenants associations, squatters groups and Claimants Unions (see Simpkin, 1979) that were described as 'communities of resistance' (Sivanandan, 1990), collectivities that serve as a base 'both to confront ... discrimination and to forge alliances to protect and support cultural, religious and national groups' (Popple 2002: 155). A very much sanitized version of 'the community' was presented in the 1982 Seebohm Report which saw *community social work* as key to the developing profession, some Labour left authorities 'went local', establishing neighbourhood offices (see Cooper, 1983, for a case example). Then came 'care in the community', built on the assumption of a closer partnership between the statutory services and the local communities.

Contemporary social work tends to be more entrenched and reactive in its relationship to local communities and Jordan and Jordan (2000) point out the irony that many of the community outreach initiatives, such as Sure Start, introduced by New Labour, rely on traditional social work skills but have been kept outside the remit of social work.

Where we are now with social work and communities is in terms of *challenging exclusion* by creating *inclusive communities* (for an example see Social Exclusion Unit Report, 2004: 22) enabling marginalized groups and communities to play a stronger role in society. A phrase that we are hearing more of is *social capital,* identifying the social networks that already exist and which can provide friendship and support, both emotional and practical and offer the potential of this being a mutual relationship (Putnam, 2000). This is of relevance to the range of service user groups and seems especially important for isolated single parents, people with mental health problems, for older people beset by problems of mobility, loss of confidence, distancing of family members and the loss of peers by death. Where social services are involved this may be simply in terms of providing domiciliary care but sub-contracting and reliance on a continual turnover of agency workers means that the 'friendly home help who ... could be regarded as a friend, seems a thing of the past' (Gray, 2006: 2).

The social work role may, then, be seen in terms of *networking,* helping develop what Trevillion terms *the enabling community,* with its emphasis on interdependency, mutuality and a challenge to stigmatizing and oppressive attitudes. In this approach the practitioner looks beyond 'formally constituted social groups or formal organisational structures of a bureaucratic nature' and works rather with 'open-ended *social fields'* (emphasis in the original) (1999: 20). Trevillion argues for a form of *community assessment* which goes beyond the customary statement about the social context of the service user, which tends to be a description of background factors or over generalized broad profiles of need. In this alternative model the worker 'always starts with a specific situation which is analysed in network terms ... it pictures individuals as active makers of their social worlds rather than helpless victims' (1999: 110). This is borne out in recent research into isolation among older people (Cattan, 2002) which first identifies the negative impact on this group of loneliness and then studies 139 projects in northern England that, through befriending and/or social activities, go some way to successfully counteracting its effects on the isolated elderly. The research goes on to identify the degree to which better transport and improved public conveniences would further encourage mobility and social contact for this vulnerable client group.

Lou a Widow Now Out in the Community

It is now 18 months since Lou was widowed.

In Chapter 5 we identified some of the ways that the social worker could intervene on an individual level, using CBT to challenge some of her negative automatic thoughts and an unplanned piece of reminiscence work based on her wedding photo.

When we last met her Lou had found her courage to get out but the shopping trip was not a good experience since the new shopping centre was large and alienating and when she took a coffee break the plastic milk container was too intricate for arthritic fingers. This only reinforced her sense of how much had changed, and how much she disliked those changes.

The next outing was more successful. The social worker had put her in touch with a social group which provided transport and the chance for a new experience, playing bingo followed by a fish-and-chip supper. The fact that it was a faith based group promised continuing contact with the church, a place of comfort and continuity.

Since that time some things have not changed: she remains in pain from her arthritis but her angina is under control and she is less scared and feels in some control of her body. Pahl (2000) talks about 'the personal community' of relatives and friends but Lou still lives alone, sees nothing of neighbours and only has intermittent contact with her children. About this she is sometimes resigned, sometimes angry, but she never directs these feelings towards them and she resists any attempt by the social worker to mediate. The social worker may maintain a commitment to getting them involved and it may not be appropriate at this point when, as Trevillion indicates, changing values of the wider family 'can often seem anachronistic, unhelpful and even oppressive' (1999: 20) and this has some resonance with Lou's situation.

The social worker, then, if s/he is to shift this sense of isolation has to act as a *broker* or *gatekeeper* within the wider social network, recognizing that professionals and service users alike are interdependent within their *social field*. The social worker has already evidenced a willingness to take this on board, recognizing the interdisciplinary dimension in ensuring that Lou gets an appointment with the doctor. This leads to a careful diagnosis and management of her symptoms and the continuing involvement with the district nurse. Given the lack of support that Lou received throughout her husband's illness, and how he was whisked away to hospital for an assessment from which he never returned, it is especially important that she stays informed about her own condition and feels in control of her destiny. A Home Help and meals on wheels are also provided and these are cited as important *mediators* between a service user, the wider community and social services (Trevillion, 1999).

Looking beyond the statutory sector the social worker initiates a visit to the *faith based voluntary day centre* and this becomes a regular feature in Lou's life. They have a regular reminiscence group, allowing the work that she started with the social worker to develop into a more systematic engagement with her personal and social history. Lou is able to recall very vividly memories of the area, this includes stories her father told her about the 1926 General Strike when he had been a leading trade unionist and activist, and about the Second World War, which is within her own direct experience and which comes alive for her again. In this process Lou is able to regain and value her sense of the community in which she has lived all her life. The club has African-Caribbean members, a group Lou has carefully avoided over the years, but her contact with them here helps her begin to change some of her racist ideas and appreciate their stories. One potent moment is when one of these women talks about her distress about her husband's dementia and Lou is able to share her own experiences, and in doing so value what she achieved and feels, in the advice and support she offered, that she had something to offer this woman. The potential of *reciprocity* is a core element of networking.

People she meets at the Centre remain as acquaintances for the moment, rather than friends but the links are strengthened through other activities such as bridge and chess games, a discussion group and poetry and reading groups. In addition there are the volunteer befrienders, some younger than Lou which she appreciates, given the importance of cross-generational contact (Gray, 2006; Social Exclusion Unit, 2006).

Lou, having got back in touch with her father's activism, is thinking about linking up with the Pensioners Forum, a borough wide advocacy and campaigning group which takes up issues both locally, sitting on users panels, etc, and nationally, with demonstrations calling for an increase in pensions (see Foote and Stanners (2002) for other examples of users groups involving older people). This is another example of reciprocity, where Lou can feel herself as an active part of the community, *brokering change* as Trevillion expresses it (1999:72).

In the opening chapter, in discussing the ways of assessing loss, *unsupportive communities* were cited as a key factor. Young and Cullen referred to the need for the bereaved individual to draw on 'communal existence' (1996: 161), where the story of the death can be heard and 'human solidarity' offered (1996: 183) and this reinforces the idea of grief as a 'social process' with the need of the community to come together to construct 'an enduring and shared memory of the dead' (Walter, 1996: 14). In Lou's increasing involvement in her community, she would be shocked to think that she is explicitly seeking 'solidarity' for her situation. Nonetheless one can begin to see how that is emerging, that she is finding a social system, a fixed locality and a quality of relationship (to return to Popple's definition) which allows her to experience her losses in a way that honours what she has been through and find a new meaning for them.

Points for practice

- Social work is not just about work with individuals but is about recognizing that most people gain their support and sense of well-being from their family and community.
- Social workers need to work consciously with the existing networks while also recognizing that there may be tensions here, that service users are often cut off in some ways from their family and/or community.
- If service users are not able to re-establish links with their own families and communities they can be helped to make new links.
- Social workers need to develop skills in working with families, communities and groups.

Further reading

For systems:
Evans, D. and Kearney, J. (1996) *Working in Social Care: A Systemic Approach.*

For systemic work with families:
Gorrell Barnes, G. (1998) *Family Therapy in Changing Times.*

For family constellations:
Franke, U. (2003) *In the Mind's Eye,* as it can be used in one-to-one work.
Also Sutcliffe, P., Tufnell, G. and Cornish, U. (1998) *Working with the Dying and the Bereaved. Systemic Approaches to Therapeutic Work.*

For group work:
There are a number of texts but the best introductory text for social workers is Brown, A. (1992) *Groupwork.*
Also the journal *Groupwork* published by Whiting and Birch.

For community work:
Trevillion, S. (1999) *Networking and Community Partnership.*

7 The Evidence Base

Chapter contents

- Research mindedness: its importance in social work in developing the role of the reflective and critical practitioner
- The practical and the philosophical underpinnings of qualitative and quantitative research
- Different research studies: what is revealed behind the findings relating to the choice of methodologies, the potential and problems of the approach and what it reveals about the researcher's value base
- The writer's own experience as a researcher and how the process allowed new perspectives to be heard

Introduction

This chapter returns to the various theories that have been presented in the previous chapters, reflecting on their validity in terms of the research that informs them. This requires a discussion about the nature of *evidence* and *research mindedness*, the differences between qualitative and quantitative methodologies and how we stand back from our assumptions, and unknow what we think we know and to 'make strange what is utterly familiar' (Reimann, 2005: 90). This is a delicate and contentious issue within social work generally where research findings are often marginalized.

Along with analysing the research methodology underlining a number of texts there is an examination of how research nourished the development of a new concept, narrative theory and lastly a case study of a research project, on the effectiveness of bereavement counselling, and how the respondents took the research down other, unexpected, paths.

The Problems and Potential of Research in Social Work Practice

Social workers are expected to be *research minded*, not necessarily active but, nonetheless, sufficiently familiar with the various methodologies to equip us to critically read relevant papers and draw on that research in our daily practice. Later, this chapter will look at a range of papers and approaches but the immediate concern is to summarise some of the debates within social work about relevant research methodologies.

Exercise 7.1   The Research Minded Practitioner

- What does 'research' mean to you in your daily practice?
- Is there a particular piece of research that guides you in your work with service users?
- What makes you confidant about this research:

  - Is it because it is cited by people you respect?
  - Does it back up the ideas you already have or does it challenge your way of thinking?
  - Have you read the actual research paper or relied on what other people say about it?

The Argument for Quantitative Research

The research process is not, of course, unproblematic. There are frustrations when findings based on small numbers of respondents are not easily generalizable and findings cannot be replicated when research projects differ in terms of definitions, outcome measures and methodologies and, as a result, contradict each other. Studies and reports frequently fail to define the need for counselling or specify goals (Raphael et al., 1993), they differ in terms of type of bereavement, geographical location, age distribution, religion and socio-economic status of the population, size of sample, measures of outcome and the types of counselling offered, whether professionally run, voluntary groups or self-help groups. 'They also vary in the magnitude of the differences observed, some results reaching high levels of significance and others showing few or no differences between groups' (Parkes, 1980: 4).

To redress these problems there is an emphasis on what is termed *gold standard* research, *evidence based* quantitative studies taking a scientific, positivist stance and using randomized controlled trials (RCT) and empirical studies rigorously testing and retesting clinically relevant treatment and outcome measures. Trinder (2000) reminds us that these were the underlying practice principles of the American Social Work Research Group, formed in the 1950s, so this is far from being a new approach but it has recently taken on new significance, especially in the arena of child care and child protection.

Macdonald (1997) welcomes evidence based practice as part of the move within social work to increased concerns with effectiveness and 'value for money'. She acknowledges the tensions here, given the 'unbounded' nature of social work with the research topic probably complex and influenced by a wide range of factors: personal, interpersonal, genetic, societal, and institutional. As an example, research may suggest that an individual's much improved ability to parent a child corresponds to their participation in an innovative ten week anger management programme. Equally important, however, might be factors not discovered as part of the research project: a new teacher who helps calm the child, the parent being rehoused to improved accommodation or finding a new, and more supportive relationship, etc. From Macdonald's perspective this only supports her case for the widest possible generalized picture as provided by systematic, large scale, randomized controlled trials using experimental groups, those who get the intervention, and those who do not. This would serve as a control for the types of confounding factors mentioned above, such as improvements being due to a change in some factor(s) external to the intervention. She accepts, however, that such approaches 'will not necessarily work in the same direction as professional values would point us in but (it) offers an opportunity for the concerns of the latter (note: values) to inform the former' (note: the approach) (Macdonald, 1997: 58).

The Argument for Qualitative Research

The discussion above offers some insight, perhaps, into why social workers might be often suspicious of anything but pragmatic, 'common sense' solutions, and may be more drawn to qualitative research: studies which rely, generally, on small numbers of respondents whose views are gained from in-depth interviews, either one-to-one or in focus groups, systematic observation of behaviour or analysis of documentary data. Broad and Fletcher (1993) characterize this as *practitioner research*, which they distinguish from *academic research* because of its emphasis on practical, rather than theoretical, problems; on personal and professional involvement rather than impersonal methods; on social forces and legislation rather than concepts; on arguments and recommendations rather than illumination and proof; on stories, the media and handbooks rather than journals and texts.

Such research studies are tempting since they are seen as drawing on the transferable skills of social work, such as communication skills within the interviews, and reflecting the subjectivity that is taken as the hallmark of social work, as opposed to the objectivity prized in quantitative research.

Qualitative research is valued for its bottom up approach, as reflected in the phrase *grounded theory* where the researcher tries to bracket off what is already known about a topic and becomes *saturated* in the material so as to be attentive to the new, emerging categories. Interestingly this approach was developed through the research on death and dying by Glaser and Strauss (1965, 1967). If interviews are used these are often *semi-structured* which allows for the researcher to balance the knowledge they do carry with them with an opportunity for respondents to expand on their own insights. This style has been described as *minimalist passive interviewing,* which then allows for 'a narrative knowing of persons' (Jones, 2004).

This perspective links well with the anti-racist and anti-discriminatory emphasis of social work, the endeavour not to marginalize groups, or prioritize the views of professionals. Trinder spells out the implications of a critical standpoint within research, insisting that service users can only find their own voice when there is a full acknowledgment of the power dynamics within the research relationship (2000: 44). This is a reminder of the radical tradition within social work (see also Humphries and Truman, 1994; Chahal, 1999) where, to paraphrase Marx, other researchers have sought to understand the world; the point is to change it.

Relating Research to the Debates within Loss, Death and Bereavement

It is the nature of debate that protagonists take sharp and opposing positions. Darlington and Scott use Schon's (1983) comparison of 'the high, hard ground' of quantitative research with the 'swampy lowland' of qualitative studies, where life is messy, uncertain, and which is the world inhabited by our service users, and those who seek to help them. Darlington and Scott resist such polarities, asserting the importance of researchers in the human services to be 'creating terraces which link the two parts of the terrain, not creating territorial disputes' (2002: 1). The next section of the chapter sees how this applies to the dynamics and detail of the research process within the specific focus of loss, death and bereavement, to track how research has challenged some ideas and allowed others to emerge.

The degree to which controversy dogs the views as to what constitutes the 'evidence base', is borne out by the way we consider Freud. We have seen how his theories run as a thread throughout the discussion about psychological approaches to loss, death and bereavement, inevitably so given his pre-eminence and the way they have become the 'common sense' of the way we think about the world. And Freud's original intention was to establish psychoanalysis as an empirical science of what it means to be human. For some (see Masson, 1984, 1997; Webster, 1995) this reliance on heavily edited case studies is enough to reject his whole way of thinking while others, like Casement can stand proudly in his tradition while also acknowledging the degree to which Freud protected himself against challenges, from patients and colleagues alike, by determinedly standing by the certainty of his own sureness (2002: 3).

Certainly contemporary commentators and practitioners, looking for what is termed as reliable, or robust, research have a richness of studies to draw upon; for example, Parkes is consistently clear and accessible as illustrated in his seminal text *Bereavement, Studies in Adult Grief* (1998). Other key texts, incorporating a range of original research papers, include Klass et al. (1996) and Stroebe and Stroebe (1987). In the discussion below the intention is to return to research studies that may be less well known or which have been cited in previous chapters, and to use these as test cases, to explore the sort of evidence authors can use to support their developing theses.

Exercise 7.2 Gordon's Study of Family Violence

In Chapter 3 as part of a wider discussion about child protection work, and the subsequent individual, familial and societal losses, reference is made to Gordon's study of family violence in the USA between 1880 and 1960 *Heroes of their Own Lives: the politics and history of family violence* (1989). This draws from the case files of social work agencies and Gordon identifies, at the turn of the twentieth century, a deeply moralistic, condescending and parent blaming culture. Gordon argues the importance of her findings in that if 'we lack a sense of history this can lead to inevitable distortions in public discussion' (1989: 2).

- What do you need to know about her methodology?
- Where lies the potential in her approach, and where the problems?
- What is the researcher's value base?

Gordon describes her *methodology* as a *case study approach*, a detailed analysis of case records of three social work agencies. A team of five researchers read 1,500 cases, 502 of which were coded and allowing an analysis of over 2,000 incidents of family violence. The codes include the family history, its economic and social circumstances and the agency response leading to 600 plus variables which were then analysed through a statistical computer program (SPSS).

Half the cases were chosen to be more fully written-up because their content revealed a level of detail or indicated themes of special interest. There is therefore an important element of non-random sampling.

Given the number of cases scrutinized and the use of the SPSS program there is a clear quantitative element but Gordon notes that the qualitative data is the more reliable because of the inconsistencies of terminology and the information recorded makes it difficult to compare like with like. 'In relying on qualitative evidence, and sacrificing often the possibility of specifying how many cases were similar, I am acting in the belief that what is revealing of deeper patterns is more significant than what is representative' (1989: 306).

Here Gordon is indicating some of the problems in her methodology. She further acknowledges that her study is a partial view, focusing on a few agencies in one part of a city, Boston, in one small part of the United States. Similarly the clients, as they would have then been called, are predominantly poor immigrants of 'non-elite ethnic and racial backgrounds', which says less about the wider prevalence of serious domestic discord, only that these deprived Italians, African-Americans and Irish were more 'likely to be "caught"' (1989: 8). But the research remains valid, she argues, because for all the demographic and social peculiarities, the wider environmental factors pertaining to family violence are likely to be typical of other urban areas over this time.

Gordon is also clear that her original intention had been to analyse family violence criminal records but this was thwarted by the absence of court recordings, and the records of life in almshouses and asylums were missing, having never been kept or destroyed. Consequently she focuses on those agencies whose records she judges to contain the fullest details and to be the most representative. Gordon came to realize that while these are, indeed, 'rich in detail about family life and personal relations' they are not 'universally reliable, understandable or easy to use' (1989: 12). Each set of records also shapes the story of the families according to the priorities of that particular agency, one dealing with statutory child protection, another arranging and supporting placements, another, exclusively therapeutic. Some records are sketchy, hard to read because of their illegibility and the taken-for-granted class and racial prejudices of the period. Overall they reflect less the actual views of the client, more the social worker's interpretation of them; the records were 'often the basis of the worker's evaluation by her superior and she needed, therefore, to note what she ought to have done, not what she did do' (1989: 17).

Gordon's *value base* draws on her clear commitment to rescuing the individuals from the judgements of the professional agencies, to provide a feminist and historical framework that explains the individuals within their political and social context and to allow them to emerge, as the title has it, as 'heroes of their own lives'. To facilitate this, Gordon provides whole case studies, rather than highlights, because she hopes that this provides fuller access to the data so that those reading the text can develop their own insights.

Exercise 7.3   Lawton's Hospice Study

In Chapter 3 as part of a wider discussion about attitudes towards 'the Good Death', Julia Lawton's study of a hospice *The Dying Process: patients' experiences of palliative care* (2000) is cited. It relates how she comes to the view that there is a gap between the ideology that the hospice adheres to of 'an aware death', and the actual practice. She notes visitors treating their dying relatives as already 'socially dead' while patients also resist in their own way. She describes how patients do everything possible to avoid one hospice worker, known to be especially committed to wanting patients 'to talk openly and frankly about the incurable nature of their illness'. When she appears 'a wave of tension used to hit the room' (2000: 68).

- What do you need to know about her methodology?
- Where lies the potential in her approach, and where the problems?
- What is the researcher's value base?

Lawton's methodology is *ethnographic:* she chose to be 'naïve', entering the world of a hospice as unknowing as any early explorer coming across a previously unstudied tribal society. Lawton's field work took her from a day care service for those with a recently diagnosed terminal illness, through to the inpatient wards on the hospice where patients are in their final stages of life. As a *participant observer,* she worked as a volunteer in both settings, befriending patients and relatives, undertaking practical activities, such as arranging flowers or making beds. She also sat in on staff hand-overs, multi-disciplinary team meetings and case conferences allowing her to see the lived reality of the patients' experiences and the 'significant discrepancy between the formal goals and objectives of the service ... and an informal model of care which had gradually evolved' (2000: 25). She witnessed 'the lethargy and despondency of patients ... . And the burnout and exhaustion experienced by their families and friends' (2000: vii) which counter the concept of 'the aware death'.

The *potential* of this research lies in its richly detailed view of the work of the hospice at every level and this is a bottom up perspective, contrasting with the existing theory and literature which, she argues, is dominated by hospice professionals and their over idealized rationale for their working philosophy.

The *problems*, as Lawton herself identifies, lie in many directions. Some staff commented that her very presence distorts what she is recording and that on some occasions they had felt 'inhibited ... from talking openly of feelings of impotence and anguish they experienced' (2000: 33). Other problems relate to her *value base*. As part of her open inquiry she gained the trust of vulnerable individuals, those who are terminally ill or their relatives. On a practical level, she debates how to introduce her role to people and whether, when she is with a patient, they see her first as a volunteer or a researcher. The patients are pleased to have someone to talk to but what can Lawton do with confidences that are shared with her when her role as researcher has been 'forgotten'. Consequently, despite the protection of anonymity of hospice and patients, she decides to use quotes gained in such circumstances selectively.

Another concern is that she had been given access by the hospice, and came to respect the staff, witnessing the pressures they are under, and struggled with the fact that they may experience her findings as very critical. She was relieved that the feedback she got tells her that, overall, her presence was seen as positive, certainly practical in terms of being a useful extra pair of hands but also as a researcher,

Finally, for Lawton the research project is never just an academic piece of work. It carries an emotional toll as she becomes involved, to a greater or lesser extent, with the over 200 people who, during her fieldwork, die in the hospice.

Narrative Theory: How Research Helps the Theory Emerge

Another way to appreciate the research process is to explore the ways that research nourishes the development of new ideas.

In Chapter 3, *narrative* was introduced as a way of conceptualizing the stories that people tell about their lives. It is important here to remind ourselves that the term 'narrative' might be relatively new but the approach and the skills are not. As we have seen in earlier discussions, when working with vulnerable groups of service users who are being helped to confront and come to new understandings about losses in their life, there is *life story work* with children and *reminiscence work* with older people.

Narrative, as a concept, allows the theory and practice to be offered not just to specific service user groups at either end of the age spectrum but to be brought into the mainstream. The hypothesis is that service users need to mitigate the impact of the *dominant narratives* of various professionals, including social workers, and *re-author* their story. They can even be helped, to recall Gordon's (1989) potent phrase, borrowed from Dickens, to become 'heroes of their own lives'.

And narrative is important also for social workers, countering the tendency for us to become 'organisational functionaries' with 'little time to enter other worlds of meaning in order to offer help' (Parton and O'Byrne, 2000: 2). Narrative allows us to recognize and put aside our own preoccupations with overly prescribed theories or abstract categories, or *paradigmatic knowing*, and focus instead on what the service user is trying to tell us, or *narrative knowing*, drawing on stories which may not be historically true but do resonate enough with what may or could be (McLeod, 2003).

The importance of this perspective is strengthened given the number of research studies which indicate the degree to which service users are denied opportunities to tell their stories, or, having found their words, they are disregarded.

Mayer and Timms' *The Client Speaks* (1970) was in its time a classic and influential text in social work, an early form of consumer research, which asked 61 clients of the Family Welfare Association (FWA) about their levels of satisfaction with the service they had received. These comments are contrasted with the views of social workers.

The resulting document is a powerful picture of misunderstanding since the FWA operated within a psychodynamic framework which was clear to its workers, but not always to those who came to use its services. The latter often saw the FWA as essentially an extension of 'the social', so it proved a shock when their requests for practical and financial help were met with questions about how they feel about their marriage. If clients became angry with what they saw as unnecessary intrusive questioning, social workers interpreted this as defensiveness and resistance, reinforcing the professional judgement that the money problems were merely 'the presenting symptom'. Clients were further blamed for being part of a working-class culture which has 'a unicausal-moralistic-suppressive approach to problem solving' (1970: 2).

The study also revealed a striking example of individuals learning only too well the process of 'becoming a client'.

> Once when I was going [to the office of the FWA] Mum said to me, 'Take the boy with you but don't put that coat on him – she'll think you're well off, that you're only there for the extra money.' Mum said 'Don't get him done up. You're supposed to look rough when you get to those places.' ... Well, it's right, isn't it? I think it's right ... Mum should know, because she's been out in the world. So I took her advice. I took his coat off and put on his old one. And I got help. (1970: 125–6)

This text is not simply an historical curiousity. Whether they are called 'client' or 'service user' what remains consistent is the way that the stories of individuals are not listened to by professionals and it is these studies which are subject to a closer scrutiny below.

Conversational Analysis: A Study of Unanswered Questions in Meetings Between Patients and Psychiatrists. McCabe et al., 2002

A team of researchers became interested in the development, within the NHS, of assertive outreach teams which seek to expand services offered to patients with severe and enduring mental health problems. There is the implication, based on research findings from research in general practice settings, that such initiatives lead to increased treatment compliance, improved satisfaction and decreased emotional distress and sense of burden from the symptoms, but the researchers comment on the lack of information about what professionals might actually do to produce these positive outcomes.

Consequently they decided to use *ethnomethodology* and *conversation analysis,* which they describe as examining, 'through naturalistic interactions ... the practice through which participants produce, recognise and coordinate their actions and activities' (McCabe et al., 2002: 1148). They videoed 32 routine consultations in two psychiatric outpatient clinics, involving 7 psychiatrists (six of whom were consultants) and 32 patients with schizophrenia or schizoaffective disorder.

The consultations lasted, on average, 15 minutes and took the form of a review of the patient's mental state, drugs and side effects, contacts with family, friends and/or other professionals, finance, etc. It was noted that 'Patients' participation ... predominantly involved responding to psychiatrists questions' (2002: 1149) although patients could be more proactive, sometimes making 'active and repeated attempts' to ask about the content of their psychotic symptoms, which seem a source of real concern for them. At such moments the doctors 'hesitated, responded with a question rather than an answer, and smiled and laughed. ... Indicating that they were reluctant to engage with patient's concerns' (2002: 1148). One particular exchange is reported where a patient explained that he felt afraid because he is convinced that everyone hates him. The psychiatrist, at this point, looked down to write his notes, alternating between silence or minimal responses, such as 'mm'.

The researchers have some interesting observations on the use of humour by the psychiatrists, which they describe as 'problematic' and suggest 'embarrassment when faced with such delicate questions from patients about the causes of their distress' (2002: 1150).

Interestingly, although the researchers indicate that half the patients were non-white and 44% are female while the psychiatrists were all white men, there is no comment in the paper as to whether these differences had any bearing on the failures to hear the stories patients are trying to tell.

In a commentary to the McCabe et al. article, Skelton acknowledges that the findings from conversation analysis are not easily generalizable so that the data might seem 'vulnerable' but its strength lies in it not offering 'simple, straightforward messages. Rather ... it offers the reader a way of thinking about the obvious and rediscovering it as profound' (Skelton, 2002: 1151).

Social Constructivism: A Study of 'Changing Identities of Motherhood' in Meetings Between Clients and Social Workers. Hall et al., 2003b

In the book *Constructing Clienthood in Social Work and Human Services* (Hall et al., 2003b) a couple of the papers, with their detailed analysis of client–professional meetings, return us to the topic of parents relinquishing their children. While the findings do not read as oppressive as the examples given in Chapter 3 – 'half caste' children forcibly removed to camps or unwed mothers having to give their child up for adoption – nonetheless there is evidence of the mothers' stories being unheard and/or subtly manipulated into fitting into an identity more tenable to the social worker's perceptions.

The text takes a *social constructivist* approach to the process of 'becoming a client', arguing that it is not an objective, fixed role but rather is the result of the interactions between the different actors, and the power dynamics of their meeting. It is 'constantly being negotiated, justified and argued' (Hall et al., 2003b: 20). The authors see themselves as qualitative, empirical researchers and the paper, 'Legitimating the Rejecting of Your Child in a Social Work Meeting' (2003b) is typical in basing its findings on a line by line transcript of two case conferences, noting and coding every inflection of every word, every pause and stumble, and so allowing the closest of analyses. The paper provides a level of detail that it is not possible to reflect here but, in essence, what is noted is the way that social workers struggle with the idea that a mother is choosing to give up custody of her child. The position of the mother is not allowed to go unchallenged since it undermines all the expectations that are held about women and family roles. 'Motherhood is a category you cannot quit' (2003a: 35) so, through careful phrasing of questions and verbal nudges, the mother comes to a position acceptable to the professionals.

> Her [*note: the mother's*] opening position that it was her decision as to what is best has been ignored in the requirement to produce a damaged identity of an abused woman living with a violent and alcoholic husband. In these circumstances it is not only legitimate to give up her children but also probably in the children's best interests. (2003a: 35)

Meaning Reconstruction Theory: The Bereaved Finding a New Sense of Themselves by Writing Down Their Experiences. Neimayer and Anderson (2002)

Returning to the world of death and dying, in a research paper referred to in Chapter 3, Neimayer and Anderson (2002) describe how the authors came to an approach that they term *meaning reconstruction theory*. They were struck by the contrasting, and, for them unexpected reactions of two women, both of whom have had a child die. One appeared 'shrunken' and she described how rapidly she had aged and how little comfort she got from friends and family, or from her religious beliefs, previously strong but now not able to sustain her. Meanwhile, the other mother found her Christian faith renewed, as were her links to her husband, her other children and to the wider community. Where the first mother had lost her moral compass, the second said she was living a life charged with meaning (2002: 46).

The researchers tried to make sense of this data: two women experiencing the same loss and coming from broadly similar economic and social circumstances but nonetheless responding in quite contrasting ways. This appeared to counter the received wisdom of existing concepts, such as the various stages models, so they developed a new hypothesis: namely that the key factor is the meaning that a person gives to their loss, and their answer to that often asked question, 'why?', works at a profound level, on 'deeply personal and intricately social levels simultaneously'. These encompass the practical through to the spiritual. Individuals could be helped if they were able to 'reconstruct meaning', to 'reconfigure a viable self and world' and that this could be done through 'the healing power of narration' (Neimayer and Anderson, 2002: 47).

The researchers' interest lay in aiding this process, accordingly their *methodology* involved identifying what they term as the *active ingredients* in narrative and they used a quantitative experimental design. One hundred and forty recently bereaved individuals were asked to write an account of their loss. One group was told to simply list, haphazardly, the various thoughts that came to them, what is termed a *low narrative structure*, while others were encouraged to follow a *high narrative structure*, using a clear beginning, middle and end for their story. Some wrote about the facts pertaining to their life after the death, being *external/objective*, others were *internal/reflective,* exploring the subjective meaning for them. The researchers then assessed the level of problematic or traumatic loss, along with standard measures of depression, health behaviour, etc. prior to, immediately following and several weeks after three writing sessions.

The *potential* of the approach lies in the striking examples provided in the paper: individuals found that a strong narrative and reflective approach allowed them 'to work towards profound transformation ... [finding] new significance in a world transformed by loss' (2002: 63).

A Study of the Carers of Dying Patients: Cultural Scripts and Interviews as a Means of 'Reality Maintenance and Reintegration'. Seale (1998)

Seale (1998) comes to the discussion from a different angle. He is a physician who analysed interviews with the relatives, friends and caregivers of 639 adults who died and his prime endeavour was to discover their perceptions on the quality of health care. To increase reliability two perspectives were sought, the accounts compared to those of healthcare staff who were questioned about various aspects of the deceased, e.g. their symptoms, number of admissions, effectiveness of pain relief. One fascinating aspect of the study is that his initial assumption, that his analysis could take full account of 'veracity, bias and validity', then gave way to a growing sense of 'the interview as a topic, primarily concerned with events during the interview' and the degree to which theories of language and self identity led the researchers to an anthropological view of the world in which they live and the 'cultural scripts' by which we abide. This led to 'a questioning of accepted views about the needs of the dying people and their carers' (1998: 1518).

The *methodology* of the research consisted of a series of fixed and open ended questions, with the emphasis on the respondents being facilitated to tell, in their own words, their individual stories. The inter-viewers accompanied this with detailed notes on the respondent's talk which was then fed into a computer program, ETHNOGRAPH, one of a number available to researchers to help manage and analyse both the actual interviews and the attendant observations. From the data came a sense of the interviews as a means of 'reality maintenance and rein-tegration' as respondents sought to defend themselves and their 'moral reputations', especially where the deceased had died alone and/or had been placed in institutional care, and so the survivors might be seen as blame worthy. To counter this, they retold their stories according to *a cultural script* that emphasized how they had struggled to get to the death bed or sought signs that the death had been a peaceful one. Seale suggests that the need to find coherence and meaning is especially important for those who had experienced the loss of a close family member or friend since they felt forced into confronting their own death and 'eventual obliteration of self-identity' (1998: 1519).

Of great significance is the sense that many people need to have 'an aware death' and that this is described in terms of 'a heroic journey', that phrase again, using, often quite explicitly, the Kübler-Ross stages model as signposts along the way.

A Personal Research Story

Seale's report reflects this writer's own small scale, hospice based, research study (Weinstein, 2005, 2007), where the focus is on the stories told by respondents about the dying and grieving process. Although each story is unique to that person what did emerge very strongly was a sense of shared themes, as epitomized by *Sam* (see Chapter 3) and which can be identified as follows:

1. The well person suddenly discovers that they are 'A Patient' and then 'A Cancer Patient'. Patient and carers alike are then involved in a story about 'Fighting the Illness'.
2. The patient and carer become involved in the hospice and now they are part of that organization's ideology of 'The Good Death';
3. After the death the mourner draws on various rituals, whether memorial services or counselling, to help them recall the well person as they once were, to re-member them by bringing them back into the family and letting them go.

What seems especially significant in this process, and is an essential aspect of the enjoyment and excitement of research, is that the findings arose despite any original intentions of the project which had been specifically to explore the effectiveness of bereavement counselling. The hospice provided an unusual opportunity to research this since counselling was offered routinely as an extension of its bereavement services. This allowed for a ready identification of those who had received counselling and a control group of people who had not taken up the offer. This control group is an important dimension of the research process given that its absence has been identified as a problem in previous research within this area (Parkes, 1980).

Methodology

The methodology combined quantitative and qualitative approaches. The *quantitative* aspect is in the questionnaire which was circulated to 50 individuals, each identified as the main carer of a hospice patient who had died at least one year earlier, a small sample since this was planned as a pilot project. Half the sample consisted of a spouse/ partner and half an adult child of the deceased, half had received coun-selling, half had not. Questions focused on their support and contact with the hospice with the intention of exploring what influences indi-viduals in choosing to have, or not have, counselling and to tease out the tangible differences in bereavement outcomes between the two groups.

The questionnaire followed the familiar Lickert scale (Robson, 1993) where respondents are asked to tick a box depending on whether they 'strongly agree', 'agree', 'are not sure', 'disagree' or 'strongly disagree'. In this way the questionnaire sought to possess *face and content validity*, in other words, to include questions on all the relevant aspects of the topic and provide the information that is required. There was a combination of questions concerning the nature of the bereavement, quantitative material focusing on health and process questions exploring the respon-dent's experience of the counselling that they had, or why they had not taken up the offer of counselling, and how they consequently felt about themselves. Within this essentially quantitative strategy there was also a qualitative element with respondents invited to write in comments on the questionnaire if they wished to expand their thoughts, an opportunity which many took and this was built upon by asking respondents to volunteer to meet with the researcher for a more in-depth discussion.

This opportunity to add their own views, either by writing on the questionnaire or being interviewed, was an explicit attempt to give more weight to the respondents' perspectives, allowing them space to elaborate their views in whatever way seemed appropriate. It was an acknowledgment that questionnaires, however carefully constructed, can be limiting and top-down in their emphasis with the questions inevitably influenced by the researcher's own, prior understandings of the issues, based on personal and professional experience and wider reading. But, as McLeod comments, 'knowledge of the literature is valuable in so far as it can be used to sensitise the researcher to potential dimensions of meaning (and) it is an impediment ... if it gets in the way of discovery' (1994: 93). Indeed, as Lawton (2000) argues, the existing literature does seem to be based mainly on researchers' and practitioners' interpretations of the mourning process, less on the direct experiences of ordinary people. Equally clearly, these are not entirely separate populations, see the moving preface to the Young and Cullen research (1996) where one of the authors describes his own experience of grieving his wife. Nonetheless the response of professionals in this field is likely to be different from that of the respondent coming relatively fresh and unknowing to the experience.

Ethical Issues

However much care is taken, this area of research is fraught in terms of ethical issues and this was explored in a number of ways, through supervision, discussion with a support group at the hospice and the submission of a research proposal to the appropriate Ethics Committee which had to give its formal approval before any work could proceed. There was also a clear commitment to confidentiality, if not for the hospice whose management was happy to be named as collaborators in the research, then for the respondents. Assurance was given that not just names but other identifying details would be changed at the point of publication.

The issues that needed to be addressed were several. The 'target' group was people who had suffered a bereavement of a close relative and the letter inviting them to take part in the research was uninvited and unexpected and so in danger of reviving any number of painful memories. When respondents were encouraged to contact the researcher for a follow-up interview this could be construed as an opportunity for a further counselling session, albeit not with the original counsellor, or the interview could have turned into one as the discussion developed. Fortunately the aftercare services at the hospice offered their continuing services to any respondent who requested it and there was some reassurance in the findings of Cook and Bosley (1995), namely that individuals find satisfaction in being research respondents on the topic of bereavement. By not approaching anyone whose bereavement was less than a year old, it was anticipated that their feelings were no longer as raw as they might have been earlier in their mourning. The individuals were selected by hospice staff, who had access to files, and so could remove from the sample those that they anticipated might respond badly. The letters, and attached questionnaires, were sent from the hospice and in that sense were 'normalized' since the hospice in any event maintained contact with past service users, keeping them in touch with news, activities, etc. The questionnaire was accompanied by a covering letter from the Principal Social Worker and an introductory letter from the researcher, emphasising the voluntary nature of the project. This also appealed to the altruism of the potential respondents, given the intention of the research to improve services for those using the hospice. A hospice contact number was provided if anyone wanted further information and/or reassurance.

Those individuals who volunteered their names for follow-up interviews were written to again, further stressing that they did not need to proceed if this no longer felt appropriate to them. Two people did, in fact, withdraw at this stage, one following a conversation with the hospice contact person.

In the follow up interviews, individuals signed a consent form and the point was made, in writing and verbally, that they could request that the interview be stopped at any point. Subsequently each respondent was sent a copy of the transcript and it was explained that they could add any further points that had occurred to them, or remove or amend any comments that they were unhappy seeing in print.

In this way the research sought to work within the clearest possible ethical guidelines and those respondents interviewed frequently referred to the comfort in being able to return to and reflect on these issues.

Findings

The findings focused on three main areas:

1   The effectiveness of bereavement counselling

The findings were very positive overall, evidencing the ability of counsellors to develop successful therapeutic relationships with individuals, even those who were clearly initially wary, even hostile, and to provide what one interviewee valued as 'a shoulder to support me, not a shoulder to cry on'.

In the *quantitative analysis* the highest ratings, expressed by all of the respondents, were given for the qualities of being taken seriously, being provided with a safe atmosphere and being helped to express their feelings.

Comparing those who had been counselled with those who had not, the former came over as significantly more certain about their current feelings and sense of recovery. This included visits to doctors and use of medication through to relationships with family and friends. There was also a significant difference in family relationships: nearly three quarters agreed these had improved while a very much lower proportion of non-counselling respondents agreed, with just over half not being sure or not considering this relevant.

The research reinforced the importance given by Walter (1999) to individuals needing to retain 'an enduring sense' of the person who died, rather than moving on by breaking the emotional bonds.

The findings offered limited information about the detail of the counselling, perhaps because the ethical considerations meant there had been a deliberate time lag between the bereavement, and thus the counselling and the research, so most of the respondents were unable to specifically identify what they had appreciated or might have wanted to be different.

2   The clear endorsement by carers of the work of the hospice movement especially when compared to hospital care and, simultaneously, their apparent resistance to a central tenet of the hospice movement. In the face of the fatal illness, all respondents managed more by denying than accepting the fact of impending death

In the *qualitative analysis* the respondents all expressed varying degrees of anger about the insensitivity of hospitals to the needs of both the dying patients and themselves as carers, and it was interesting to note their subsequent, equally strongly held, appreciation of hospice care. In the *quantitative analysis* respondents strongly endorsed the work of the hospice in terms, generally, of their support for the patient (100%), for the carer (89%) and, specifically, at the point of death (88%). The interviews allowed an elaboration of these views and what was then named was confidence in the medical care of the patients, choice of treatment, lack of confining rules and a positive atmosphere.

Following on from these findings, there was an apparent contradiction at the heart of this support. Hospices are committed to a particular approach to palliative care, their concept of 'a Good Death' emphasizes a full awareness rather than a denial of dying. Nonetheless, in the interviews all the respondents offered ringing endorsements of the hospice while simultaneously apparently resisting the central tenet of the hospice movement, as represented in Sam's telling phrase about putting discussion about the dying 'into the bottom drawer'.

3   The importance for the respondents to sustain a continuing sense of the individuality of the person who died

This returns us to the debates about the purpose of bereavement with the previously prevailing Freudian orthodoxy, of reaching closure and moving on, being challenged by those who argue that healthy mourning instead demands gaining a fuller and enduring sense of them. This latter position seems to be supported in this research. In the *quantitative analysis* respondents who received counselling were more likely to still think of the person who died but to be less upset when they do so. In the *qualitative analysis* we can see that, whether managing the early stages of the illness, accompanying the patient through to their final moments, mourning them subsequently and engaging, or not, in counselling, the individual interviewees evidenced their moving attempts to retain a sustaining sense of self of their loved ones first during their illness, and despite first their physical diminishment, and then after their death. Those who did not take up counselling regretted this decision, in part, because they believed that this would have helped them clear away the barriers from seeing their loved ones more clearly.

Conclusions and Implications of the Research

The findings have to be treated with caution. The sample was very small since, as indicated above, it was intended as a pilot project but the follow-up, a far larger analysis, never materialized because of changing research priorities at the hospice. Even with these limitations, the research raised some important provisional findings of interest in terms of practice and policy for a range of health and social care professionals, not just counsellors.

Some conclusions appear as relatively straightforward and relate to the importance of providing space for those caught up in the drama and trauma of the dying and death of a close family member. Counselling seems to provide that space. Further, because it is offered as an automatic element of the hospice bereavement services, rather than having to be sought out, the figures suggest that those normally under represented in counselling, men and older people, felt freer in accessing this help. Such findings remain speculative at this point and a larger sample might have provided further evidence about these factors, plus data on how this relates to individuals from ethnic minority groups other than the majority white European population who made up this sample. One could also complement this service user perspective with an exploration of the counsellors' perspectives and understandings: a combination of self-report questionnaires and interviews, either one-to-one or focus groups, could provide important data on the relationship between service user satisfaction and particular counselling approaches, including theoretical stance and personal/ professional style.

The other major conclusion lies in the fierceness of the respondents when recalling the responses of the hospitals. This suggests that the prevailing medical ethos of 'fighting' and denying death, which the interviewees experienced as marked by misdiagnosis and ultimate failure, provoked in them a similar fight response, but directed at the hospital. In the hospice something quite profoundly shifted. There it seemed the hospice, with contrasting clarity and confidence, held the reality of the dying which allowed the pain, physical and psychological, to be contained in the system. The carers permitted themselves to stop fighting and to relax into the dying process even while not naming it. Perhaps bereavement counselling would not be such an urgent concern if more health and social care professionals could follow the, earlier cited, advice of Zinker to:

> stay with the process and listen, not push for outcomes, show respect for what is there, see the usefulness and even the beauty of the way others express their mourning and sense of loss and allow oneself to be the firm ground on which the other stands. (1994: 262).

Points for practice

- The GSCC requires all social workers to undertake continuous professional development in order to remain registered as a professional.
- One way to do this is to undertake some research or writing of your own, investigating in more detail something that you have noticed or that interests you in your work or by writing up some interesting or innovative work that you have done.
- If you do not have the confidence or opportunity to do this yourself you can still develop the skills of 'research mindedness' by reading existing literature more critically.
- With the computerization of information, it is now much easier to keep yourself up-to-date with the relevant evidence about effective practice.
- Regularly visit the key websites such as the Social Care Institute of Excellence, and the Department of Health which will offer or sign-post you to the latest papers and documents. Use Google scholar to track down books and articles on your subject of interest.

Further reading

A comprehensive introduction to research methodology is provided in:

Robson, C. (1993) *Real World Research, a Resource for Social Scientists and Practitioner-Researchers.*

Social workers have a growing body of literature available to them. Of these see:

Corby, B. (2006) *Applying Research in Social Work*. Maidenhead: OUP.

Darlington, Y. and Scott, D. (eds) (2002) *Qualitative Research in Practice, Stories from the Field.*

Fuller, R. and Petch, A. (1995) *Practitioner Research, the Reflexive Social Worker.*

8 Social Workers within our Agencies: The Need for 'Relentless' Self-care

---

Chapter contents

- The social worker's need for support, or 'containment'
- The nature of organizational 'defences against anxiety'
- Stress in social work and 'the fear of feeling'
- The need for 'relentless self-care'
- Models of supervision
- The place of hope, for ourselves and service users

Introduction

Throughout this text there has been example after example of confusion in the wider world in the face of loss, death and bereavement. Inevitably social workers are not exempt from being personally affected in various ways, will share these wider difficulties, and have some that are uniquely ours. This chapter explores the degree to which our employing agencies struggle to support and/or offer containment to their workers, building on the insights of Menzies Lyth (1959/1988), and her classic research into how a hospital sought, and failed, to defend nurses against anxiety, and relating this to social work's literature. We explore what is meant by stress, and other related terms and concepts, and the degree to which these relate to the fear of feeling deep within the culture of modern state welfare (Cooper and Lousada, 2005).

Social workers are quoted with examples of how they were faced with death and dying. This elaborates the need for 'relentless self-care' (Renzenbrick, 2004) and how this might be found within our organizational, professional and personal support systems. Emphasis is given to the importance of supervision and the *seven eyed model* developed by

Hawkins and Shohet (2006) is followed. The chapter ends by revisiting the scenarios and advocating the place of *hope* in our work.

How professionals cope, or not

In the introductory chapter the text's core aim is set out as helping to recognize, rescue and revive the social work role within our work with loss, death and bereavement. To fulfil this ambitious target subsequent chapters have elaborated and critiqued the body of skills, the range of theories, the underpinning value base and the body of research that is available but we are still left with a hard truth: individuals from across the professions will struggle with the emotions raised in this work. This was illustrated, in the introductory chapter, in various ways.

The New York paramedic, Frank, is obsessed with the young woman he fails to save (Scorsese, 1999) and the suddenly bereaved psychotherapist is out of patience with what now seem the minor problems of his patients (Moretti, 2001). There are the real life examples: Nuland, visiting his terminally ill brother, experiences the hospital doctors as 'untouchably aloof and self-absorbed … too distanced from the truth of their own emotions to have any sense of ours' (1994: 226) while Laungani recalls the doctor who, in his repeated statements '"I don't want to alarm you … there's nothing to be frightened of" … scared the living daylights out of me!' (1992: 13).

Presumably no professional, including social workers, enters their vocation intending to become so 'distanced' from their service users or wanting to scare them so profoundly. The fact that it happens, nonetheless, means that there is an urgent need to examine the how, where and why of this phenomena and how it might be worked with more effectively and so avoided.

> ### Example 8.1   Social Worker Dealing With Loss – a Hospital Social Worker With Older People
>
> Malcolm, in his forties, is manager of a multi-disciplinary 'rapid response' team mainly working with older people and those with disabilities to help them get discharged from the hospital back into the community. The work is short term, usually not more than six weeks.
>
> 'We had this guy who was a cancer patient and the doctors told us that he had six months to live but hadn't told him yet. And the student (a young white woman, aged 21) had to go and introduce herself so how can she go easy with him on that? I can deal with it, and it can be difficult. I come
>
> *(Continued)*

(Continued)

from Ireland and am used to these big funerals where the whole village will turn out, there's the wake and at the funeral the family sits in the front pews and everyone comes up and says "I'm sorry for your troubles". But over here? I've been to cremations where if more than 20 mourners come they have to go out and bring in extra chairs! I was brought up with death and loss, I can talk to people because of my background ... We had one woman who was described as having "taken to her bed". I thought that was quite disrespectful. Her husband had died 18 months earlier, and perhaps she'd always been a bit depressed but to lose your husband like that, after all the things they had been through together, I might want to "take to my bed" in a situation like that. It's not so unusual.'

Example 8.2 Social Worker Dealing With Loss – a Manager of Adult Services

Josephine, is the operational manager of adult services (mental health, physical disabilities, older people) in a voluntary agency working principally with the Jewish community.

(After a death of a resident) 'ideally, the key workers should be able to get special attention, they should be able to go the funeral if they want, and sometimes they do. And that can be very difficult if staff had been off duty for a few days and come back to find the funeral had been and gone. I hope that the manager would give them time and place to talk about it ... (and) It's like what happens in hospital – you're already planning for the next person. There's not the time or space. With the younger residents, certainly it was a bit more shared, with staff and residents. There was an opportunity to go to the funeral or they'd light a candle, they'd say the prayers at the home, it was formally marked. That happened when we had the suicide, and that was more complicated. Staff and residents both separately, and collectively had the chance to mark what was a very traumatic experience. When something was pretty dreadful we'd get someone from outside involved, we'd get the hospice movement involved.'

Example 8.3 Social Worker Dealing With Loss – an Approved Social Worker

George is a social worker in a community mental health team and experienced two deaths within a fortnight, one of a young black woman, Jan, who was admitted against her will and then died on the ward from an undiagnosed

(Continued)

(Continued)

medical condition. The second, Penny, an older woman who, he decided, need not be admitted and then died later that evening in her own home, of a heart attack.

'The "support" was that we had to go to a Serious Untoward Incident Panel, chaired by a senior manager. It was like a little inquiry. That was the support we were given … I felt very stressed, I didn't know what to do … It's a Victorian organization, it's got a Victorian bureaucracy … There's no supervision although the policy is that we have supervision monthly so the organization covers itself … So, it's getting your own supervision. People go through stages of getting burnt out … we're like the sponge of society.'

What these examples suggest is the powerful impact of such situations on social workers and the degree to which the professionals involved go outside of the formal structures to get support, sometimes to agencies seen as specialists, such as the hospice in Josephine's case, or, for George, informally to colleagues despite the fact that they seem to be in a similar stage of 'burn out'. Malcolm, critical of his colleagues, instead draws deep on his own early experiences in his native Ireland of how a community mourns, and Josephine, too, cites the values of the faith community from which her service users come, almost as a counterpoint to the organizational imperatives of 'no time, no space'.

The next exercise invites you to put yourself into the picture.

Exercise 8.1   Unexpected Personal and Professional Feelings of Loss

Take yourself back to a situation where the strong feelings of a service user, related to their sense of loss, or losses, brought up powerful, and perhaps unexpected, feelings for you.

- Why do you think you were affected so powerfully?
- What support did you need and what support did you get to help you in your work?
- Renzenbrick (2004) refers to the need for social workers to subject themselves to 'relentless self-care'. What does this mean for you? What might this consist of?

Stress in Work within Welfare

What we are dealing with here is the potential for social workers to experience strong, even disabling feelings given the demands of the diverse, and often deeply traumatized, individuals who make up our caseloads, those who have experienced 'actual and emotional injustice, and actual and psychic injury' (Davies, 1998: 19). To be effective we need to 'draw extensively on our own personal resources' when striving 'to understand and support the personal, social and emotional needs of service users' (Hafford-Letchfield, 2006: 108). But this is tested given that we bring to our work 'our personalities; our past and some of our less integrated experiences' (Appleby, 1998: 91), indeed it may have been the latter that brought us to the work, our acting as 'wounded healers' (see discussion in McLeod, 2003: 490–1).

When, as a consequence, our feelings become too much this is variously described as *burnout, compassion fatigue, vicarious trauma* or more simply *stress*. This last term, as Menzies Lyth (1998:7) reminds us, is no more than a technical word, based in physics where it describes the application of force on an object. She goes on to emphasize that, in the work of health and social care, professionals will often feel under pressure but this can be a positive factor. She cites research that shows that when organizational changes bring nursery nurses into more immediate and intimate contact with distressed patients and their families the nurses actually flourish, they 'enjoyed the new challenge, valued their new skills and grew more confidant'. The issue, is not about being overwhelmed by the more demanding work: the nurses actually thrive because of:

> the careful management of the circumstances in which the role-change took place; clear definition of the roles of all concerned and of the nature of delegation, support and training where necessary, the development of a culture where people talked. (Menzies Lyth, 1998: 7)

In this analysis, Menzies Lyth is reiterating her previous, ground breaking research (1959/1988) of the low retention rates of student nurses, which identified high levels of distress and anxiety across the hospital. The research revealed complex responses, or defence mechanisms, mostly unconscious which were apparently effective in the short term but ultimately proved very damaging. Menzies Lyth argues that nurses are very distressed by the unusually emotional and painful nature of the work and the hospital, instead of recognizing, and responding to these feelings, actually exacerbated the situation through an organizational culture which left nurses less able to cope with anxiety than before they became students.

Defences Against Anxiety (Menzies Lyth, 1959/1988)

- Caring for patients and decision making is turned into *ritual task performance* which discourages discretion and initiative and serves to come between the nurse and the patient.
- *Professional detachment*: the patient is depersonalized and categorized, as is the nurse who can be moved from ward to ward as a way of denying or resisting attachment and over involvement. The consequent psychological distancing can come over as a 'don't care' attitude and lack of team sprit,
- *Feelings are not allowed* and *interpersonal repressive techniques culturally required*: nurses are encouraged to have a 'stiff upper lip' or to 'pull yourself together'.
- *Decisions and tasks are forced upwards*: nursing staff and students carry out lower level of tasks in relation to their personal ability, skill and position in the hierarchy, which protects them from difficult decisions but also leaves them with feelings of frustration and stress.
- *Intra-personal struggles turned into interpersonal conflict*: the individual copes with their own uncertainties and difficulties by blaming others, a process of denial, splitting, and projection. Managers take good work for granted meaning that nurses are more likely to be reprimanded than praised and the nurses mirror this by criticizing other nurses, or a whole category of nurses, normally the grade immediately below or above them, for being careless, irresponsible, insubordinate. The accusation can become a self-fulfilling prophecy, 'people act objectively on the psychic roles assigned to them' (1959/1988: 57).
- *Teamwork is discounted*: given their sense of impermanence, individuals act in isolation from each other and in ignorance of other people's tasks and skills.
- *Avoidance of change*: as a way of avoiding anxiety 'the service tends to cling to the familiar even when the familiar has ceased to be appropriate or relevant' (1959/1988: 62).

All of these defences against the feelings of anxiety, guilt, doubt and uncertainty absorb enormous energy and represent an uneasy compromise that cannot hold.

Cooper and Lousada (2005) stay within a psychoanalytical frame but incorporate a political dimension for the problems confronting welfare professionals such as social workers. When the Welfare State was established after the Second World War it was assumed that rational and expert professionals could take on 'the giants' of Idleness, Ignorance, Want, Squalor and Disease. This was, in political terms, a paternalistic, social democratic, top down approach which served to 'hive off its (the wider society's) awareness of the worst of its social and personal ills' (2005: 10) to specialized professional groups who were expected to hold these unbearable tensions, to be society's container. But if social workers are then to deal with the messiness, uncertainty and risk which our work puts us in touch with we need the space for our difficult feelings to be voiced. Our increasingly centralized and regularized organizations of welfare, however, are places marked by 'a fear of feeling', consequently 'welfare organisations' become 'puzzling, contradictory and uncomfortable' places where people's feelings are dealt with but not acknowledged (2005: 3).

Stress and Social Workers

Certainly this has been recognized as a consistent theme in commentaries about social work. The Victoria Climbié report (Home Office, 2003) repeats the findings of many earlier such documents when identifying over pressured workforces muddling through by means of unconsidered interventions, poor supervision and bureaucratic back covering.

Various researchers are equally telling when they write not in retrospect concerning obvious failures, like the death of a child, but about more routine, every day situations.

Pithouse's (1987) grounded theory research in a child care team relies on both formal interviews and listening in on meetings, supervision sessions and conversations. What he records is a pattern of social workers defensively protecting themselves against potential problems and manipulating complex issues so that colleagues and managers can recognize what has been turned into 'an approved reality' (1987: 39). Critical analysis of each other's work is avoided since that 'would mean criticism of perhaps a colleague and we don't do that. We sort of play the happy family' (1987: 53). Pithouse does not regard the social workers as cynical but rather, in seeking to manage the contradictory nature of their work and the limited resources which they have available, adopting a stance of 'interactive distance, that is the control of actual contact and conduct ... This allows the worker to ration her time and skills in relation to the competing demands made upon her' (1987: 94–5).

Social workers within a mental health setting are the subject of a rather different research project, a qualitative study of a questionnaire response and work diary returned by 237 frontline mental health social workers alongside two focus groups (Huxley et al., 2005). 'Stress and pressures' are explored and the themes that emerge are: *pressure of work*, especially having to complete paper work; *staffing matters*, related to covering for absences and unfilled vacancies; *job satisfaction and well-being*, and where this is lacking because of role confusion and the constant changes accompanying reorganizations; *recruitment and retention issues*, with 49% either very much wanting to move on or actually with plans in hand to do so. Some are seeking posts within social work, where they hope to be better supported, others want to leave the profession altogether. The last category relates to *being valued* and respondents are most vulnerable when they are not valued by their employers, with whom they feel 'out of sympathy' (2005: 1075), and the wider society, a category not discussed further. Over half (55%) of the respondents have stress levels as high as to indicate a probable common mental disorder.

Motivation is sustained through the support of their supervisors and team members along with direct contact with their service users who provide a sense that they are able to make a difference. The paper concludes that 'on the whole they stay because of professional commitment to the goals and values of the profession, to serve their users' (2005: 1077).

Seeking Solutions

Stress or pressures are, then, not the problem per se. Working to and being stretched beyond one's limits 'can create a "buzz" or act as a motivating factor' (Hafford-Letchfield, 2006: 108), it is there in the job spec 'along with the contract, salary and car loan' (Davies: 1998: 14). The issue is how to manage the pressures, to stay with doubt and uncertainty within levels that keep both the worker and the client safe.

One possible strategy lies in the gestalt concept of *self-support* (Clarkson, 1989), the intra-personal space, or inner self-confidence, that allows the individual to understand and then ask for the support they need from their wider environment. Psychoanalysis talks in terms of how workers can be *contained* (Speck, 1994), as opposed to constrained with Hawkins and Shohet (2006) citing Winnicott's concept of *good enough parenting*. The main carer, normally the mother, can only provide appropriate care if she is, in turn, held and supported by another adult, normally the father. In our context, the social worker can be there for the service user if supported by the agency, as represented by the supervisor and/or manager.

Renzenbrick (2004), basing her experiences on palliative care, urges on the social worker the need for what she terms 'relentless self-care' which consists of:

- *Supervision*: that 'safe place for sharing of both personal and professional struggles' (2004: 861).
- *Therapy*: when colleagues, managers, friends and/or lovers are not enough.
- *Values*: whether professional, secular or religious, or in any combination, they reflect the need for 'a strong sense of positive growth, transformation and healing' (2004: 861).
- *Balance*: between work and home and community and within the workplace with moves allowed between direct work with service users and other personal and professional developments involving further training, writing and outreach work.
- *Education*: 'engage the intellect' (2004: 861).
- *Going from the personal to the political*: holding onto the sense that you can make a difference out there in the wide world.

You may find it useful to check back on your own list on self-care (in Exercise 8.1. above) and see what is consistent or different between Renzenbrick's and yours. The ordering as set out above is important since good supervision can encompass all that follows.

Super-vision

Supervision is a given in any organization but it may be far from the 'safe place for sharing of both personal and professional struggles' envisaged by Renzenbrick (2004: 861). As George, the mental health social worker who has experienced two recent deaths of service users, comments: 'There's no supervision although the policy is that we have supervision monthly so the organization covers itself'. In the report on the death of Victoria Climbié, with reference to the social worker holding the case, it is noted that there 'was no systematic evaluation of the way she handled Victoria's case ... her supervision sessions amounted to "me telling them what was happening in the case and then I was just handed a list of actions"' (evidence by the social worker to the independent inquiry (Selwyn, 2001)).

Below is a social worker's account of his own early experiences as a supervisee.

Personal Experiences as a Supervisee

I came straight off my training course into an agency which was undergoing yet another, radical reorganization. Various key staff had left so we were over reliant on agency people and there was an influx of new cases, or so it seemed. In the press there was a flurry of 'shock, horror' stories about the latest child death which was unsettling.

In the office the managers seemed preoccupied and uncertain so it was the team where we pulled together, offered mutual support and moaned and we also organized collectively in the union as a form of alternative authority and strength. There was little challenge, constructive criticism or detailed discussion of case material. Certainty was encouraged, for example, in giving evidence in court and so I tended to not admit or value my not knowing.

Formal, regular supervision was offered but was essentially managerial, 'policing' me to ensure that I was 'policing' my clients. So, I became adept at looking after myself but because this was premature I rushed to judgement and learned to put a spin on case material to get from managers what I wanted for my service users, mainly in terms of material goods. Since I was conscientious, hard working and considered good at my work, and well able to express myself confidently, whether in court reports, supervision or team meetings, I was basically unchallenged. My bluff was not called. The fact that I had only just qualified and was obviously on a steep learning curve was not acknowledged, either by my managers, or me.

This difficult experience of supervision continued, with some honourable exceptions, into my subsequent career. One supervisor would regularly fall asleep during our sessions so I made sure I always had my newspaper to read until he came to. Discussing this with colleagues, who experienced the same phenomena, we decided that he suffered from petit mal but this was never personally discussed or acknowledged with the individual concerned. Another supervisor was a mainly silent figure who never responded to my suggestions about developing my work but would then bring my ideas back to me, six months later, as his initiatives. Again I did not question this but adapted to this managerial style while complaining about him behind his back.

There are many ways to explain supervision, or *super-vision* as the word is played with by the gestaltist Houston who goes on to describe it as focusing on the wider context and finding a place to acknowledge emotions, suspicions, hunches, doubts and whatever may have been suppressed at the time (1990: 2). Casement (1985) suggests that super-vision offers the opportunity for *hindsight*, looking back on a session, *foresight*, anticipating what may happen in a future session and *insight*, the capacity to function with more immediate understanding within the momentum of the therapeutic encounter. The whole process involves a shift from needing an outside source of wisdom and support to developing an *internalized supervisor*, your own authority and 'an island of intellectual contemplation' to which the worker can go during a session and from which you can watch yourself critically (1985: 29).

These concepts are intended principally for counsellors and psy-chotherapists and, although their understandings can be applied to a purely social work perspective, Hafford-Letchfield (2006), surveying the current literature, emphasizes the focus on the organizational aspects with the attendant hierarchies of administrative authority and multiple accountabilities:

> Supervision involves four parties: the agency, the supervisor, the super-visee and service users. It should be an enabling process which mirrors direct social work practice and parallels social work intervention. Short-term objectives of social work supervision are to improve the worker's capacity to do the job effectively by providing a healthy work environ-ment, stimulate professional knowledge, practice skills and provide practical and emotional support. (2006: 124)

One approach that fully acknowledges the organizational dimension and the process issues is Hawkins and Shohet's (2006) *seven-eyed model*. In the outline below it has been modified to focus on the social worker.

'The Seven-Eyed' Model of Supervision (Adapted from Hawkins and Shohet, 2006)

Each time a social worker and a supervisor meet their work should include:

Mode 1 The content of the social worker–client session
Mode 2 Focusing on strategies and interventions
Mode 3 Focusing on the social worker–service user relationship

(Continued)

(Continued)

Mode 4 Focusing on the social worker's process
Mode 5 Focusing on the supervisory relationship
Mode 6 Focusing on the supervisor's own process
Mode 7 Focusing on the wider context

- Reflect on your own experience of being supervised. How far do your meetings go in terms of moving between the modes?

To explore the usefulness of this model let us return to the mental health social worker, George, but this time assuming good practice, namely that he is having regular supervision and this is taking place shortly after the two deaths and before the Serious Untoward Incident Panel. Let us also bear in mind the earlier statistics cited in the research by Huxley et al. (2005); according to these findings, if George is not to be one of the 49% planning to leave or one of the 55% with stress levels so high that they indicate a probable common mental disorder he needs to be helped with:

- *pressure of work*, especially having to complete paper work;
- *staffing matters*, related to covering for absences and unfilled vacancies;
- *job satisfaction and well-being* and where this is lacking because of role confusion and the constant changes accompanying reorganizations;
- *being valued,* staff are most vulnerable when they feel undervalued by their employers, with whom they feel 'out of sympathy' (2005: 1075), and the wider society.

Motivation is sustained through the support of their supervisors and team members along with direct contact with their service users who provide a sense that they are able to make a difference. The paper concludes that 'on the whole they stay because of professional commitment to the goals and values of the profession, to serve the users' (Huxley et al., 2005: 1077).

Mode 1 The Content of the Social Worker–Client Session

This is about what actually happened in the meeting between the worker and the service user, what the service user chose to share, what aspect of their lives they brought to the discussion and how this links back to the content of previous sessions. The aim and goal here is to help the worker pay attention to the service user and the choices that they are making and how this links to other aspects of their life.

For George there are two service users, both strangers to him before he had to do the emergency assessments which were followed by their deaths. One death is put down to 'natural causes' so there are no wider organizational waves; the other is controversial. George needs to be asked whether, because of these wider pressures, he wants to bring just the younger black woman, Jan, or also Penny, the older woman. George is pleased to be reminded that both individuals are of equal importance to him, even though they are getting disproportionate attention from the organization. In both circumstances it is important for George to go back to the content of what happened, to check what he heard and observed in a way that is not influenced by what happened next. He needs to be clear as to whether, in the focus on the psychological symptoms, he had missed any obvious physical conditions.

This helps George clarify that on neither occasion could he reasonably be expected to have detected the physical problems. Clearly both individuals were distressed at being confronted with the risk of losing their liberty and being sectioned but he had talked in the flat with Penny's GP who was the professional responsible for the patient's medical condition.

Mode 2 Focusing on Strategies and Interventions

The main goal here is to consider the skills in and choices of intervention, what was done, and why and what might have been the alternatives.

George notices the dynamics in each situation, what was brought by the individual service user, the other family members who were present and the other professionals, such as doctors and, in Jan's case, the police. Again George is helped to see that he drew on his wealth of experience to help him make his decisions. With Penny he had been careful to honour her own feelings about her illness and resist the pressures of others. He wishes now that he had checked more carefully with the GP about her physical condition and will do so when such situations arise in the future. With Jan, George is aware of how caught up he became in supporting the anger and anxieties of the family members who had summoned the help because of their concerns for Jan's mental health but were then panicking when this led to police officers at the door. George is helped to see that he had used all his skills to secure a voluntary admission, and that once Jan refused this there was no painless way out of the predicament.

Mode 3 Focusing on the Social
Worker–Service User Relationship

This phase focuses on the unconscious and conscious aspects, 'what happened around the edges; (the) metaphors and images that emerged ... (allowing for) greater insight and understandings of the dynamics of the ... relationship' (2006: 70).

Given the organizational and functional imperative of social work, and taking George's needs at face value, the supervision could have ended by now, both supervisor and supervisee reassured that all had been covered in organizational terms. George would certainly have got more from this than in the actual situation. But there are also opportunities to explore further, while staying this side of the supervisor going into 'therapist' mode with George. The clue that George might need more is there in the image of the desperate look Jan gave him as the police took her out, still resisting, through the door and her comment earlier in the session that she felt trapped by her disturbing images of the world. Her fantasies had become reality and George is left feeling at fault. She had said that she was going to fight her illness but had ended up fighting the police. Penny provoked other images, of a deeply alone woman. Although George had gone along with her wishes, not sectioning her, his last impression is of leaving the flat with all the other professionals, relieved not to be involved in any follow-up paper work, pleased at having supported her in her wishes but catching, and then avoiding, a very defeated look in her eyes. He fantasizes that he was the last person to see her alive, that where he saw her sitting in the corner of the sofa is where she was later found dead, that if he had insisted on her going to hospital she would have got life saving medical attention when she started her heart attack.

Mode 4 Focusing on the
Social Worker's Process

Since much of the above is George's imagination he might want to at least acknowledge, if not explore his projections, what he is carrying, consciously and unconsciously, which leaves him feeling responsible for all that occurred. George is haunted by the fact that all of Jan's family members are black and all the professionals white and he feels, in that moment, sickened by the emptiness of the anti-racist and anti-discriminatory stance he professes. He is distressed by the aloneness of Penny and wonders if leaving her in her flat was less about caring for her than simply another form of discrimination, ageism, assuming that her solitude and confusion were a normal part of being old rather than something that could be addressed. He is also distressed as he recalls his energy, when starting in social work, 'to make things better' and he wonders what this younger self would say to the George who now spends so much of his time dashing into crisis situations with the police and psychiatrists in tow. To echo the call of the radical social work conference, he is not sure if he is in a profession 'worth fighting for'.

The supervisor might respond to such thoughts with reassuring words: 'you did the best you could', 'we have to live in the real world' and George might benefit if it is acknowledged just how desperate dealing with mental distress can be, that some people cannot be helped, even if their problems come earlier to our attention, that the wider world can be a pitiless place, that being aware of discrimination does not always mean we can rise above it. George can come to see that sometimes service users can be so powerful that their desperate, 'mad' feelings, can end up 'in' the social worker. This may help him to step back from the emotions, to give back responsibility for what belongs elsewhere. For a careful and accessible discussion of how these compli-cated feelings, which can be termed *projective identification,* occur within social work see Fleming (1998) on 'the inner impact of work with disturbance'.

Good supervision would also help acknowledge the range of losses that are being brought to supervision. The obvious loss in the deaths of two individuals and also the loss, for the service users, of mental faculties, of freedom in terms of whether they will be sectioned or not, of dignity as professionals gather around them and neighbours twitch their curtains, and, for George, the loss of his sense of being a skilled, caring worker committed to a clear value base.

Mode 5 Focusing on the Supervisory Relationship and Mode 6 Focusing on the Supervisor's Own Process

These two modes are based on the understanding that what happens between the social worker and the service user(s) will be *mirrored* in the meeting between the social worker and the supervisor, there is an impact which cannot but change the relationship. Another way of describing this is in terms of *a parallel process.* In the session described here we can follow the supervisor as s/he manages the boundaries of the work, allows and contains the strong feelings and is neither defen-sive nor overwhelmed. In other words s/he is mirroring good practice, what should take place between the social worker and the service user. There was the possibility of the supervisor allowing the session to end after modes 2 and 3, with the immediate reassurances that George had done all basics and would have a good account ready for the Incident Panel but this may only have unhelpfully mirrored how George left Penny. Instead the supervisor notices the 'defeated look' in George's eyes and stays with it, with some subsequent important learning and support for George.

Mode 7 Focusing on the Wider Context

This is the recognition that in Hawkins and Shohet's model the triad of service user–social worker–supervisor does not 'exist on an island', there is a 'wider context which impinges upon and colours the process within it ... There are professional codes and ethics, organizational requirements and constrictions, as well as relationships with other involved agencies' (2006: 71). The social worker and the supervisor need to be aware of these dynamics, as a manager taking back to their own supervisor concerns about the pressures, whether of job vacancies or more long-term uncertainties about restructuring. In the team the supervisor as manager can think systemically, checking out the degree to which other team members are aware of what George is facing; what is real and what is circulating in the gossip around the water cooler; if George wants the issues brought to a team meeting or if more informal networks need to be supported and for it not to be assumed that just George, as the social worker directly involved, needs support. George just happened to be on duty that day so others may be pondering that 'there but for the grace of God go I'.

All this is in recognition of the fact that 'the deaths' unsettle not just George but the team as a whole. In an interesting paper on responding to a death of a child in a school, Cornish (1998) notes that while such a tragic death may 'remind some of their own mortality ... evoke unpleasant memories associated with previous painful life experiences' nonetheless it is a qualitatively different experience from the death of friend or relative and is unlikely to have long-lasting repercussions. For all that there will be 'a considerable impact' on the community that makes up that organization, time needs to be taken 'to adjust to the loss and its implications' (1998: 99).

The supervisor/manager will need also to keep an eye on the media and ensure that the agency responds clearly and honestly to any criticisms about their interventions. This will not in itself be sufficient to guarantee a wider, societal appreciation for the difficult work in which George is engaged, that is a wider political project, but it may mean that George avoids what has occurred to other workers caught up in tragedies, where they feel vilified rather than valued (see Ruddock, 1998).

In conclusion what is being offered here is a combination of managerial and clinical supervision which in some settings, such as nursing, are carefully separated off functions but which are combined in social work. The 'seven-eyed' model is an approach that offers the opportunity for careful reflection without neglecting the more organizational demands: the next steps of how to deal with the inquiry, manage the paper work, anticipate the possible or probable outcomes. It will also be helpful to address George's professional and personal development, whether further training would help or some personal counselling, those aspects identified by Renzenbrick as part of the 'relentless self-care' we all need.

Sustaining Hope in Our Work, for Ourselves and for Service Users

In the above discussion there is the image of the 'defeated look', in the eye of both the service user and the social worker, and the strong temptation we have to avoid such an uncomfortable gaze. The supervisor, as noted, does not turn away. If George is to be helped to feel that he can 'make a difference' (identified as important in Huxley et al., 2005) the hope for this has to be held in terms of honouring what he has done and will continue to do in his professional life. *Hope* is an important ingredient in any aspect of social work but especially perhaps when we are confronting loss.

A persuasive case for 'the essential, positive' nature of hope in our work is made by Itzhaky and Lipschitz-Elhawi (2004). Drawing on the wider literature, the argument is for *learned hopefulness* and that:

> unlike denial, hope does not distort reality. Hope involves recognition of reality and the difficulties it involves and an effort to cope with and overcome them by offering a more effective behavioral alternative for coping. (2004: 47)

This text has sought to provide social workers with a rich repertoire of skills and theories, underpinned by practice examples and accessible research findings, but none of this will be effective if we fail to sustain hope, in our service users and in ourselves, that what we do is important and effective, that those who turn to us need not avoid the genuine feelings in the face of real losses and that we can help them to confront them fully and come to a new understanding.

Points for practice

- You need to recognize that social work, especially when working with issues of loss, death and bereavement is stressful and you have a right to express your feelings, whatever they may be.
- You cannot support service users unless you are yourself getting support, mainly through supervision.
- Make sure that you know what your own signs of stress are. If you don't think you have any – ask someone who knows you well. Make sure you become aware of when stress is building up and that you develop strategies to ease your stress.
- Use supervision effectively. Raise issues of concern and take the opportunity to reflect on your own practice and development.
- If you are not receiving adequate supervision, make sure you notify a more senior manager.

Further reading

For a modern text on social work organizations see:
Hafford-Letchfield, T. (2006) *Management and Organisations in Social Work.*

For a critique of the wider atmosphere within which social worker and other welfare professionals work, see:
Cooper, A. and Lousada, J. (2005) *Borderline Welfare: Feeling and Fear of Feeling in Modern Welfare agencies.*

For a discussion of pressures on social workers see:
Davies, R. (ed.) (1998) *Stress in Social Work,* especially the chapter, 'Yes, and But, and Then Again Maybe' by Ruddock, M.

References

Adams, R. (2002) 'Developing Critical Practice in Social Work' in R. Adams, L. Dominelli and M. Payne (ed.) *Critical Practice in Social Work*. Hampshire: Palgrave. pp. 83–95.

Age Concern (2005) *Dying and Death*. London: Policy Unit, Age Concern England.

Alderman, N. (2006) *Disobedience*. London: Viking Books.

Allan, C. (2007) *Poppy Shakespeare*. London: Bloomsbury Publishing.

Allot, P. (2004) 'What is Mental Health, Illness and Recovery?' in T. Ryan and J. Pritchard (eds) *Good Practice in Adult Mental Health*. London: Jessica Kingsley. pp. 13–31.

Aldridge, D. (2000) *Spirituality, Healing and Medicine, Return to the Silence*. London: Jessica Kingsley.

Anderson, D. and Mullen, P. (eds) (1998) *Faking It: The Sentimentalisation of Modern Society*. London: Penguin Books.

Angst, D.B. (eds) (2001) 'School-age Children' in M. Bluebond-Langner, B. Lask, and D.B. Angst *Psychosocial Aspects Of Cystic Fibrosis*. London: Arnold. pp. 125–38.

Appleby, S. (1998) 'Being Different: A Black Experience' in R. Davies, *Stress in Social Work*. London: Jessica Kingsley. pp. 83–92.

Ariès, P. (1981) *The Hour of Our Death*. London: Allen Lane.

Armstrong-Coster, A. (2004) *Living and Dying with Cancer*. Cambridge: Cambridge University Press.

Armstrong, S. (2006) 'Modern Death, People are Killing Themselves and Their Children and No one Seems to Notice', The *Guardian,* 14 January accessed www.guardian/co.uk/comment/story 27.01.06.

Aymer, C. (2000) 'Teaching and Learning Anti-racist and Anti-discriminatory Practice' in R. Pierce and J. Weinstein (eds) *Innovative Education and Training for Care Professionals, A Provider's Guide*. London: Jessica Kingsley. pp. 121–36.

Balfour, A. (2006) 'Thinking about the Experience of Dementia: The Importance of the Unconscious', *Journal of Social Work Practice,* 20(3): 329–46.

Barclay Report (1982) *Social Workers: Their Role and Tasks*. London: Bedford Square Press.

Barker, J. (1983) *Volunteer Bereavement Counselling Schemes: A Report on a Monitoring Exercise Research Perspectives on Ageing, 3*. London: Age Concern Research Unit.

Barker, P. (ed.) (1999) *Talking Cures: A Guide to the Psychotherapies for Health Care Professionals*. London: Nursing Times Books.

Barnes, C. and Mercer, G. *Exploring the Divide, Illness and Disability*. Leeds: The Disability Press.

Bartol, G.M. and Richardson, L. (1998) 'Using Literature to Create Cultural Competence', *Journal of Nursing Scholarship*, 30: 75–9.

Bayley, J. (1999) *Iris: A Memoir of Iris Murdoch*. London: Abacus.

Beck, A.T. (1989) *Cognitive Therapy and the Emotional Disorders*. Harmondsworth: Penguin.

Becker, H. (1973) *The Denial of Death*. Harmondsworth: Penguin.

Beckett, C. and Maynard, A. (2005) *Values and Ethics in Social Work.* London: Sage.

Beresford, P., Adshead, L. and Croft, S. (2006) *Palliative Care, Social Work and Service Users.* London: Jessica Kingsley.

Berger, P. and Luckmann, T. (1967) *The Social Construction of Reality: A Treatise in the Sociology of Knowledge.* New York: Double Day.

Berzoff, J. and Silverman, P.R. (eds) (2004) *Living with Dying: A Handbook for End-of-Life Healthcare Practitioners.* New York: Columbia University Press.

Bettelheim, B. (1991) *The Uses of Enchantment: The Meaning and Importance of Fairy Tales.* London: Penguin.

Biestek, F.P. (1961) *The Casework Relationship.* London: Allen and Unwin.

Biggs, S. (1993) *Understanding Ageing: Images, Attitudes and Professional Practice.* Buckingham: OUP.

Bleyen, J. (2005) 'Changing Contexts of Stillbirth: Towards an Oral History of "Empty Cradles" and "Hidden Sorrow" since 1940', paper presented at the Death, Dying and Disposal 7 Conference, Bath.

Bluebond-Langner, M., Lask, B and Angst, D.B. (eds) (2001) *Psychosocial Aspects Of Cystic Fibrosis.* London: Arnold.

Blythe, R. (1979) *The View in Winter, Reflections on Old Age.* London: Harcourt Brace Jovanovich.

Borg, S. and Lasker, J. (1982) *When Pregnancy Fails, Coping with Miscarriage, Stillbirth and Infant Death.* London: Routledge & Kegan Paul.

Bowlby, J. (1991) *Loss: Sadness and Depression, vol. 3 of 'Attachment and Loss'.* London: Penguin.

Breakwell, G. (1986) *Coping With Threatened Identities.* London: Methuen.

Briskman, L. (2003) *The Black Grapevine, Aboriginal Activism and the Stolen Generations.* Annan dale, NSW: Federation Press.

Broad, B. and Fletcher, C. (eds) (1993) *Practitioner Social Work Research In Action.* London: Whiting and Birch.

Broad, B. (ed.) (1999) *The Politics of Social Work Research and Evaluation.* Birmingham: Venture Press.

Brown, A. (1992) *Groupwork,* 3rd edn. Aldershot Hants: Ashgate.

Browning, D. (2004) 'Fragments of Love: Explorations in the Ethnography of Suffering and Professional Caregiving' in J. Berzoff, and P.R. Silverman (eds) *Living with Dying: A Handbook for End-of-Life Healthcare Practitioners.* New York: Columbia University Press. pp. 21–42.

Bush, A. (2001) 'Cystic Fibrosis: Cause, Course and Treatment' in M. Bluebond-Langner, B. Lask, and D.B. Angst (eds) *Psychosocial Aspects Of Cystic Fibrosis.* London: Arnold. pp. 1–25.

Carpentier, J.D. (ed.) (2006) *Old Heads on Young Shoulders.* London: NSPCC.

Casement, P. (1985) *On Learning from the Patient.* London: Routledge.

Casement, P. (2002) *Learning from our Mistakes, Beyond Dogma in Psychoanalysis and Psychotherapy.* Hove Sussex: Brunner-Routledge.

Cattan, M. (2002) *Supporting Older People to Overcome Social Isolation and Loneliness.* London: Help the Aged.

Chahal, K. (1999) 'Researching Ethnicity: Experiences and Concerns', in B. Broad (ed.) *The Politics of Social Work Research and Evaluation.* Birmingham: Venture Press. pp. 59–74.

Christie, G.H. (2005) 'Interventions with Bereaved Children' in P. Firth, G, Luff and D. Oliviere (eds) *Loss, Change and Bereavement in Palliative Care.* Berkshire: OUP. pp. 96–118.

Clarkson, P. (1989) *Gestalt Counselling in Action.* London: Sage.

Cline, S. (1995) *Lifting the Taboo, Women, Death and Dying.* London: Little, Brown and Company.

Coleman, P.G. (1986) *Ageing and Reminiscence Processes: Social and Clinical Implications.* Chichester: Wiley.

Colōn, Y. (2004) 'Technology-Based Groups and End-of-Life Social Work Practice' in J. Berzoff, and P.R. Silverman (eds) *Living with Dying: A Handbook for End-of-Life Healthcare Practitioners.* New York: Columbia University Press. pp. 535–47.

Cook, A.S. and Bosley, G. (1995) 'The Experience of Participating in Bereavement Research: Stressful or Therapeutic?', *Death Studies,* 19: 157–70.

Cooper, M. (1983) 'Community Social Work' in B. Jordan and N. Parton (eds) *The Political Dimensions of Social Work.* Oxford: Blackwell. pp. 146–63.

Cooper, A. and Lousada, J. (2005) *Borderline Welfare: Feeling and Fear of Feeling in Modern Welfare.* London: Karnac Books.

Corby, B. (2006) *Applying Research in Social Work.* Maidenhead: OUP.

Cornish, U. (1998) 'Death of a Pupil in School' in P. Sutcliffe, G. Tufnell and U. Cornish (eds) *Working with the Dying and Bereaved.* Hampshire: Macmillan. pp. 98–128.

CPS (Canadian Paediatric Society) Fetus and Newborn Committee (2001) 'Guidelines for health care professionals supporting families experiencing a perinatal loss', *Paediatrics and Child Health,* 6(71): 469–77.

Crawford, K. and Walker, J. (2004) *Social Work with Older People.* Exeter: Learning Matters Ltd.

Crow, L. (1996) 'Including all of our Lives' in C. Barnes, and G. Mercer (eds) *Exploring the Divide: Illness.* Leeds: Disability Press. pp. 55–73.

Cummings, E. and Henry, W.E. (1961) *Growing Old: The Process of Disengagement.* New York: Basic Books.

Currer, C. (2001) *Responding to Grief, Dying, Bereavement and Social Care.* Hampshire: Palgrave.

Cwikel, J. and Oron, A. (1991) 'A Long-Term Support Group for Chronic Schizophrenic Outpatients', *Groupwork,* 4(2): 163–77.

Dale, P., Davies, M., Morrison, T. and Waters, J. (1986*) Dangerous Families, Assessment and Treatment of Child Abuse.* London: Tavistock.

Danbury, H. (1996) *Bereavement Counselling Effectiveness: A Client Opinion Study.* Aldershot: Avebury.

Darlington, Y. and Scott, D. (2002) *Qualitative Research in Practice, Stories from the Field.* Buckingham: OUP.

Davies, D.J. (2005) *A Brief History of Death.* Oxford: Blackwell.

Davies, R. (ed.) (1998) *Stress in Social Work.* London: Jessica Kingsley.

Dawes, J. (2002) 'Losses and Justice: An Australian Perspective' in N. Thompson (ed.) *Loss and Grief, a Guide for Human Services Practitioners.* London: Palgrave. pp. 174–89.

Dean, C. (1993) *The Arguments for and Against Transracial Placements.* Norwich: Social Work Monographs.

Dearden, C. and Becker, S. (1997) *Children in Care, Children who Care: Parental Illness and Disability and the Child Care System.* Loughborough: Calouste Gulbenkian Foundation, Young Carers Research Group.

Department of Health (1990) *Caring for People: The Care Programme Approach for People with a Mental Illness Referred to Specialist Health Services.* London: Department of Health.

Department of Health (1999) *National Service Framework for Mental Health.* London: Department of Health.

Department of Health (2001) *National Service Framework for Older People.* London: Department of Health.

Department of Health (2002) *Guidance on the Single Assessment Process for Older People.* London: Department of Health.

Department of Health (2006) *Our Health, Our Care, Our Say: A New Direction for Community Services.* London: Department of Health.

Desai, S. and Bevan, D. (2002) 'Race and Culture' in N. Thompson (ed.) *Loss and Grief, a Guide for Human Services.* London: Palgrave. pp. 65–78.

de Shazer, S. (1985) *Keys to Solutions in Brief Therapy.* New York and London: Norton.

Diamond, G.S., Serrano, A.C., Dickey, M. and Sonis, W.A. (1996) 'Current Status of Family-based Outcome and Process Research', *Journal of the American Academy of Child and Adolescent Psychiatry',* 35(1): 6(11).

Diamond, J. (1998) *C, Because Cowards get Cancer too ...* London: Vermillion.

Dickenson, D., Johnson, M. and Katz, J.S. (eds) (2000) *Death, Dying and Bereavement.* London: Sage/OUP.

Dickinson, G.E. (2005) 'Baby Boomers and Personalized Death Trends', paper presented at the Death, Dying and Disposal 7 Conference, Bath.

Didion, J. (2006) *The Year of Magical Thinking.* London: Harper Perennial.

Dinnage, R. (1992) *The Ruffian on the Stair: Reflections on Death.* London: Penguin Books.

Doel, M. and Sawdon, C. (2001) 'What Makes for Successful Groupwork? A Survey of Agencies in the UK', *British Journal of Social Work,* 31: 437–63.

Doka, K.J. (ed.) (2002) *Disenfranchised Grief, New Directions, Challenges, and Strategies for Practice.* Champaign, IL: Research Press.

Doka, K.J. and Aber, R.A. (2002) 'Psychosocial Loss and Grief' in K.J. Doka (ed.) *Disenfranchised Grief, New Directions, Challenges, and Strategies for Practice.* Champaign, IL: Research Press. pp. 217–31.

Dominelli, L. (2002) *Feminist Social Work Theory and Practice.* Basingstoke: Palgrave Macmillan.

Don, A. (2005) *Fathers Feel Too.* London: Bosun Publishing on behalf of SANDS.

Donald, J. and Rattansi, A. (eds) (1992) *'Race', Culture and Difference.* London, Sage/OUP.

Donne, J. (1994) *The Complete Works and Selected Prose of John Donne.* Modern Library Series. New York, NY: Random House.

Duerzen-Smith, van E. (1995) 'Psychology and Counselling' in W. Dryden (ed.) *Hard-Earned Lessons from Counselling in Action.* London: Sage. pp. 129–35.

Eisenbruch, M. (1984) 'Cross-Cultural Aspects of Bereavement, I and II', *Culture, Medicine and Psychiatry,* 8: 283–309, 315–47.

Engebrigsten, G.K. and Heap, K. (1988) 'Short Term Groupwork in the Treatment of Chronic Sorrow', *Groupwork* 1.3: 197–214.

Erikson, E.H. (1965) *Childhood and Society.* London: Hogarth Press.

Evans, D. and Kearney, J. (1996) *Working in Social Care: A Systemic Approach.* Bury St. Edmunds: Arena.

Fanon, F. (1970) *Black Skin White Masks.* London: Paladin.

Farber, S., Egnew, T. and Farber, A. (2004) 'What is a Respectful Death' in J. Berzoff, and P.R. Silverman (eds) *Living with Dying: A Handbook for End-of-Life Healthcare Practitioners.* New York: Columbia University Press. pp. 102–27.

Faulks, S. (2005) *Human Traces*. London: Hutchison.

Firestone, R.W. and Seiden, R.H. (1987) 'Microsuicide and Suicidal Threats of Everyday Life', *Psychotherapy*, 24(1): 31–9.

Firth, P., Luff, G. and Oliviere, D. (2005) *Loss, Change and Bereavement in Palliative Care*. Berkshire: OUP.

Fleming, R. (1998) 'The Inner Impact of Work with Disturbance' in R. Davies (ed.) *Stress in Social Work*. London: Jessica Kingsley. pp. 153–63.

Fook, J. (1999) 'Critical Reflectivity in Education and Practice' in B. Pease and J. Fook (eds) *Transforming Social Work Practice: Postmodern Critical Perspectives*. London: Routledge. pp. 195–208.

Foote, C. and Stanners, C. (2002) *Integrating Care for Older People, New Care for Old – A Systems Approach*. London: Jessica Kingsley.

Frank, A.W. (1995) *The Wounded Storyteller: Body, Illness and Ethics*. Chicago: University of Chicago Press.

Franke, U. (2003) *In My Mind's Eye: Family Constellations in Individual Therapy and Counseling*. Heidelberg: Carl-Auer-Systeme Verlag.

Freud, S. (1915/1993) 'Death and Us' in D. Meghnagi (ed.) *Freud and Judaism*. London: Karnac Books.

Freud, S. (1917/1984) 'Mourning and Melancholia' in *On Metapsychology, the Theory of Psychoanalysis, Vol. 11, The Pelican Freud Library*. Middlesex: Penguin. pp. 245–68.

Freud, S. (1920/1984) 'Beyond The Pleasure Principle' in *On Metapsychology, the Theory of Psychoanalysis, Vol. 11, The Pelican Freud Library*. Middlesex: Penguin. pp. 275–338.

Frost, N. and Stein, M. (1989) *The Politics of Child Welfare: Inequality, Power and Change*. Herts: Harvester Wheatsheaf.

Furedi, F. (2004) *Therapy Culture, Cultivating Vulnerability in an Uncertain Age*. London and New York: Routledge.

(GSCC) (General Social Care Council) (2002) *Codes of Practice*. London, GSCC.

Gibson, F. (1992) 'Reminiscence Groupwork With Older People', *Groupwork* 5(3): 28–40.

Gibson, M. (2001) 'Death Scenes: Ethics of the Face and Cinematic Death', *Mortality*, 6: 306–20.

Gilroy, P. (1992) 'The End of Antiracism' in J. Donald and A. Rattansi (eds) *'Race', Culture and Difference*. London: Sage/OUP. pp. 49–61.

Glaser, B. and Strauss, A. (1965) *Awareness of Dying*. Chicago: Aldine.

Glaser, B. and Strauss, A. (1967) *The Discovery of Grounded Theory*. Chicago: Aldine.

Gordon, L. (1989) *Heroes of Their Own Lives: the Politics and History of Family Violence*. London: Virago Press.

Gork, R.V. (2006) 'Death Rituals in Sunni Societies in Turkey', paper presented at the 4th Global Conference on Death and Dying, Cambridge.

Gorell Barnes, G. (1998) *Family Therapy in Changing Times*. Basingstoke: Macmillan Press.

Grant, L. (1998) *Remind Me Who I Am Again*. London: Granta Books.

Gray, A. (2006) *Growing Old in a London Borough: The Shrinking Personal Community and How Volunteers Help to Maintain it*. Families & Social Capital ESRC Research Group: London South Bank University.

Greenberg, J. and Mitchell, S. (1983) *Object Relations in Psychoanalytical Theory*. Cambridge, MA: Harvard University Press.

Grenier, A. (2005) 'Older Women Negotiating Uncertainty in Everyday Life: Contesting Risk Management System' in L. Davies and P. Leonard (eds) *Social Work in a Corporate Era*. London: Ashgate. pp. 111–27.

Hafford-Letchfield, T. (2006) *Management and Organisations in Social Work.* Exeter: Learning Matters.

Haimes, E. and Timms, N. (1985) *Adoption, Identity and Social Policy: The Search for Distant Relatives.* Hants, England and Vermont, USA: Gower.

Hall, C. (2004) 'Survivors of cancer live longer if they're rich', *The Daily Telegraph.* 10 March 2004.

Hall, C., Jokinen, A. and Suoninen, E. (2003a) 'Legitimating the Rejecting of Your Child in a Social Work Meeting' in C. Hall et al. (eds) *Constructing Clienthood in Social Work and Human Services.* London: Jessica Kingsley. pp. 27–43.

Hall, C., Juhila, K., Parton, N. and Poso, T. (eds) (2003b) *Constructing Clienthood in Social Work and Human Service, Interaction, Identities and Practices.* London: Jessica Kingsley.

Hall, P., Weaver, L., Fothergill-Bourbonnais, F., Amos, S., Whiting, N., Barnes, P. and Legault, F. (2006) 'Interprofessional Education in Palliative Care: A Pilot Project Using Popular Literature', *Journal of Interprofessional Care,* 20(1): 51–9.

Harrison, L. and Harrington, R. (2001) 'Adolescents' Bereavement Experiences: Prevalence, Association with Depressive Symptoms and Use of Services', *Journal of Adolescence,* 24(2): 159–69.

Hart, B., Sainsbury, P. and Short, S. (1998) 'Whose Dying? A Sociological Critique of the 'Good Death', *Mortality,* 3(1): 65–77.

Hawkins, P. and Shohet, R. (2006) *Supervision in the Helping Professions,* 3rd edn. Buckingham: OUP.

Hearn, F. (2005) 'Excluded and Vulnerable Groups of Service Users' in P. Firth, G. Luff and D. Oliviere (eds) *Loss, Change and Bereavement in Palliative Care.* Berkshire: OUP. pp. 133–49.

Hedtke, L. and Winslade, J. (2003) *Re-membering Lives: Conversations with the Dying and the Bereaved.* New York: Baywood.

Hellinger, B. (2002) *Insights, Lectures and Stories.* Heidelberg: Carl-Auer-Systeme Publishers.

Hellinger, B. (2003) *To the Heart of the Matter, Brief Therapies.* Heidelberg: Carl-Auer-Systeme Verlag Publishers.

Hellinger, B. with Weber, G. and Beaumont, H. (1998) *Love's Hidden Symmetry, What Makes Love Work in Relationships.* Heidelberg: Carl-Auer-Systeme Publishers.

Hill, A. and Brettle, A. (2006) 'Counselling Older People: What Can we Learn from Research Evidence?' *Journal of Social Work Practice,* 20(3): 281–98.

Hoggett, P. (1993) 'What is Community Mental Health?', *Journal of Interprofessional Care,* 7(3): 201–19.

Holland, S. (1992) 'From Social Abuse to Social Action: A Neighbourhood Psychotherapy and Social Action Project for Women' in J.A. Ussher and P. Nicolson (eds) *Gender Issues in Clinical Psychology.* London: Routledge. pp. 68–77.

Hollis, F. (1964) *Casework: A Psychosocial Therapy.* New York: Random House.

Holmes, T.H. and Rahe, R.H. (1967) 'Social Readjustment Rating Scale', *Journal of Psychosomatic Research,* 11: 213–16.

Home Office (2003) *The Victoria Climbié Inquiry Report.* London: The Stationery Office.

Houston, G. (1990) *Supervision and Counselling.* London: Rochester Foundation.

Howe, D. (1995) *Attachment Theory for Social Workers.* Basingstoke: Macmillan.

Howe, D. (1996) 'Surface and Depth in Social Work Practice' in N. Parton (ed.) *Social Theory, Social Change and Social Work.* London: Routledge. pp. 77–97.

Humphries, B. and Truman, C. (1994) *Re-thinking Social Research.* Aldershot: Avebury.

Hutton, D. (2005) *What Can I Do To Help? 75 Practical Ideas for Family and Friends from Cancer's Frontline.* London: Short Books.

Huxley, P., Evans, S., Gately, C., Webber, M., Mears, A., Pajak, S., Kendall, T., Medina, J. and Katona, C. (2005) 'Stress and Pressures in Mental Health Social Work: The Worker Speaks', *British Journal of Social Work*, 35: 1063–79.

Itzhaky, H. and Lipschitz-Elhawi, R. (2004) 'Hope as a Strategy in Supervising Social Workers of Terminally Ill Patients', *Health and Social Work,* 29(1): 46–55.

Jacobs, C. (2004) 'Spirituality and End-of-Life Care Practice' in J. Berzoff, and P.R. Silverman (eds) *Living with Dying: A Handbook for End-of Life Healthcare Practitioners.* New York: Columbia University Press. pp. 188–205.

Jeffries, S. (2005) 'I have stage four cancer. There is no stage five'. The *Guardian*. 12 July 2005.

Jones, E. (1957) *Sigmund Freud, Vol. 111. The Last Phase, 1919–1939.* London: Hogarth Press.

Jones, K. (2004) 'The Turn to a Narrative Knowing of Persons: Minimalist Passive Interviewing Technique and Team Analysis of Narrative Qualitative Data' in F. Rapport (ed.) *New Qualitative Methodologies in Health and Social Care Research.* London and New York: Routledge, pp. 35–54.

Jordan, B. (1983) *Invitation to Social Work.* Oxford: Martin Robertson.

Jordan, B. (1990) *Social Work in an Unjust Society.* Hemel Hempstead: Harvester Wheatsheaf.

Jordan, B. with Jordan, C. (2000) *Social Work and the Third Way, Tough Love As Social Policy.* London: Sage.

Jung, C.G. (1967) *Memories, Dreams, Reflections.* London: Collins.

Kalish, R.A. and Reynolds, D.K. (1981) *Death and Ethnicity: A Psychosocial Study.* New York: Baywood.

Kasher, A. (ed.) (2007) *Making Sense of Dying and Death*, 3. Amsterdam/New York: Rodopi.

Katz, J. (2002) 'Ill-health' in N. Thompson (ed.) *Loss and Grief: A Guide for Human Services Practitioners.* Basingstoke: Palgrave. pp. 149–161.

Kenny, C. (1998) *A Thanatology of the Child.* Dinton: Quay Books.

Kesey, K. (2003) *One Flew Over the Cuckoo's Nest.* London: Marion Boyars.

Kirchenbaum, H. and Henderson, U.L. (ed.) (1990) *The Carl Rogers Reader.* London: Constable.

Kirton, D. (2000) *'Race', Ethnicity and Adoption.* Buckingham: OUP.

Kitwood, T. (1997) *Dementia Reconsidered.* Buckingham: OUP.

Klass, D. (1996) 'Spiritual Aspects of the Resolution of Grief' in D. Klass, P.R. Silverman and S.L. Nickman, S.L. (eds) *Continuing Bonds, New Understandings of Grief.* Philadelphia, PA: Taylor & Francis. pp. 243–68.

Klass, D., Silverman, P.R. and Nickman, S.L. (eds) (1996) *Continuing Bonds, New Understandings of Grief.* Philadelphia, PA: Taylor & Francis.

Kohner, N. (2000) 'Pregnancy Loss and the Death of a Baby, Parent's Choices', in D. Dickenson, M. Johnson and J.S. Katz (eds) *Death, Dying and Bereavement.* London: Sage/OUP. pp. 356–59.

Krueger, G. (2005) 'The Death Scene Investigation in Sudden Infant Death Syndrome (SIDS); An analysis using a surveillance model', paper presented at the Death, Dying and Disposal 7 Conference, Bath.

Kübler-Ross, E. (1969) *On Death and Dying.* New York: Macmillan.

Lafond, V. (2002) *Grieving Mental Illness.* Toronto: University of Toronto Press.

Laing, R.D. (1959) *The Divided Self.* Harmondsworth: Penguin.

Laing, R.D. and Esterson, A. (1964) *Sanity, Madness and the Family.* Harmondsworth: Penguin.

Lambert, M.J. and Cattani-Thompson, K. (1996) 'Current Findings Regarding the Effectiveness of Counseling: Implications for Practice', *Journal of Counseling and Development,* 74: 601–8.

Larkin, P. (1988) *Collected Poems.* London: The Marvell Press and Faber and Faber.

Latner, J. (1986) *The Gestalt Therapy Book.* Gouldsboro, ME: The Gestalt Journal Press.

Laungani, P. (1992) *It Shouldn't Happen to a Patient: A Survivor's Guide to Fighting Life-threatening Illness.* London: Whiting and Birch.

Laurence, J. (2003) *Pure Madness, How Fear Drives the Mental Health System.* London and New York: Routledge.

Lavalette, M., Penketh, L. and Ferguson, I. (2006) 'For help and solidarity', Letter in *Socialist Worker,* 22.04.06.

Lawton, J. (2000) *The Dying Process: Patients' Experiences of Palliative Care.* London: Routledge.

Lazarus, A.A. (1971) *Behaviour Therapy and Beyond.* New York: McGraw Hill.

Leick, N. and Davidsen-Nielsen, M. (1991) *Healing Pain, Attachment, Loss and Grief Therapy.* London: Routledge.

Lendrum, S. and Syme, G. (2004) *Gift of Tears: A Practical Approach to Loss and Bereavement in Counselling and Psychotherapy,* 2nd edn. London: Routledge.

Lenny, J. (1993) 'Do Disabled People Need Counselling?' in J. Swain, V. Finkelstein, S. French and M. Oliver (eds) *Disabling Barriers-enabling Environment'.* London: Sage/and OUP. 233–40.

Lindemann, E. (1944) 'The Symptomatology and Management of Acute Grief', *American Journal of Psychiatry,* 101: 141–48.

Littlewood, R. and Lipsedge, M. (1997) *Aliens and Alienists, Ethnic Minorities and Psychiatry,* 3rd edn. London: Unwin Hymen.

Lloyd, L. (2006) 'A Caring Profession? The Ethics of Care and Social Work with Older People', *British Journal of Social Work,* 36: 1171–85.

Lousada, J. (1993) 'Self-defence is no Offence', *Journal of Social Work Practice,* 7(2): 103–13.

Lymbery, M. (2005) *Social Work with Older People: Context, Policy and Practice.* London: Sage.

Lynch, T. (1998) *The Undertaking, Life Studies from the Dismal Trade.* London: Vintage Books.

MacAttram, M. (2006) 'Faith, Hope and Recovery', *Mental Health Today:* April. 10–11.

Macdonald, G. (1997) 'Social Work Research: The State We're In', *Journal of Interprofessional Care,* 11(1): 57–65.

McCabe, R., Heath, C., Burns, T. and Priebe, S. (2002) 'Engagement of Patients with Psychosis in the Consultation: Conversation Analytical Study', *British Medical Journal,* 325: 1148–51.

McCarthy, J.R. with Jessop, J. (2005) *Young People, Bereavement and Loss: Disruptive Transitions?* London: Joseph Rowntree Foundation/National Children's Bureau.

McCarthy, R. (2006) 'Goodbye to Iraq', The *Guardian,* 11 August.

McCubbin, M.A., McCubbin, H.I., Mischler, E. and Svavarsdottir, E. (2001) 'Family relationships' in M. Bluebond-Langner, B. Lask, and D. B. Angst (eds) *Psychosocial Aspects Of Cystic Fibrosis.* London: Arnold. pp. 211–37.

McLaren, J. (1998) 'A New Understanding of Grief: A Counsellor's Perspective', *Mortality,* 3(3): 275–90.

McLaren, J. (2005) 'The Death of a Child' in P. Firth, G. Luff and D. Oliviere (eds) *Loss, Change and Bereavement in Palliative Care.* Berkshire: OUP. pp. 80–95.

McLaughlin, R. (2001) 'The Father's Perspective: "Different from the Start"' in M. Bluebond-Langner, B. Lask, and D. B. Angst (eds) *Psychosocial Aspects Of Cystic Fibrosis.* London: Arnold. pp. 44–61.

McLeod, J. (1994) *Doing Counselling Research.* London: Sage.

McLeod, J . (2000) 'Narrative Therapy' in C. Feltham and I. Horton (eds) *Handbook of Counselling and Psychotherapy.* London: Sage. pp. 343–47.

McLeod, J. (2003) *An Introduction to Counselling,* 3rd edn. Buckingham. OUP.

Madge, S. (2001) 'The Role of Group Work and Support' in M. Bluebond-Langner, B. Lask, and D.B. Angst (eds) *Psychosocial Aspects Of Cystic Fibrosis.* London: Arnold. pp. 307–17.

Mander, R. (1995) *The Care of the Mother Grieving a Baby Relinquished for Adoption.* Aldershot: Avebury.

Manor, O. (ed.) (1984) *Family Work in Action.* London: Tavistock Publications.

Mantel, H. (2005) *Beyond Black.* London: Harper Perennial.

Manthorpe, J. and Iliffe, S. (2005) *Depression in Later Life.* London: Jessica Kingsley.

Markovitz, M.S. (2001) 'Death and Dying in Cystic Fibrosis: Considerations in the Terminal Phase' in M. Bluebond- Langner, B. Lask, and D.B. Angst (eds) *Psychosocial Aspects Of Cystic Fibrosis.* London: Arnold. pp. 380–89.

Marris, P. (1974) *Loss and Change.* London: Routledge Kegan Paul.

Marris, P. (1996) *The Politics of Uncertainty: Attachment in Private and Public Life.* London: Routledge.

Maslow, A. (1968) *Towards a Psychology of Being.* New York: Van Nostrand.

Masson, J. (1984) *Freud: The Assault on Truth.* London, Faber & Faber.

Masson, J. (1997) *Against Therapy.* London: Harper Collins.

Mayer, J.E. and Timms, N. (1970) *The Client Speaks: Working-Class Impressions of Casework.* London: Routledge & Kegan Paul.

Mearns, D. and Thorne, B. (2000) *Person-Centred Therapy Today: New Frontiers in Theory and Practice.* London: Sage.

Meddings, S., Walley, L., Collins, T., Tullett, F. and McEwan, B. (2006) 'The Voices don't like it …', *Mental Health Today,* September: 26–30.

Meghnagi, D. (ed.) (1993) *Freud and Judaism.* London: Karnac Books.

Menzies Lyth, I. (1959/1988) 'The Functioning of Social Systems as a Defence Against Anxiety: A Report on a Study of the Nursing Service of a General Hospital' in I. Menzies Lyth *Containing Anxiety in Institutions, Selected Essays.* London: FAB, pp. 43–85.

Menzies Lyth, I. (1998) 'Foreword' in R. Davies (ed.) *Stress in Social Work.* London: Jessica Kingsley. pp. 7–8.

Miller, L. (2006) *Counselling Skills for Social Work.* London: Sage.

Morris, J. (ed.) (1989) *Able Lives, Women's Experience of Paralysis.* London: The Women's Press.

Morrison, B. (1998) *And When Did You Last See Your Father?* London: Granta Books.

Moss, B. (2007) *Values.* Lyme Regis: Russell House Publishing.

Neimeyer, R.A. and Anderson, A. (2002) 'Meaning Reconstruction Theory' in N. Thompson (ed.) *Loss and Grief, A Guide for Human Services Practitioners.* London: Palgrave. pp. 45–64.

Neimeyer, R.A. and Jordan, J.R. (2002) 'Disenfranchisement as Empathic Failure: Grief Therapy and the Co-Construction of Meaning' in K.J. Doka (ed.) *Disenfranchised Grief, New Directions, Challenges, and Strategies for Practice.* Champaign, IL: Research Press. pp. 96–117.

Neuberger, J. (2004) *Caring for People of Different Faiths,* 4th edn. Oxford: Radcliffe Medical Press.

Newman, T. (2003) *Children of Disabled Parents, New Thinking about Families Affected by Disability and Illness.* Lyme Regis: Russell House Publishing.

Nickman, S.L. (1996) 'Retroactive Loss in Adopted Persons' in D. Klass, P.R. Silverman and S.L. Nickman (eds) *Continuing Bonds, New Understandings of Grief.* Philadelphia, PA: Taylor & Francis. pp. 257–72.

Nuland, S.B. (1994) *How We Die.* London: Chatto and Windus.

O'Hanlon, B. and Beadle, S. (1994) *A Field Guide to Possibility.* Hummelstown, PA: Possibility Press.

Okitikpi, T. (ed.) (2005) *Working with Children of Mixed Parentage.* Lyme Regis: Russell House Publishing.

O'Leary. E. and Barry, N. (1998) 'Reminiscence Therapy with Older Adults', *Journal of Social Work Practice,* 12(2): 159–65.

Oliver, M. (1990) *The Politics of Disablement.* Basingstoke: Macmillan.

Oliver, M. and Sapey, B. (2006) *Social Work with Disabled People,* 3rd edn. Basingstoke: Palgrave Macmillan.

Orbach, A. (1999) *Life, Psychotherapy and Death. The End of our Exploring.* London: Jessica Kingsley.

Orbach, S. (1979) *Fat is a Feminist Issue.* London: Hamlyn.

Pahl, R. (2000) *On Friendship.* Cambridge: Polity Press.

Papell, C. and Rothman, B. (1966) 'Social Groupwork Models: Possession and Heritage', *Journal for Education for Social Work,* 2(2), reprinted in H. Specht and A. Vickery (eds) (1977) *Integrated Social Work Methods.* London: George Allen and Unwin.

Parkes, C.M. (1975) 'Determinants of Outcomes Following Bereavement', *Omega,* 6: 303–23.

Parkes, C.M. (1980) 'Bereavement Counselling: Does it Work?', *British Medical Journal,* 281: 3–6.

Parkes, C.M. (1998) *Bereavement, Studies of Grief in Adult Life,* 3rd edn. London: Penguin.

Parton, N. (1985) *The Politics of Child Abuse.* Basingstoke: Macmillan.

Parton, N. and O'Byrne, P. (2000) *Constructive Social Work: Towards a New Practice.* Basingstoke: Macmillan.

Payne, M. (2005) *Modern Social Work Theory,* 3rd. edn. Basingstoke: Palgrave Macmillan.

Payne, S., Horn, S. and Relf, M. (1999) *Loss and Bereavement.* Buckingham: OUP.

Peek, D. (2001) 'The Adult's Perspective' in M. Bluebond-Langner, B. Lask, and D.B. Angst (eds) *Psychosocial Aspects Of Cystic Fibrosis.* London: Arnold. pp. 29–36.

Perls, F. (1969) *Gestalt Therapy Verbatim.* Moab, UT: Real People Press.

Philpot, T. (1989) *Last Things, Social Work with the Dying and Bereaved.* Wallington: Community Care.

Piaget, J. (1952) *The Origins of Intelligence in Children.* New York: International Universities Press.

Picardie, J. (2001) *If the Spirit Moves You.* London: Macmillan.

Picardie, R. (1998) *Before I Say Goodbye.* London: Penguin.

Pilgrim, D. (1999) 'Care, Control and Evidence in British Mental Health Policy' in D. Tomlinson and K. Allen (eds) *Crisis Services and Hospital Crises: Mental Health at a Turning Point.* Aldershot: Ashgate. pp. 25–38.

Pincus, A. and Minahan, A. (1973) *Social Work Practice: Models and Method.* Ithaca, IL: Peacock.

Pincus, L. (1978) *Life and Death, Coming to Terms with Death in the Family.* London: Sphere Books.

Pithouse, A. (1987) *Social Work: The Social Organisation of an Invisible Trade.* Aldershot: Avebury.

Polster, E. (1990) *Every Person's Life is Worth a Novel.* New York: W.W. Norton.

Polster, E. (1995) *A Population of Selves, A Therapeutic Exploration of Personal Diversity.* San Francisco: Jossey-Bass Publishers.

Popple, K. (2002) 'Community Work' in R. Adams, L. Dominelli and M. Payne (eds) *Critical Practice in Social Work.* Basingstoke: Palgrave. pp. 149–58.

Powis, K. (2005) 'Words Fail? The Capacity and Incapacity of Language in Experiencing the Self in Terminal Illness', paper presented at the Death, Dying and Disposal 7 Conference, Bath.

Puchalski, C.M. (2000) 'FICA: A Spiritual Assessment Tool', *Journal of Palliative Care* 3(1): 131.

Putnam, R.D. (2000) *Bowling Alone.* New York: Simon and Schuster.

Raiff, S. and Shore, V. (1993) *Advanced Case Management: New Strategies for the Nineties.* London: Sage Human Services Guide.

Randall, L. and Walker, W. (1988) 'Supporting Voices: Groupwork with People Suffering from Schizophrenia', *Groupwork* (1)1: 60–6.

Raphael, B. (1977) 'Preventative Intervention with the Recently Bereaved', *Archives of General Psychiatry Gen,* 34: 1450–4.

Raphael, B., Middleton, W., Martinek, N. and Misso, V. (1993) 'Counselling and Therapy of the Bereaved' in M.S. Stroebe, W. Stroebe and R. Hansonn (eds) *Handbook of Bereavement, Theory, Research and Intervention.* Cambridge: Cambridge University Press. pp. 427–56.

Rattenbury, C. and Stones, M.J. (1989) 'A Controlled Evaluation of Reminiscence and Current Topics Discussion Groups in a Nursing Home Context', *Gerontologist,* 29: 768–71.

Reeve, D. (2000) 'Oppression Within the Counselling Room', *Disability & Society,* (15)4: 669–82.

Reimann, G. (2005) 'Ethnographies of Practice – Practicing Ethnography: Resources for Self-reflective Social Work', *Journal of Social Work Practice,* 19(1): 87–101.

Renzenbrick, I. (2004) 'Relentless Self-Care' in J. Berzoff and P.R. Silverman (eds) *Living with Dying: A Handbook for End-of-Life Healthcare Practitioners.* New York: Columbia University Press. pp. 848–68.

Richards, B. (1989) *Images of Freud, Cultural Responses to Psychoanalysis.* London: J.M. Dent & Sons.

Riches, G. (2002) 'Gender and Sexism' in N. Thompson (ed.) *Loss and Grief: A Guide for Human Services.* London: Palgrave. pp. 79–91.

Riches, G. and Dawson, P. (1996) '"An Intimate Loneliness": Evaluating the Impact of a Child's Death on Parental Self-identity and Marital Relationships', *Journal of Family Therapy,* 18(1): 1–22.

Robben, A.C.G.M. (ed.) (2004) *Death, Mourning and Burial: A Cross-Cultural Reader.* Oxford: Blackwell.

Robson, G. (1993) *Real World Research.* Oxford: Blackwell.

Rogers, C. (1951) *Client-Centred Therapy.* London: Constable.

Rogers, C. (1961) *On Becoming A Person: A Therapist's View of Psychotherapy.* New York: Houghton Mifflin.

Rogers, C. (1980) 'Growing Old, or Older and Growing' in H. Kirchenbaum and U.L. Henderson (1990) (eds) *The Carl Rogers Reader.* London: Constable. pp. 37–55.

Romaine, M. (2002) 'Adoption and Foster Care' in N. Thompson (ed.) *Loss and Grief: A Guide for Human Services.* London: Palgrave. pp. 125–38.

Royal College of Psychiatrists (2005) *Partners in Care, Postnatal Depression.* London: RCP.

Ruddock, M. (1998) 'Yes, and But, and Then Again Maybe' in R. Davies (ed.) *Stress in Social Work.* London: Jessica Kingsley. pp. 93–100.

Sadler, E. and Biggs, S. (2006) 'Exploring the Links between Spirituality and "Successful Ageing"', *Journal of Social Work Practice,* 20(3): 267–80.

Sample, I. (2005) 'Health Timebomb as Rising Cocaine use Threatens Heart Problems in Young', The *Guardian,* 24 October, p. 9.

Satir, V. (1978) *Poeplemaking.* London: Souvenir Press.

Schon, D.A. (1983) *The Reflective Practitioner: How Professionals Think in Action.* London: Temple Smith.

Seale, C. (1998) 'Theories and Studying the Care of Dying People', *British Medical Journal,* 28(317): 1518–20.

Sealey, L.A. (1993) 'Alone with Illness' in K.A. Nichols (ed.) *Psychological Care in Physical Illness.* London: Chapman & Hall. pp. 187–98.

Sebold, A. (2002) *The Lovely Bones.* London: Picador.

Seden, J. (1999) *Counselling Skills in Social Work Practice.* Buckingham: OUP.

Seligman, M.E.P. (1992) *Helplessness: On Depression, Bereavement and Death.* New York: W.H. Freeman.

Selwyn, J. (2001) 'Key social worker in Climbié case complained of "poor supervision"', *Community Care,* 29 November 2001 (www.communitycare.co.uk/Articles/2001/11/29/34273/key-social-worker-in-climbie-case-complained-of-poor-supervision.html).

Seymour, W. (1998) *Remaking the Body: Rehabilitation and Change.* London: Routledge.

Shah, S. and Argent, H. (2006) *Life Story Work: What it Is and What it Means.* London: BAAF.

Showalter, E. (1997) *Hystories, Hysterical Epidemics and Modern Culture.* London: Picador/Macmillan.

Silverman, P.R. (2004) 'Dying and Bereavement in Historical Perspective' in J. Berzoff, and P.R. Silverman (eds) *Living with Dying: A Handbook for End-of-Life Healthcare Practitioners.* New York: Columbia University Press. pp. 128–149.

Silverman, P.R. (2005) 'Mourning: A Changing View' in P. Firth, G. Luff and D. Oliviere, (eds) *Loss, Change and Bereavement in Palliative Care.* Berkshire: OUP. pp. 18–37.

Silverman, P.R. and Klass, D. (1996) 'Introduction: What's the Problem?' in D. Klass, P.R. Silverman and S.L. Nickman (eds) *Continuing Bonds, New Understandings of Grief.* Philadelphia: Taylor & Francis. pp. 3–23.

Simpkin, M. (1979) *Trapped Within Welfare: Surviving Social Work.* London: Macmillan.

Sivanandan, A. (1990) *Communities of Resistance: Writings on the Black Struggles for Socialism.* London: Verso.

Skelton, J. (2002) 'Commentary: Understanding Conversation', *British Medical Journal,* 325: 1151.

Smale, G., Tuson, G., Biehal, N. and Marsh, P. (1993) *Empowerment, Assessment, Care Management and the Skilled Worker.* London: HMSO.

Social Exclusion Unit Report (2004) *Mental Health and Social Exclusion.* London: ODPM.

Social Exclusion Unit Report (2006) *A Sure Start to Later Life: Ending Inequalities for Older People.* London: ODPM.

Solnit, A.J. (1993) 'Preparing for Uncertainty: Family Reactions to a Seriously Impaired Child' in B.W. Weller, L.M. Flohr and L.S. Zeguns (eds) *Psychosocial Interventions with Physically Disabled Persons.* Jessica Kingsley: London. pp. 29–42.

Sontag, S. (1993) *Illness as Metaphor.* London: Allen Lane.

Specht, H. and Vickery, A. (eds) (1977) *Integrated Social Work Methods.* London: George Allen and Unwin.

Speck, P. (1994) 'Working with Dying People: On Being Good Enough' in A. Obholzer and V. Roberts (eds) *The Unconscious at Work: Individual and Organizational Stress in the Human Services.* London: Routledge. pp. 94–100.

Spiegel, Y. (1977) *The Grief Process.* London: SCF.

Stanley, N., Penhale, B., Riordan, D., Barbour, R.S. and Holden, S. (2003) *Child Protection and Mental Health Services: Interprofessional Responses to the Needs of Mothers.* Bristol: The Policy Press.

Stanton, A.N. (2003) 'Sudden Unexpected Death in Infancy Associated with Maltreatment: Evidence from Long-term Follow up of Siblings', *Archives of Disease in Childhood,* 88: 699–701.

Stillion, J.M. (1995) 'Death in the Lives of Adults: Responding to the Tolling of the Bell' in H. Wass and R.A. Neimeyer (eds) *Dying: Facing the Facts.* Washington: Taylor & Francis. pp. 303–22.

Strauss, B. and Howe, R. (1995) 'Generations: The History of America's Future 1584 to 2069'. New York: William Morrow.

Stroebe, M.S. and Schut, H. (1999) 'The Dual Process Model of Coping with Bereavement: Rationale and Description', *Death Studies,* 23: 197–224.

Stroebe, W. and Stroebe, M.S. (1987) *Bereavement and Health: The Psychological and Physical Consequences of Partner Loss.* Cambridge: Cambridge University Press.

Sutton, A.L. and Liechty, D. (2004) 'Clinical Practice with Groups in End-of-Life' in J. Berzoff and P.R. Silverman (eds) (2004) *Living with Dying: A Handbook for End-of-Life Healthcare Practitioners.* New York: Columbia University Press. pp. 508–34.

Swift, G. (1996) *Last Orders.* London: Picador.

Swinton, J. (1986) *Spirituality and Mental Health Care: Rediscovering a 'Forgotten' Dimension.* London: Jessica Kingsley.

Taylor, S.F. (2005) 'Between the Idea and the Reality: A Study of the Counselling Experiences of Bereaved People who Sense the Presence of the Deceased', *Counselling & Psychotherapy Research,* (5)1: 53–62.

Teague, A. (1989) *Social Change, Social Work and the Adoption of Children.* Aldershot: Avebury.

Thompson, B. (2003) 'Lazarus Phenomena: An Exploratory Study of Gay Men Living with HIV', *Social Work in Health Care,* 37(1): 87–114.

Thompson, N. (2001) *Anti-Discriminatory Practice,* 3rd edn. Basingstoke: Palgrave.

Thompson, N. (ed.) (2002) *Loss and Grief: A Guide for Human Services Practitioners.* London: Palgrave.

Thompson, S. (1996) 'Living with Loss: A Bereavement Support Group', *Groupwork,* (9)1: 5–14.

Thompson, S. (2002) 'Older People' in N. Thompson (ed.) *Loss and Grief, a Guide for Human Services Practitioners.* London: Palgrave. pp. 162–73.

Tobin, S.A. (1975) 'Saying Goodbye' in J. Stevens (ed.) *Gestalt Is.* Moab, UT: Real People Press. pp. 117–28.

Tomlinson, D. and Allen, K. (eds) (1999) *Crisis Services and Hospital Crises: Mental Health at a Turning Point.* Aldershot: Ashgate.

Trevillion, S. (1999) *Networking and Community Partnership,* 2nd edn. Aldershot: Arena.

Trinder, L. (2000) 'Reading the Texts: Postmodern Feminism and the "Doing" of Research' in B. Fawcett, B. Featherstone, J. Fook and A. Rossiter (eds) *Practice and*

Research in Social Work, Postmodern Feminist Perspectives. London: Routledge. pp. 39–61.

Turton, P., Badenhorst, W., Hughes, P., Ward, J., Riches, S. and White, S. (2006) 'Psychological Impact of Stillbirth on Fathers in the Subsequent Pregnancy and Puerperium', *British Journal of Psychiatry,* 188: 165–72.

Van den Hoonaard, D.K. (2001) *The Widowed Self: The Older Woman's Journey through Widowhood.* New Brunswick: Wilfrid Laurier University Press.

Viorst, J. (1987) *Necessary Losses.* New York: Ballantine Books.

Wallcraft, J. (2005) 'Recovery from Mental Breakdown' in J. Tew (ed.) *Social Perspectives in Mental Health, Developing Social Models to Understand and Work with Mental Distress.* London: Jessica Kingsley. pp. 200–15.

Walter, T. (1996) 'A New Model of Grief: Bereavement and Biography', *Mortality,* 1(1): 7–25.

Walter, T. (1999) *On Bereavement, the Culture of Grief.* Buckingham: OUP.

Walter, T. (2005) 'Mediator Deathwork', *Death Studies,* 29: 383–412.

Walters, M. (1990) 'A Feminist Perspective in Family Therapy' in R.J. Perelberg and A.C. Miller (eds) *Gender and Power in Families.* London: Tavistock/Routledge. pp. 13–33.

Warren, K. (2003) *Exploring the Concept of Recovery from the Perspective of People with Mental Health Problems.* Social Work Monographs. Norwich: University of East Anglia.

Wass, H. and Neimeyer, R.A. (1995) *Dying: Facing the Facts.* Washington, DC: Taylor & Francis.

Webster, R. (1995) *Why Freud Was Wrong: Sin, Science and Psychoanalysis.* London: Harper Collins.

Weinstein, J. (1998a) 'A Proper Haunting: The Need in Mourning to Maintain a Continuing Relationship with the Dead', *Journal of Social Work Practice,* (12)1: 93–102.

Weinstein, J. (1998b) *My Safe Place: A Report on the Work of the Havering and Brentwood Bereavement Counselling Service.* London: South Bank University.

Weinstein, J. (2005) *'A Shoulder To Support Me, Not A Shoulder To Cry On'.* London South Bank University, Institute of Primary Care and Public Health.

Weinstein, J. (2007) 'So That's a Completely Different Story: Competing Narratives in the Lives of Relatives Caring for Dying Patients' in A. Kasher (ed.) *Making Sense of Dying and Death,* 3. Amsterdam/New York: Rodopi.

Welsh, I. (1993) *Trainspotting.* London: Minerva.

West, P. (2004) *Conspicuous Compassion.* London: Civitas.

Wilkinson, J. (1998) 'Danger on the Streets: Mental Illness, Community Care and Ingratitude' in A. Symonds and A. Kelly (eds) *Social Construction of Community Care.* Basingstoke: Macmillan. pp. 208–19.

Wilks, T. (2005) 'Social Work and Narrative Ethics', *British Journal of Social Work,* 35: 1249–64.

Woodgate, R. and Chernick, V. (2001) 'The Professional Caregivers' Perspective', in M. Bluebond-Langner, B. Lask and D. B. Angst (eds) *Psychosocial Aspects Of Cystic Fibrosis.* London: Arnold. pp. 86–94.

Worden, W. J. (1991) *Grief Counselling and Grief Therapy: A Handbook for the Mental Health Practitioner,* 2nd edn. London: Routledge.

Wortman, C.B. and Silver, R.C. (1989) 'The Myth of Coping with Loss', *Journal of Clinical Consulting Psychology,* 57: 349–57.

Yalom, I.D. (1980) *Existential Psychotherapy.* New York: Basic Books.

Yalom, I.D. (1985) *The Theory and Practice of Group Psychotherapy,* 2nd edn. New York: Basic Books.

Yalom, I.D. (1989) *Love's Executioner and Other Tales of Psychotherapy.* London: Penguin,

Young, M. and Cullen, L. (1996) *A Good Death: Conversations with East Londoners.* London: Routledge.

Zinker, J. (1978) *Creative Process in Gestalt Therapy.* New York: Basic Books.

Zinker, J. (1994) *In Search of Good Form.* San Francisco: Josey-Bass.

Zinner, E.S. (2002) 'Incorporating Disenfranchised Grief in the Death Education Classroom' in K.J. Doka (ed.) *Disenfranchised Grief, New Directions, Challenges, and Strategies for Practice.* Champaign, IL: Research Press. pp. 389–404.

Films

Burton, T. (2005) *Corpse Bride.*

Cole, N. (2003) *Calendar Girls.*

Curtis, R. (2003) *Love Actually.*

Eyre, R. (2002) *Iris.*

Forman, M. (1975) *One Flew Over the Cuckoo's Nest.*

Leigh, M. (1996) *Secrets and Lies.*

Loach, K. (1994) *Ladybird, Ladybird.*

Madden, J. (1997) *Mrs. Brown.*

Minghella, A. (1991) *Truly, Madly, Deeply.*

Moretti, N. (2001) *The Son's Room.*

Newell, M. (1994) *Four Weddings and a Funeral.*

Noyce, P. (2002) *Rabbit Proof Fence.*

Robinson, P. (1989) *Field of Dreams.*

Scorsese, M. (1999) *Bringing Out the Dead.*

Schepsi, F. (2002) *Last Orders.*

Music

Dylan, B. (1965) 'It's alright, ma (I'm only bleeding)'. Bringing it All Back Home. USA: Columbia Records.

Television

Ball, A. (2001–2005) *Six Feet Under.*

Bleasdale, A. (1982) *The Boys from the Blackstuff.*

Faulkner, J. and Foster, R. (2004) *Someone to Watch Over Me.*

Fox, E. (2006) *Ghost Whisperers.*

Holgate, P. (1989) *The Talking Cure.*

Loach, K. (1966) *Cathy Come Home.*

Volk, S. (2005–2006) *Afterlife.*

Index

This index is in word by word order. Page numbers in **bold** indicate 'Points for practice' boxes.